THE TEDDY BOY WARS

THE YOUTH CULT THAT SHOCKED BRITAIN

Michael Macilwee

MILO BOOKS LTD

ISBN 978-1-908479-86-0

Typeset by etype

Printed and bound by CPI Group (UK) Ltd, Croydon, CR0 4YY

MILO BOOKS LTD
www.milobooks.com

Dedicated to Pat and Sheila Keeley

CONTENTS

PREFACE

'I do not know how the population of this town allows this Teddyism to go on. Drainpipe trousers and funny hair-cuts – they are absurd. In my opinion it is the height of badness. I think they should be dealt with severely.'

(Father of a Somerset Teddy Boy, 1957)

Early in the 21st century, British newspapers would periodically report that inhabitants of the remote Falkland Islands still shared the much-missed values and lifestyle of Britain in the 1950s. The locals, it was wistfully asserted, enjoyed low crime rates, neighbourliness and industriousness. The 1950s was preserved in the imagination as a golden age of good behaviour: an era of post-war diligence in a law-abiding land with crime-free streets, discipline in schools, bobbies on the beat and the ultimate deterrent of hanging making murder a rare event. Its passing is still lamented.

A trawl through the newspapers of the 1950s, however, tells a very different story, for the nation appeared to be in the grip of a crime wave. 'What's Gone Wrong With Us?' asked a headline in the *News of the World* in September 1958. The accompanying article warned of the 'growing army of vicious hooligans and cowardly mobsters', and a peaceful, conservative society was shocked and bewildered at this unprecedented rise in crime. The number of people aged seventeen to twenty-one convicted of crimes of violence in England and Wales jumped from 745 in 1954 to over 2,000 by 1958; in 1938, it had stood at just 147. In a single year, 1956–57, recorded juvenile crime rose from 430,000 to 545,000. Overall violent crime almost doubled from 1955 to 1960. Something seemed to have gone seriously wrong. Politicians, journalists and churchmen searched desperately for an answer.

Most importantly, the 1950s was the decade that gave rise to the Teddy Boys. Although the rise of the Ted cannot be blamed for all of the violence, this new youth phenomenon was responsible for more than its fair share. And it is to the Teds that we must turn in search of answers as to what went wrong.

The story traditionally begins at the start of the decade when working-class London youths began to enjoy the fruits of full employment. With money in their pockets to spend on clothes, they latched onto and customised the fashionable Edwardian look being worn by upper-class gentlemen of the time. This look was undergoing a revival in the West End following years of wartime austerity and shapeless clothing. In a nod to the golden age of the English aristocracy during the reign of Edward VII (1901–10), guardsmen and young bloods had begun sporting long, narrow, single-breasted jackets with turned-back velvet cuffs worn with tapered trousers. Working-class teenagers began modifying the style by adding American influences such as bootlace ties and silk brocade waistcoats, so that it became a hybrid of Wild West gambler and English gentleman. Not that there was anything gentlemanly in the behaviour of some of these tough boys from the bomb-scarred, crime-ridden districts of the capital.

The fashion might well have faded away, or at least remained a London phenomenon, had it not hit the national headlines in July 1953 when a boy was stabbed to death by a group of youths near Clapham Common. As the culprits had been wearing Edwardian-style clothing, the press began to make a connection between the peculiar fashions of these young South Londoners and a culture of casual violence. It wasn't long before these Edwardian hooligans would be referred to as 'Teddy Boys', or simply 'Teds'.

After the Clapham murder, Teddy Boys began dominating newspaper headlines and acres of newsprint were devoted to describing their violent exploits. As the fashion and accompanying anti-social behaviour spread throughout the country, Teds came to represent the breakdown of society's moral fabric and the collapse of law and order. Newspaper readers recoiled in horror as they read of Teds arming themselves with axes, coshes, flick-knives, razors, knuckle-dusters, studded belts and bicycle chains. Victims included not only other Teds but innocent members of the public. Knife fights broke out on buses, cafes were smashed up and cinemas were taken over by youths dancing, shouting and carving up the seats. Teds in Nottingham and London were involved in racial attacks on black immigrants and there were large-scale battles between rival gangs in many city centres. Even quiet towns and villages such as Calstock in Cornwall and Sandiacre in Derbyshire were invaded and terrorised. The new cult was reinforced by the spirit of youthful rebellion from America where James Dean and Marlon Brando were popular screen idols. In 1955 the exciting new music genre, rock 'n' roll, also crossed the Atlantic, further fanning the flames of teenage revolt. Tosco R. Fyvel was a London-based journalist at the time and the author of *The Insecure Offenders: Rebellious Youth in the Welfare State* (1961), one of the first books to analyse the Teddy Boys. He claimed that no other group of youths in modern England had found itself the focus of so much intense dislike. Teds were the 'hoodies' of their day.

Why did the country produce this disturbing new generation of delinquents? This book, in attempting to find the answer, looks at how this initially small, fashion-led movement, started by a group of working-class lads, initiated the modern world of youth culture, became a byword for hooliganism and helped transform British society. It examines Teddy Boys in newspaper articles, official reports, novels, plays, autobiographies and films. The following chapters look not only at what the Teddy Boys did, but also why they were supposed to have acted as they did – and how the authorities, including politicians, magistrates, teachers, policemen, clergymen and youth workers, tried desperately to stop them.

1

THE CLAPHAM COMMON MURDER

'The boy stabbed to death on Clapham Common was a symbol of what the public had expected the Teddy Boys to be capable of.'

(Stanley Cohen, sociologist)

'Walk around the other side, you flash c—t!' These shocking words were to spark a teenage revolution. They were spoken by one of four lads who objected when a smartly dressed youth asked them to move their legs from a park bench, so that he and his girlfriend could walk past. Minutes later, knives had been drawn and a seventeen-year-old was bleeding to death on a pavement near Clapham Common in South West London. It was the first in a string of senseless acts of violence that was to define the rest of the decade. The Clapham Common murder of July 1953 brought to national attention the existence of what became known as the Teddy Boy.

Local concern about the number of incidents of gang warfare on the Common had already been growing. Fights were sporadic and usually broke up when the police approached. The lads largely fought against each other and were sometimes left to get on with it. The police did not seem too concerned. Occasionally a member of the public was caught up in the fighting but it was often difficult to identify the culprits since they were usually all dressed in a similar Edwardian fashion.

In those days the area was rough. In the bombed-out buildings and streets surrounding the Common, one of the largest open spaces in London, weapons were concealed in various spots. They belonged to a local gang known as the Plough Boys, named after the public house of the same name on nearby Clapham High Street, and were kept ready for use against 'foreigners': rival gangs from other areas. London boasted several mobs, including the nearby Latchmere Lot, plus the Brixton Boys and the Elephant Mob, based a few miles away. Despite his young age (he was not yet sixteen), Ronald Coleman was the leader of this local gang of young thugs, and the so-called 'King of the Common'. He had a conviction for using insulting words and behaviour on the Common, but nothing more. As a schoolboy he had stabbed a fellow pupil with a nail file after an argument but no charges were brought. In July 1952 he was identified as one of twenty youths who would persistently push and abuse people who got in their way.

One of the Plough Boys explained that their rough behaviour had started getting them barred from local cinemas and cafes and, as their reputation grew, they were refused entry to places they had not even visited before. The one place that wasn't out of bounds was Clapham Common and this became their home: it was as if they owned it. If strangers dared to trespass on the Common it was seen as an open act of warfare. They were lads who were simply looking for trouble and it was against this background of territorialism, anti-social behaviour and violence that the murder took place.

* * *

At 9 p.m. on the warm evening of Thursday 2 July 1953, about 200 youths had gathered around the bandstand on the Common to hear musicians play covers of popular hits by the likes of Frankie Laine and Dickie Valentine. Some drank lemonade at the nearby cafe, others sat under the trees amid wafts of Brylcreem and aftershave, chatting while girls danced to the music. The boys mostly strutted and preened themselves, keeping a disinterested eye on the girls, some of whom were wearing short-fitting jackets worn over skin-tight sweaters and long skirts, the look emphasising the bust and hips. Many of the lads were dressed smartly with long, greased-back hair falling in an often-combed wave over their foreheads and sideburns. They wore long jackets with deep lapels, sometimes of velvet, together with white shirts, tapered trousers without turn-ups and thick crepe-soled shoes called 'creepers'.

Along with young Ronald Coleman, others on the Common that evening included a powerfully built labourer called Michael Davies, who was twenty, another labourer called John Allan, aged twenty-one, Terence Woodman, a sixteen-year-old street-trader, a carpenter called Allan Lawson, aged eighteen, and unemployed Terence Power, aged seventeen. The girls who frequented the Common and followed the Plough Boys around sometimes fought among themselves for the honour of going out with them. Some were said to be as ruthless as the lads.

Around 9.30 p.m. the band stopped playing and the crowd began to disperse. Four boys from outside the area, and not wearing the Edwardian fashion, were sitting in pairs on two benches, facing each other with their feet resting on the opposite seats. They were an apprentice electrical engineer called John Beckley, who was seventeen, from Walworth; Brian Carter, an eighteen-year-old sheet-metal worker from Southwark; Mathew Chandler, eighteen, a Bermondsey bank clerk; and John Ryan, nineteen, from Lambeth. Ronald Coleman approached with his girlfriend, seventeen-year-old Sylvia Clubb, and asked the four boys to move their feet so that they could pass. There was plenty of space on either side of the benches, which were not even on the public footpath, meaning there was no reason – except bloody-mindedness – why the couple could not detour round the youths. Coleman instead tried provocatively to push his way through but the lads refused to budge and the outnumbered Coleman turned away, only to receive that stinging insult from Ryan.

Coleman turned back to look at the four before going over to his mate, Michael Davies, who was standing with a girl called Sylvia Pilkington and her boyfriend, Bernard Wood, to tell him what had happened. Coleman warned that he would summon a couple of boys. Witness James Leaver claimed that at this point Davies produced a knife from his pocket and said, 'I will be all right with this.' Leaver was a friend of Wood and later in court it was suggested by Davies' defence that Leaver had invented his story to protect Wood, who had played a greater role in the incident.

The four friends wisely got up from the benches and walked off but as they reached a drinking fountain, north of the bandstand, they realised that they were being chased by about eight youths. Egged on by some girls, the Plough Boys laid into their rivals. It was later claimed that John Beckley was 'nominated' by one of the girls to be stabbed. As the frenzied mob closed in on him girls were said to have screamed, 'Knife him! Knife the —!'

At first the outnumbered group held their own. One of the four lashed out and decked one of his pursuers. A Plough Boy also threw a punch and felled one of the four, only for his victim to jump up and knock another one down. But two of the Plough Boys soon had him on the floor again, where he was kicked. Another two of the four went down and also took a kicking before struggling back up and knocking down their attackers. Then somebody shouted, 'Get out the knives.' Despite Ryan being stabbed in the shoulder, all four lads managed to flee. One sprinted to the right of the path onto the grass. Another went along a different path towards the far corner of the Common. Beckley and Chandler stayed together, continuing along the path towards Cedar Road. Their attackers split up to chase the boys in different directions.

Carter, who had veered to the right, was safe and managed to catch the train home. Ryan, who had headed for the far corner, also escaped after a desperate chase and caught a bus home. The other two came to a main road and were lucky to jump on a number 137 bus temporarily caught at traffic lights. As it began to move away they stood on the platform catching their breath, no doubt thankful for a lucky escape. The double-decker then turned into the main road, travelled about fifty yards and pulled up at the next bus stop. Waiting there were their attackers.

The pair were dragged off the bus and viciously assaulted. Two beat Chandler while the others focused on Beckley. Chandler managed to catch hold of the handrail and pull himself back on the bus, unaware that he had been stabbed in the stomach and groin. Beckley broke away and began to run towards Clapham Old Town, but after 100 yards he stopped, exhausted, and leaned back against a low wall outside a fashionable apartment block called Okeover Manor. In court, the prosecution alleged that he shouted: 'Go on then, stab me, stab me!' His attackers did just that: Beckley received two cuts to his scalp and six wounds to the body, one of which penetrated the main artery to his heart. He eventually sagged down the wall, ending up slumped in a half-sitting position on the pavement. The gang scarpered.

With the bus now stopped, a passenger made a phone call from a flat in Okeover Manor while another turned a folded coat into a makeshift pillow for Beckley. At 9.42 p.m., a policeman arrived and stayed with the teenager until the ambulance arrived and rushed him to Bolingbroke Hospital, not far from the Common. Beckley received a blood transfusion, but he died from a haemorrhage caused by stab wounds to the chest and abdomen. A newspaper subsequently spoke of 'the true shame of Clapham Common', for out of fifty passengers on the bus only four later came forward to testify about a murder which many of them, some seated on the top deck, must have witnessed.

A boy claimed that Davies afterwards ran to a church and said, 'I've got rid of the knife. There's no claret on it.' It was also alleged that later that night Davies went to a coffee stall where he demonstrated how he had used the blade. Another allegation was that, two days after the killing, Sylvia Clubb, Coleman's girlfriend, was standing near The Plough talking to Power and Davies about the fact that Coleman was being questioned by the police. Clubb said that if her boyfriend was charged she would go to the police to tell them who was the real murderer. Davies was then supposed to have threatened her, telling her that he would make sure that he was in prison for a minor offence, such as drunk and disorderly, when an attack upon her would take place, so that he could not be blamed. Power was also said to have threatened her if she dared go to the police.

After questioning local gangs, the police swiftly narrowed the field down to six likely suspects. All were arrested and charged with John Beckley's murder. 'You won't pin anything on me,' said one. However, after persistent questioning, all later confessed to having taken some part in the attack, though all denied using a knife. 'I was there but I didn't use any knife,' declared Michael Davies. Shown a tie taken from his home, he admitted that he had worn it on the fatal night; he was to find out later why the police considered his neckwear to be important. Ronald Coleman claimed to have been elsewhere with his girlfriend, before admitting, 'I was in the fight on the Common but not at the bus stop. I didn't stab him.' At first Terence Woodman denied any knowledge but then confessed, 'All right, I'll come clean but I didn't use the knife.' Allan Lawson claimed not to have seen any fight but then admitted involvement. Terence Power also denied that he was on the Common: 'If any bastard said that I was there, he is a liar. I don't want to say anything more. You prove it.' In a later interview with the police he confided, 'I want to tell you about it. Mickey Davies told you I was there. The — won't live long after he comes out from this because I'll do him. I only booted the fellow. I was not the one with the knife.' Another suspect, John Allan, was then arrested and admitted to being involved in the brawl at the fountain where he assaulted a lad – but not in the fight at the bus stop. He later owned up to a role in the scrap at the bus stop but denied using any knife.

* * *

After a three-day local hearing, the case was sent to the Central Criminal Court – the Old Bailey – for trial. On Monday, 14 September 1953, all six appeared before Mr Justice Pearson. Coleman and Davies pleaded not guilty to murdering John Beckley. Christmas Humphreys, prosecuting for the Crown, said that there was insufficient evidence against the other four on the indictment and they were formally acquitted. However, he said that there was a second indictment against them of committing common assault, and they were remanded in custody. After considering a verdict for over three hours, the jury could not reach a decision on Coleman and Davies, and the jury foreman said there was no hope of them doing so. Maxwell Turner, appearing for the Crown, then said that the prosecution no longer proposed putting Coleman on trial again on the charge of murder.

Appearing in the dock the next day, Coleman was told that no evidence would be offered against him. A new jury was sworn in and, on the direction of the judge, returned a formal verdict of not guilty. Coleman, however, was now charged with common assault along with the other four lads. All were found guilty. Lawson received six months' imprisonment, while his colleagues received nine months for what the judge described as 'miniature gang warfare'. Despite his young age, Ronald Coleman, who had started the whole affair, was considered too dangerous for borstal and was also imprisoned.

During the trial, the prosecution showed an interest in the strange-looking clothes the defendants had been wearing, asking if they had worn tight trousers and coats with a slit down the back. Coleman was asked by his defence, 'You were not completely Edwardian?' He explained that he was in 'narrow trousers' but not as narrow as the usual style. Because of this focus on youth fashions, the press, for the first time, began to associate the Edwardian style with violence. The *Daily Mirror* on 15 September 1953 summed up: 'Edwardian Suits, Dance Music and a Dagger'. The first proper reference to the existence of a new teenage phenomenon was in the *Evening Standard* of 23 September which spoke of gangs of teenage hooligans sporting 'Edwardian-style suits', who had become a regular nuisance every evening on Clapham Common. Coleman was described as 'the leader of the Edwardians'. The more popular name was officially born on the same day, after the *Daily Express* shortened Edward to Teddy and coined the term 'Teddy Boy' (which was later shortened again to 'Ted'). The newspaper acknowledged that this was a term already used by the youths' girlfriends.

Michael Davies was left to face the music on his own and went on trial at the Bailey between 19 and 22 October, before Mr Justice Hilbery. One crucial witness was Mary Frayling, a secretary, who claimed to have seen the attack from the top deck of the bus. She told the police that she had seen a particular youth, whom she described as the principal attacker, put what appeared to be a green-handled knife into his right breast pocket. He was wearing a gaudy tie, which he removed, putting it in another pocket. She later identified him as Davies.

His preoccupation with looking good was Davies' undoing. When he first appeared in the newspapers, his dress sense was mentioned but no significance attached to it – he was seen merely as a thug who happened to be obsessed by clothes. The newspapers then began to portray Davies as a dandy. Even from a young age, he was said to have been fanatical about flashy clothes. Just before the murder he had allegedly borrowed £12 from an uncle to buy a new suit. In his defence, Davies explained the presence of blood in his inside breast pocket by admitting to punching the bloodied Ryan and then reaching for his comb, which was in the pocket. Damningly, the judge, in his closing speech, remarked, 'He pauses, while a boy is lying crumpled up against the wall, to comb his hair. You might think that is the lowest moment of the defence.' This act of vanity was in fact pretty normal for lads fastidious about their appearance. For Teddy Boys, regular hair-combing was almost a nervous reflex.

Perhaps Miss Frayling was mistaken about what she had seen. It was, after all, late in the evening and her view on the moving bus, with its internal lights on, might have been obscured by both the relatively small windows and the large trees alongside the road. Indeed, Frayling had first picked out Davies as the main attacker while he was standing in the dock of a local South London court and not in an organised identity parade. Nevertheless, she kept exactly to the same story on the four occasions she appeared as a witness. After the trial she was commended by both police and the prosecution for her consistency.

It emerged that Davies had previous convictions. Aged nine he had appeared before a juvenile court and been bound over after entering an empty house with some mates. Later he was bound over again for shop-breaking and receiving. He spent a year in the Merchant Navy, making two voyages, before being called up for service in the Royal Air Force, from which he was discharged in April 1953. In February of that year he was conditionally discharged after receiving a pair of trousers. In May he was put on probation for two years after being found guilty of receiving two electric razors. The prosecution, in summing up, stressed that Davies had previously given evidence in court on his own behalf and yet had been found guilty, therefore making him an unreliable witness.

Although no murder weapon was ever found and no one – including the victim's friends – had seen Davies use a knife on the fateful night, the jury took just two hours to return a guilty verdict. The judge placed the black cap upon his head and told Davies that he would be taken to prison and hanged by the neck until he was dead, and may the Lord have mercy upon his soul.

Almost immediately after the verdict, many suspected that there had been a gross miscarriage of justice. Davies had been the only one of the original suspects to admit to the police that he had been present on the Common and involved in the brawl. His co-accused had wrongly suspected that he had grassed on them (it was in fact someone else). For their part, they and their friends almost certainly colluded and made subtle statements that suggested that Davies had carried a knife that evening. A few years later one of Davies' fellow suspects admitted that Davies was not a fighter but that when they were charged with the offence they had realised that he seemed to revel in the notoriety. His colleagues decided that if he wanted to take the blame then he could. They nevertheless knew that he was not the murderer.

Davies was sent to Wandsworth Prison, the site of 135 executions between 1878 and 1961, and put in a special cell for condemned prisoners. This was, in fact, three cells knocked into one and there were three lights in the ceiling, a bed and a wooden table with some chairs. On the table were books, magazines, a chess set and jigsaws, as if they could take a man's mind off his impending doom. The once stylishly dressed Davies was reduced to wearing loose, sloppy clothes, including carpet slippers and a shirt with no buttons, just knobs of cloth that went through the button holes. Davies came to realise that the plain metal door on the opposite wall was the one he had entered on his first night. He had originally thought that the space beyond was a cloakroom – it was, in fact, the execution chamber. It had a moveable wall like a shutter which was drawn back to become a larger room used to conduct the hanging. Just to the side of the door was a cross, strategically placed so that it was the last thing the prisoner saw before he met his maker. The day of execution was fixed for 11 November 1953 but later postponed as the case was due before the Court of Criminal Appeal on 1 December.

When the appeal failed, a new execution date was set for 18 December, a week before Christmas. On two occasions Davies was moved out of the condemned cell so that other prisoners could be hanged, before being returned. His date of execution was postponed once again as the appeal went up to the House of Lords. A petition pleading for clemency was raised containing over thirty thousand signatures. On 21 January 1954, Davies was reprieved and sentenced instead to life imprisonment. He had spent ninety-two days in the condemned cell, including his twenty-first birthday. Overjoyed that he could now look smart again, albeit in different prison clothes, the first words that the fashion-conscious Davies said to his mother and sister were, 'Look, they're letting me wear a collar and tie.'

* * *

While Davies served out his sentence, the Labour politician and social reformer Frank Pakenham, better known as Lord Longford, offered his help. However, such was the public feeling against his interest in the case that when an article appeared in the *Sunday Empire News*, Lord Longford received anonymous letters warning that he would be razor-slashed and scarred for life. In 1958, despite the ongoing campaign and after considering so-called 'breakthroughs' from Davies' supporters, the Home Secretary, R.A. ('Rab') Butler, could still find nothing to alter his opinion of the case. He did, however, decide to limit the period of imprisonment which Davies had to serve so that, with good behaviour, he would be released in two years. By now there were statements from many of the original suspects stating that Davies was not the murderer, along with written evidence that one of the original suspects had swapped a bloody suit with a friend.

Although he was not officially pardoned, Davies was finally released from prison in October 1960 after serving seven years, while Longford continued his battle to obtain a Queen's pardon. Now a free man, Davies said that he did not want money or compensation; he merely wanted to clear his name for the sake of his family. In the eyes of the law, however, he was still a murderer. Nobody else was ever charged with the murder of John Beckley. Davies, who eventually married and bought a house, later told a journalist that he had met the actual killer in a public house while on parole.

It was a senseless killing that had a massive social and cultural impact. The usual motivations or mitigations did not seem to apply. Both the Clapham accused and his victim came from seemingly happy homes. For writer Jeff Nuttall, 'The murder was not done for gain or revenge or the hand of a girl. It was the first casualty in the excitement game, the first of an unending series of teenage killings.' Nuttall puts it all down to a love of excitement. 'Theft was understandable. Revenge was understandable but the principle of excitement was not.' Disturbingly, this love of excitement was what drove post-war youth.

Tony Parker, in his published account of the trial, wrote that Michael Davies was not the first person to have been condemned to death not so much for his alleged crime as for representing something which the public found both detestable and threatening to their secure way of life. In Davies' case he became a symbol of the phenomenon known as the Teddy Boy, even if his clothes and hairstyle weren't the best possible example.

The sensationalist newspaper headlines meant that not only was Davies on trial but also all that he and his stylishly dressed companions represented. The Clapham Common murder launched the violent public image of the Teddy Boy far and wide. From now on Teds were not just rebellious youths who liked to dress in gaudy clothes; they were capable of killing people. Yet the truth was that, while the Teds' clothes made them stand out from the drab post-war crowd of faceless conformity, the phenomenon of fashion-conscious, aggressive young men was actually nothing new.

2

COSH BOYS

'Ever since that night when a boy called Craig crouched on the roof of a warehouse and began to blaze away with a gun, killing a policeman, people have been seriously asking themselves if there is something wrong with the whole teenage generation.'

Illustrated magazine, 1953

Standing before a court in 1954, three Teddy Boys accused of burglary were told, 'You seem only to ape Edwardians in their dress. It would be far better if you adopted their code of honour.' This view, from the chairman of Liverpool Juvenile Court, was far from unique in the criminal justice system. The following year, at the trial of a Nottingham Ted who was alleged to have slashed four youths, Mr Justice Stable stated: 'If these young men instead of imitating the garments of forty years ago imitated how people behaved then they would do much better.' J.T. Jackson, a Crewe county councillor, also felt that the Edwardian label was not in keeping with the age it was supposed to represent, for the original Edwardians had been noted for the virtues of good clean living and service to God and man.

Did such an earlier golden age of high moral standards ever exist? It could be argued that the new Edwardians of the 1950s had a great deal in common with their namesakes from the beginning of the century, particularly the working-class hooligan element of the urban slums. In one sense the Teds were nothing new. If their sense of fashion belonged to an earlier age, so did their behaviour, for the Teddy Boys were not the first generation of youths to adopt a uniform and a fighting spirit. The bloody street-warfare, weapon-carrying and territorialism all had their origins in the previous century at least. In 1963 the *Daily Mirror* suggested that the Teds were merely a modern-day version of the Peaky Blinders, gangs of youths from Birmingham who were active in the late nineteenth and early twentieth century. Their name derived from their caps worn with the peak pulled down, done not only for fashion purposes but to avoid recognition by witnesses to their misdemeanours in a similar way that 21st century youths wore hooded tops.

The *Salford City Reporter* considered the Teds to be descendants of the 'scuttlers' and it is true to say that the first fashion-conscious street gangs were not the Teds but these late-Victorian working-class teenagers from the rough districts of Manchester and Salford. Rival mobs such as the Bungall Boys, Buffalo Bill's gang and the Bengal Tigers would engage in neighbourhood-based fights or 'scuttles'. Their uniform consisted of bell-bottomed trousers, a loose white scarf worn around the neck, hair plastered down on the forehead and a cap, tilted to display what was known as a 'donkey fringe'. Brass-tipped pointed clogs, hidden under the flared ends of the trousers, were ideal for kicking opponents, while the scuttling sound made by hobnails on cobbles probably gave them their name.

While scuttling was on its way out by the late 1890s, another worrying phase of youth disorder was about to begin in London. 'Hooligan' gangs made their media debut after an August Bank Holiday festival in 1898. Like the scuttlers, they not only fought against each other but they also wore a similar uniform of bell-bottomed trousers over their boots, neck scarves, and caps, sometimes of velvet or plaid, depending on the particular gang affiliation. Belts, some studded with sharp brass caps, were also adapted for fighting.

The term 'hooligan' is of Irish origin. While the Irish were usually blamed for exporting their supposedly unique brand of brutality to Victorian England, over half a century later, when Teddy Boys began springing up in Northern Ireland, a Mrs

Haughton of the Child Welfare Council stated that they were a nasty 'English invention', thereby reversing the usual mode of thinking.

Where Victorian gangs made improvised weapons out of belts, hob-nailed boots and (allegedly) razors fixed to their peaked caps, their modern heirs hid razor-blades and bicycle chains inside coat collars and used large rings as knuckle-dusters. Like earlier gangs, the Teddy Boys' best weapon was their sheer number, which they used to intimidate both their rivals and innocent members of the public. Such common factors suggest that gang behaviour is somewhat traditional, being passed down from one generation to another, and gangs of various periods and widespread locations are certainly bound together by familiar delinquent behaviours, including rituals of territorial dominance, trials of strength, gang fights, the mocking of adult authority and antagonism towards outsiders.

* * *

The Teds were also the successors of aggressive young men of the early 1950s known as 'cosh boys'. In 1949, cinemagoers flocked to see the Ealing classic *The Blue Lamp*, a film about a policeman murdered in a shoot-out, a rare crime in post-war Britain, although it would be echoed by the infamous Craig and Bentley case three years later. The audience could rest assured, however, that the culprit was caught and punished, and justice done. Despite the awful crime, the film portrays an image of law-abiding decency that was perpetuated for another two decades in its spin-off TV series, *Dixon of Dock Green*.

Away from the happy endings of the cinema, in the real world of austerity, inner-city slums and rationing, a wave of ruthless criminals, many of them young, was gathering to shatter the old order and its rosy image of a peaceful, law-abiding country. The authorities were forced to focus on the enemies within, particularly the burglars, juvenile delinquents and spivs who had thrived under wartime conditions. Like the slang term 'yob' (a reversal of 'boy'), the word spiv was a reversal of VIPs, and an ironic term for wartime traders in the black market.

It seems that Britain had won the war only to face a major social crisis at home. Crime became a political hot potato. In 1952, in the House of Commons, the Home Secretary Sir David Maxwell Fyfe was informed that people were being 'robbed, maimed and murdered daily in our towns and cities'. Throughout the early 1950s various politicians painted a terrifying picture of a lawless country. The language was meant to shock: 'lustful and savage acts of cruelty and violence', 'this terrible wave of crimes', 'the degree of violence employed is becoming more brutal', a 'growing concern felt throughout the country at the increase in crimes of violence and brutality', etc.

It could be claimed that this was merely politicians scoring points over the opposition, but the crime statistics only confirmed a deepening catastrophe. Having risen by half during the war years, recorded indictable offences had not only failed to recede in peacetime but had, in 1951, reached a new high. Although crime statistics are never accurate reflectors of criminal activity, the figures nevertheless looked appalling when compared to the pre-war years. In 1938 only one per cent of fourteen- to seventeen-year olds were convicted of an indictable offence; by 1951 that figure had doubled. In 1936, 2,533 offences of murder, attempted murder, manslaughter, wounding, indictable assault, robbery and rape were known to the police in England and Wales; in 1951 the figure had soared to 7,188.

The shocking rise in violent crime turned the spotlight on the cosh boys. Named after their choice of weapon, which included anything from a sock filled with sand to a lead pipe, they regularly appeared in the newspapers. '16 Cosh Boys Raid a Night School' ran the headline in *The Citizen* in December 1950, after a gang of youths armed with bludgeons and chains attacked the principal and damaged property in West Dulwich. By then London cosh boys were under pressure from the police, who had begun stopping suspects and searching them for weapons. Some youths responded by using a shilling's worth of coins in a knotted handkerchief; swung with force, this seemingly innocent weapon was extremely dangerous. In the Elephant & Castle area, some youths favoured the leather passenger straps with a ball-shaped end torn from the ceilings of Tube carriages on the Bakerloo line.

A particularly nasty cosh boy attack took place in 1952. Four masked lads broke into the Lancashire home of Annie Metcalfe, a 79-year-old spinster who lived alone. One of them carried an air pistol while two others had coshes. Demanding money, they burnt her face with a cigarette. The terrified woman offered them £1 in silver and promised to give them more money the next day. She duly withdrew £40 (today worth over £2,000) from the bank and handed it over at an appointed place. The boys, still carrying coshes and masks, were later captured during another robbery at a hotel. The judge called them 'disgraceful little cowards' and jailed each of them for five years.

Illustrated magazine described the typical cosh boy in 1953: 'He invariably wears buttonless clothes, and ox-blood coloured shoes ... A silk handkerchief cascades from his breast-pocket. But his flashy silk tie is his real pride and joy. He may well take ten minutes to put it on before he sets out for his headquarters – the inevitable "caff" in some brightly lit High Street.' The association between crime and clothing certainly predated the Teds. During the early 1950s it became common to relate young people's clothing to growing levels of delinquency and a general decline in moral values. What shocked police Superintendent Robert Fabian of Scotland Yard was not simply the knuckle-dusters and flick-knives found on arrested cosh boys, but their flamboyant clothing. He described two fifteen-year-olds sporting the garb of the London spiv, with drape jackets and bright bow ties, vivid thick-soled shoes and trousers hitched high to flaunt red-and-yellow socks: 'Here, in this costume, are all the ingredients of exhibitionism – peacocks strutting to attract attention,' Fabian mused.

The drape style, and post-war fears about law and order, merged to become a national issue in 1952, the year of the Craig and Bentley case. Derek Bentley and Christopher Craig were found guilty of murdering a policeman after a botched robbery at a Croydon warehouse. Bentley, who had the mental age of an eleven-year-old, was in police custody at the time the officer died and did not fire the gun; the ambiguous command he was supposed to have shouted to his armed accomplice – 'Let him have it, Chris' – has been the subject of much debate. Even if the words were uttered, was Bentley pleading for Craig to hand over the weapon or cold-bloodedly ordering the policeman's execution? The jury decided the latter. However Craig was only sixteen, leaving nineteen-year-old Bentley to face the hangman's noose alone in January 1953. Craig went on to serve ten years in prison.

The pair embodied society's worst fears about the damaging effects of American culture on Britain's youth. The press drew attention to the defendants' 'flashy' American-style clothes and demeanour. On their way to commit the crime, they were wearing wide-brimmed hats, calf-length overcoats, fingertip-length drape jackets and crepe-soled shoes. Craig also alternated between his native South London accent and a gangster-style American drawl, no doubt inspired by his three or four trips to the cinema each week. The case firmly fixed in the minds of the public the problem not only of juvenile delinquency but of fashion and the corrupting influence of American culture. The scene was set for the coming media infatuation with the new breed of young Edwardians.

The cosh boy phenomenon reached its height in 1953 with the release of a movie of the same name, directed by Lewis Gilbert. Billed as 'The Year's Most Controversial Film!' by enthusiastic cinema managers, *Cosh Boy* was the first British-made picture to be awarded an X certificate, which meant that it could only be watched by those aged over sixteen. With its stark and atmospheric shots of London's bombed-out ruins, the film captures the remains of old London, before it made way for tower blocks and walkway estates. *Cosh Boy* was well ahead of its time in its frank depiction of juvenile delinquency, unmarried teenage sex, pregnancy and abortion: all deeply shocking for most in the repressive early 1950s.

The movie charts the exploits of Roy Walsh, a sixteen-year-old thug from a decent home who is the boss of a gang of youths in Hammersmith, West London. Roy is convincingly nasty, vicious, hyperactive and insecure. He bullies anyone weaker than himself, particularly his slow-witted accomplice Alfie and his naïve girlfriend Rene, played by a young Joan Collins. The parallels with the case of Derek Bentley were not lost on the audience, or the censor.

The film was said to have inspired at least one murder. In 1953, 21-year-old George Newland, from Walthamstow, North East London, robbed and battered a pensioner to death with a claw hammer because he needed money for a new suit. Newland explained to the police, 'I am sorry I did this. What really got into my mind was a cosh boy picture I saw the other day.' He was later hanged.

Around the time of the movie's release, the *Daily Record* came up with an eye-catching front-page headline, 'Total War Against Cosh Gangs', posted gratuitously onto a story about the progression of the Prevention of Crime Bill through the House of Commons. The Prevention of Crime Act 1953 was passed primarily to deal with the cosh boys and prohibited the carrying of any offensive weapon in a public place without lawful authority or reasonable excuse.

Some claimed that the makers of *Cosh Boy* were trying to cash in on the latest criminal craze but the movie was actually based on a play called *Master Crook*, written by Bruce Walker three years before the Craig–Bentley case. The play was also later turned into a novel with the leading characters now referred to as Teddy Boys. Occasionally the Edwardian and cosh boy threats merged, as in the *Daily Mail*'s account of two London youths in Teddy Boy uniform who coshed and robbed a man in Fleet Street in 1954. By then, however, the term cosh boy had almost disappeared from the newspapers, replaced by the quaint but somehow terrifying phrase 'Teddy Boy'.

* * *

For some the terms 'Teddy Boy' and 'Edwardian' were simply new labels for something that already existed. In Parliament Sir Thomas Moore declared, 'Instead of using the word "Edwardian", would not the proper description be "young thugs", leaving it at that?' At a school speech day, R.T. Spooner, chairman of West Bromwich Education Committee, told pupils and parents that he detested the name Teddy Boy because it brought to mind something 'warm, cuddly and pleasant'. Teds were none of these things; they were 'thoroughly objectionable'. John Woolfenden, Liverpool's chief probation officer, felt the term was merely a sentimental name for louts and thieves. He also called Teddy Boys 'miserable' and 'sordid' but made a distinction between them and youth in general – claiming that the present generation of youths were the finest there had ever been, and shouldn't be confused with the Teds. In 1957 the Chief Constable of Somerset went further when he explained that young people labelled Teddy Boys were no worse than young people of his own generation.

There was still something crucially different about the Teds that set them apart from earlier working-class criminal gangs. Leicester's *Illustrated Chronicle* explained: 'The mantle of terror and violence, once worn by the gaudy spiv of post-war years, has been assumed by the Teddy Boy. But the Teddy Boy is a worse menace.' The *Brighton and Hove Herald* also considered Teddy Boys to be a greater threat than the racecourse gangs active after the First World War. These gangs were said to have fought only among themselves: they did not normally interfere with the public. Modern thugs, however, lashed out indiscriminately at innocent people who were minding their own business. Superintendent Fabian also believed Teddy Boy violence differed from that meted out by villains in the past. He felt that earlier thugs, including racecourse 'minders', would expect to be paid handsomely for dishing out a beating, when the teenage gangsters of the early 1950s would willingly use knives or chains on those who merely stood in their way.

For the Teds, violence seemed to be an end in itself with no secondary purpose. There was rarely any financial gain, merely a love of brutality. It was said that a Ted might knock an opponent into the gutter and kick him in the face but he would never stoop so low as to then steal his wallet. As one Birmingham Ted explained, 'I fight for the kicks, just for the thrill of it like.'

Inter-gang warfare was to provide many such thrills. On 11 October 1953, in the aftermath of the horror over the Clapham Common murder, a fight in a Brighton dance hall between local lads and a mob from London was referred to as 'gang warfare' between groups of Edwardian youths. It was the first outbreak of the phenomenon recorded in the press. The incident began when a sixteen-year-old barrow boy from Mitcham, Surrey, wearing a long grey Edwardian coat with a velvet collar, black drainpipe trousers and a loud scarf, punched from behind a seventeen-year-old Brighton sign-writer called John Davey, knocking him unconscious. Another youth, however, later testified that after Davey had been hit he turned around and floored his attacker before kicking him in the stomach. Whatever the exact details, the assault sparked a free-for-all in which chairs were wielded as weapons. '"Edwardian" youth on dance fight charge' was the headline in the [Brighton] *Evening Argus*.

* * *

Reverend Douglas Griffiths worked closely with London toughs at his Methodist Youth Centre in Lambeth, South London, in the early 1950s. He later reflected that there were three separate waves of adolescent gang activity in London in the post-war years. The first was the era of the cloth-capped gangs of Razor Boys, in the years immediately after the war. Next were the Teddy Boys, who carried knuckle-dusters. Griffiths said that in London the big Teddy Boy gangs broke up as the fashion spread and it became impossible to distinguish a 'true Ted'; as more youths adopted items of Edwardian clothing, the ties that bound them together were loosened, until the original gang spirit and cohesion were completely lost and the Teds were no longer a community which stood alone against society.

Finally, around 1955–56, came the third wave: more sophisticated groups of adolescents in Italian clothes who went about in smaller, more purposeful gangs. For Griffiths this was the worst. Already he sensed a moral deterioration in the heirs of the original Teddy Boys, finding in the more criminally minded among them a marked lack of standards or restraints. Almost nostalgically, he later claimed that the original Teds had their own code of conduct, including obsessive loyalty to each other; they were also kind to children and the elderly. The new gangs had no such morals, as shown by their later involvement in the Notting Hill disturbances (see chapter 16), when Teds roamed the streets indiscriminately beating up black immigrants. It was this newer generation of youths that caused the bulk of the trouble – and kept the newspapers in stories until the late 1950s and beyond.

The Teddy Boys might have been a completely unique phenomenon or they might simply have been a more smartly dressed continuation of what went before. What is certain is that their style owed a great deal to the past.

3

THE ORIGINS OF THE STYLE

'I don't know why they call them "Teddy Boys". I think it would make the late King Edward turn in his grave.'

(Superintendent Redfern, 1956)

Accounts vary as to exactly when and where the distinctive Teddy Boy look actually began. Conventional wisdom has it that the working-class adoption of Edwardian fashions started in the Elephant & Castle area of South East London around 1953. It makes sense that youths from that area, visiting Soho and the West End for their Saturday night entertainment, were so impressed by the Mayfair Edwardian look – or at least its Soho imitations – that they took it back home.

A number of factors challenge this view. The Clapham Common murder happened in South West London, and not the South East. Also, the first recorded episode of inter-gang warfare involving Edwardian-clad youths actually took place on the south coast, in the seaside resort of Brighton. Gangs from the Elephant & Castle do not appear in any of the local newspapers during 1953. The first photographs of authentic Teds were, in fact, published in a November 1953 issue of the *Daily Mirror* and taken at a dance hall in Tottenham, North London. Another theory has it that the first Teds emerged around Tottenham and Highbury. From there the style was said to have spread southwards to Streatham, Battersea and Purley, and westwards to Shepherd's Bush and Fulham.

Coincidentally, and somewhat puzzlingly, as early as October 1952 the *Sunday Pictorial* published a photo of bop fans jitterbugging in the Northumberland market town of Hexham, twenty-five miles from Newcastle. At least one lad is wearing tight trousers, a longish jacket and brothel-creeper shoes with thick soles – with his hair styled just like Tony Curtis. Something was clearly happening nationwide, although no-one could foresee what it was. It is perhaps safest to conclude that the fashion was springing up simultaneously in various places at around the same time.

* * *

The Edwardian style revival was kick-started after the Second World War by a group of Savile Row tailors, the arbiters of British upper-class style. It made a welcome change from the drab and shapeless men's fashions that hadn't altered much for decades. Of course most fashions are a reaction to something that went before; in the 1920s, 'Oxford bags' were a liberating response to the tightness of earlier trouser styles. The Edwardian style reversed this trend, although tailors confessed they did not think the fad would last as long as the craze for Oxford bags because the suits were so expensive and could not be worn for work.

Edwardian dress consisted of a long, narrow-lapelled jacket, narrow trousers (but hardly 'drainpipes'), ordinary toe-capped shoes and an ornate waistcoat. A white shirt with a cut-away collar was adorned by a tie fastened with a Windsor knot. For those who favoured a hat, the Trilby or narrow-brimmed bowler was preferred. Wealthy young men, including Guards officers, picked up on this new tailored look that harked back to the style of their fathers and grandfathers, over forty years earlier. This was arguably the last golden moment for the British aristocracy, the so-called long Edwardian summer, a time when the social classes knew their place and Britain ruled half the world. The time had come for post-war Britain to regain a sense of pride, to offset the decline of a once-powerful Empire.

These upper-class dandies were perhaps also cocking a snook at the post-war Labour government with its austerity measures and reviled social levelling. Perhaps they feared that their social position was under threat. At the end of the war the country had been promised a more classless and equal society; by wearing clothes that boldly emphasised the social distinction between upper and lower classes, it was as if these elegant men-about-town were mocking the very idea of everyone pulling together. The style also signalled a rejection of mass American culture, with its chewing gum, comics and weird distortions of the mother tongue, in favour of something uniquely English. As much as this new style looked back nostalgically to happier times, it also looked to the future, signalling that the war was over and a new era of optimism had begun.

Upper-class flirtation with Edwardian chic lasted from around 1948 to the coronation of Queen Elizabeth II in 1953. It spread from Mayfair to young city clerks, before being hijacked and modified by gangs of working-class youths with money in their pockets – at which point the upper classes quickly began to ditch what had now become a disreputable style. One ex-Guardee complained that the whole of his wardrobe had immediately become unwearable.

By 1953, Savile Row had already abandoned the look. A year later, London's leading tailors were advocating the 'Backward Look', boasting broader jacket lapels and wider trousers, in an attempt to counter the adoption of the Edwardian trend by the Teds. In the same year, second-hand Edwardian suits were to be found on sale in various markets around the capital, abandoned by their wealthy owners. The style now belonged solely to the working classes.

* * *

Something was happening too on the other side of the Atlantic. In early February 1940, a young American busboy called Clyde Duncan entered Frierson McEver's tailors in the town of Gainesville, Georgia, with an unusual request. The Blue Mountain foothills were hardly the centre of world fashion, and Duncan's demand for a particular style of suit so startled tailor A. C. McEver that he felt the need to report it to the trade journal *Men's Apparel Reporter.* So odd was the design that McEver tried to talk his customer out of it, but Duncan was adamant. The controversial style either was already, or later became, known in South Georgia as the 'Killer Diller'. It would become much more widely known as the 'zoot suit' – an overstated box-like jacket hanging halfway down to the kneecap, with outrageously padded shoulders that made the wearer look like an American footballer. The suits were worn with trousers severely tapered at the ankles.

This story, however compelling, is only one of various explanations for this revolution in American men's fashion. It is difficult to nail down the origin of the zoot. Like all fashion innovations it has several roots, including Harlem jazz culture, particularly the flamboyant style of bandleader Cab Calloway. Some speculate that it was inspired by the authentic American Civil War clothing worn by Clark Gable's Rhett Butler in *Gone With The Wind*. The timing fits, as the film had opened in Georgia two or three months before Duncan visited Frierson McEver and made his historic request. *The Chicago Defender* also attributed the style to champion boxer Henry Armstrong whose small stature required a body-enhancing suit.

The zoot suit was adopted by gangs of black and Mexican-American youths (called *pachucos*) who had migrated to Southern California; a large but mainly invisible minority group, they proudly flaunted this new and extrovert style to forge an identity separate from their parents' Hispanic culture. It was the black American Zooties, however, who made the most impact, largely because it was what many of the major jazz musicians wore.

The zoot style became a symbol of moral panic and juvenile delinquency after inspiring the Los Angeles riots in the summer of 1943. Significantly, it was the swarming military towns along the Pacific coast and the industrial districts of Detroit, Pittsburgh and Los Angeles that experienced the fiercest outbreaks of zoot suit rioting. With the entry of the United States into the Second World War in December 1941, the nation had to come to terms with the restrictions of rationing, particularly of fabrics. New regulations effectively banned the manufacture of loose-fitting zoot suits and most legitimate tailoring companies ceased to make, or advertise, any suits that fell outside the War Production Board's guidelines. However, a network of bootleg tailors based in Los Angeles and New York continued to cater for black-market demand, making the schism between servicemen and the Zooties immediately visible. If the chino shirt and military dress were the uniform of patriotism, the baggy zoot suit became an unpatriotic and provocative means of flouting the official regulations of rationing.

During weeks of rioting, servicemen re-established their authority by ritually humiliating the zoot-suiters. Gangs of US Marines thought it their duty to waylay wearers, strip them down to their underwear and leave them half-naked in the streets. In one incident, some drunken sailors ambushed two victims in the cinema, dragged them onto the stage, stripped them in front of the audience and, as a final humiliation, urinated on their suits.

An article on the zoot fashion, published in the *Daily Mail* in 1943, claimed it would not take off in Britain and would be forgotten in six months. A few years later though elements of the fashion were indeed being worn on British streets, thanks mainly to the influence of Hollywood films and the presence of black American GIs during the war, followed by the arrival of sharp-suited West Indian immigrants on the *Empire Windrush*, which docked at Tilbury, Essex, in 1948.

* * *

Another influential innovation was the 'American look' introduced by British tailor Cecil Gee around 1946. Gee was an astute East End Jewish tailor who imported colourful American kipper ties and shiny shirts to the drab streets of London's Charing Cross Road. He also made copies of drape suits. A clear break from the demob suit, the 'American look' was heavily influenced by gangster chic and had close affinities to the zoot suit. After a while though, Gee became so concerned about the negative criminal associations of his new look that he decided to ditch it and promote Italian-inspired clothing instead. He claimed that he could have made a fortune, but with murders being committed in Soho and gangs taking part in street fights, he reasoned that these weren't the sort people with whom he wanted to do business.

The Edwardian uniform, as adopted by the Teds, owes its origins as much to the American zoot as to the stylistic innovations of Savile Row. In his novel *Hurry on Down* (1953), John Wain describes an early incarnation of the Teddy Boys standing outside a London dance hall. There is an American influence, particularly in the loud tweed jackets and flannels, with broad suede shoes. Some have their long jackets unbuttoned to show off their brightly coloured American-style shirts. A few wear their hair swept back into shiny quiffs, stiff with grease. Several have brushed their hair smoothly back, without a parting, while others sport merely a thin covering of scrub, three-eighths of an inch long.

When imported to Britain, the 'American drape' style soon became associated with the 'spivs'. Easily identified by their exaggerated, wide-shouldered suits and lurid ties, spivs were also known as 'wide boys', meaning wide awake or streetwise and able to live off their wits. While the authorities disapproved of them, many people welcomed the opportunity to purchase items made scarce by rationing, such as nylons and chocolates. Spivs, along with the so-called cosh boys, were the spiritual if not stylistic ancestors of the Teds, though the chukka boots and brocade waistcoats worn by some might also have been an influence.

The distinction between English and American influences was made early on. In 1953, a contributor to the British *Tailor and Cutter* magazine explained that many press reports of hooligans wearing Edwardian clothes were incorrect: such lads were actually wearing American-style fingertip-length drapes and zoot trousers. The working-class version of the Edwardian style was more a synthesis of English and American influences, no doubt the result of watching movies about gangsters and gunslingers. The hairstyles, ever-tighter trousers, bootlace ties and crepe-soled shoes were unrelated to the original English Edwardian style.

It is also worth mentioning the claim that it was the French *Zazous* in the 1940s who invented the Teddy Boy uniform. In 1959 it was pointed out that the style was merely part of a cultural exchange between the French and English, whereby English youths borrowed and resurrected the *Zazous* look, adding the bicycle chains and flick-knives, and exporting it back to France, where it became part of a later delinquent movement known as *Blousons Noirs* (Black Windcheaters; see chapter 25).

The name *Zazous* probably derives from a line in the song 'Zah Zuh Zaz' by jazz musician Cab Calloway. Another possible inspiration was the hit song 'I'm Swing' by French crooner Johnny Hess, with its nonsense lyric 'Za zou, za zou, za zou, za zou ze'. The *Zazous* were a group of a few hundred young people, aged between seventeen and twenty, living in France during the Second World War. The Parisian quarter of Saint Germain was one of the movement's centres. The *Zazous* expressed their individuality by wearing brash, oversized jackets adorned with multiple vents and pockets, similar to the American zoot suit – the amount of material used being a defiant snub to clothing rationing issued by the German occupiers. Young men also wore narrow trousers and sported bright handkerchiefs. Their shirt collars were high and secured by gold horizontal pins. Thick-soled suede shoes were worn with white or brightly coloured socks and the lads used olive oil to fashion ornate quiffs out of their longish hair. The 'decadent' *Zazous* loved dancing wildly to swing jazz, a style of black music condemned by the occupying Germans and collaborationist press.

The movement did also have its political implications, developing into a loosely organised protest against the severity of the Vichy regime. Working-class *Zazous* stole cloth and engaged in other black-market activities in order to put together their outfits, sometimes stitching their own clothes. Just as American servicemen would defile the clothing of zoot-suiters, so, in July 1942, a collaborationist French youth group called Jeunesse Populaire Francaise was targeting and attacking the *Zazous*. Armed with hair-clippers, they set out to 'Scalp the *Zazous*'. The press also sought to have members sent to work camps, forcing some to go into hiding.

* * *

Whatever the origins of the Teddy Boy style, its wearers were certainly attracted to it because they wanted to look good and stand out from the crowd. With a mixture of aspiration, arrogance and rebelliousness, the original Teds refused to conform to the 'Sunday best' sartorial traditions of their parents and grandparents. This idea of young people having their own fashion was something unique. Before the war, adults and young people usually wore the same style of clothing, mainly because youths had little or no money. Even after the war, when some teenagers were beginning to earn good wages, there was no market for clothes, food, music or entertainment aimed specifically at them. The business world had yet to recognise and exploit the vast consumer potential of teenage custom. It was only from the mid-1950s onwards that the increased spending power of adolescents inspired the advertising and marketing industries to focus on teenage consumers.

The Teds had to create their own unique fashion by borrowing and stealing stylistic touches from elsewhere. A reader of *The Times* wondered whether the hostility they attracted was due to the fact that, for the first time in history, working-class youths had assembled their own unique look rather than directly copying the fashions of their betters. Similarly, for youth worker Elizabeth Stucley the interesting thing was that while most styles came from the upper classes and filtered down, Teddy Boys had the enterprise to reverse the trend and to design a working-class look that eventually spread upwards, so that high-end fashion brands such as Hardy Amies and Dior began to add Edwardian touches to some of their women's collections.

Since it was created from the bottom up, rather than dictated by fashion stylists and experts, the style was never fixed. Although it maintained some common elements, it was adapted, modified, customised and personalised over time and depending on the region of its wearer. Nevertheless, the early Teds looked quite different from the caricatures and cartoon representations of later years, particularly the 1970s when glam-rock-influenced bands such as Showaddywaddy helped create a completely distorted picture. For a more authentic look we must go back to the beginning.

4
THE LOOK

'To be a young man in 1955, and to aspire towards even a semblance of style, was to be a Teddy boy.'

(George Pearson, writer)

In November 1953, the *Daily Mirror* interviewed and photographed an eighteen-year-old Ted called Leonard Sims. He had designed his own suit and had his tailor make it up. It consisted of a single-breasted jacket with four buttons, high narrow lapels, turn-back cuffs and four outside pockets adorned with flaps and buttons. This set him back £20. Sims also spent £6 on high-waisted, twelve-inch-wide whipcord pants. His black ankle-boots, without toe-caps, cost another £5. He also owned two silk poplin shirts costing 65 shillings and various Slim-Jim ties with tie pins. Sims criticised colleagues who went for an over-the-top look with knee-length jackets, tight trousers and velvet collars. 'Nothing flash' was his fashion philosophy.

As Sims admitted, his style was only one version. In more detail, working from top to bottom, the Ted uniform consisted of a number of elements. First up was the hair. By the 1950s youths were letting their hair grow longer as a reaction to the National Service regulation short-back-and-sides. Many copied the look of American actor Tony Curtis. There was also the Boston, in which the hair was greased straight back into a quiff and cut square across at the nape, above a shaved neck. **A barber called Angel Rose, from Tottenham Court Road, London, claimed to have invented the quiff, the Ted's signature haircut.** Another popular feature was the DA, where the hair at the back was greased in from the sides to form the shape of a 'duck's arse' (District Attorney was a more polite use of the initials). The DA was reputedly pioneered in Britain by the Hounslow hairdresser Len Pountney. The popularity of Elvis Presley meant that his style became the norm.

Combs and grooming products such as grease and Brylcreem became essential, particularly as the quiffs became more elaborate. Towards the end of the 1950s came the 'elephant's trunk', a long quiff swept forward and left to dangle over the face. Some Teds had their hair styled once a fortnight, requiring the use of driers and hairnets. One West End barber claimed that lads paid anything between 5s 6d and 32s 6d a time; quite an expenditure for young wage-earners. Ray Gosling, who later became a journalist and broadcaster, recalls one specialist salon: after the hair was washed, the quiff would be curled with hot irons before being finished off under the drier, held in place with a hairnet. Teds maintained the look with coconut grease from Boots. Gosling recalls a particularly cold day when his hair froze stiff and he had to stand near a boiler to thaw it out, resulting in melted grease running down the back of the neck, ruining his white shirt.

One Ted revealed that some of the boys used to have their hair permed; he didn't see anything wrong with it. The ten-shilling wave was optional for Manchester lads who needed to keep the hair out of their eyes in labouring jobs. Most opted for a crew cut or Tony Curtis style for four bob, shampoo included, which lasted for two weeks. For many of the older generation, particularly those who had fought in the war, all this styling must have seemed rather effeminate. The Teds' obsession with their hair certainly shocked one newspaper gossip columnist, who found two drape-suited young men in the cloakroom of an Aberdeen dance hall, both wielding combs, carefully tending to each other's quiffs.

The decline of hat-wearing among young men was blamed on these elaborate and expensive haircuts, which cried out to be shown off. One manufacturer joked about marketing transparent hats. One hat that was popular among London Teds, however, was the flat-sided cap known as a 'cheese cutter'.

Essential to the look by the late-1950s were whiskers, in the form of sideboards or sideburns (named after American Civil War General Ambrose Burnside), sprouting well below the ear-lobes. Early Teds did not wear long sideburns; if worn at all they were ear-lobe length, as popularised by Elvis Presley, particularly after he became a Hollywood star in 1956. Younger Teds, of course, were too young to grow them. Nevertheless, when teenage boys sporting sideburns were barred from a dance hall in Newcastle in 1961 they were allowed to visit a nearby police station to shave them off. In an attempt to avoid being barred from venues, it seems they had stopped wearing their drape suits and grew sideburns as an alternative badge of Teddyism. English rock 'n' roll singer Vince Taylor was ordered to shave off his sideburns before appearing on ITV's *Oh Boy!* programme as producers thought that they made him look like a Teddy Boy.

Perhaps surprisingly Savile Row tailor Lungley Powe spoke of his admiration for the Teds. He believed that they had character and stuck to their standards like Guards officers. They also spent more money on clothes; indeed expense seemed no object for some. Nevertheless, in a world of post-war austerity and continued rationing, the decision to dress in this way was not to be taken lightly since it needed careful financial planning.

Some bought less expensive garb – and paid the price. As one Ted explained, pointing to his coat, it was 34 inches long when he first got it and, after just six cleans, was now only 30 inches. Don McCullin, the acclaimed photographer, spent his first savings on a navy blue hopsack Edwardian suit. He wore the outfit, which cost £7.7s.6d., on his first date, only for it to pour with rain. His hair hung down and he could feel the suit shrinking on his back as he escorted his girl to a dance in Highgate.

This was a time when neither cash nor credit for clothing was easy to come by. The average salary in Britain in 1950 was around £2 per week. A good suit might cost £20 and all the accessories pushed the price up further. Including everything, from the Tony Curtis hair-do to the crepe-soled shoes, the uniform might cost as much as £100. In a letter to the *Daily Express* in 1954, Lady Child of Surrey begged to discover where the cash came from to indulge their flamboyant tastes. Was it, she queried, their parents or the bountiful Welfare State that was providing the money? Sometimes it was the former. When asked by the *Daily Mirror* how he could afford his suit, Leonard Sims admitted that he couldn't: his mum paid for it.

What Lady Child didn't appreciate was that, because of plentiful employment, even those lacking qualifications were now earning relatively high wages in unskilled jobs and were able to afford their own suits. *Picture Post* journalist Hilde Marchant found that the lads in a Tottenham dance hall were all earning good wages. They paid between £17 and £20 for a suit, £2 for a poplin shirt and £3 for shoes. According to a probation officer, ninety per cent of Teds worked as labourers during the day. If they spent a lot on clothes, they probably saved money by standing on street corners while their mates were in the pub. He felt the reason their clothes cost more than ordinary suits was that the lads went to backstreet tailors who were prepared to add adornments such as coloured lapels and velvet or moleskin trim collars. Detailing on jackets varied widely. Some had patch pockets, piped pockets, flap pockets or slash ('jetted') pockets. Buttons ranged from a single-link button to six buttons.

Some frowned upon such excesses. A Hammersmith tailor called Eckler said he admired the style as long as it wasn't taken to extremes. He disliked trousers that were too tight, velvet collars and gauntlet cuffs but felt that they were on their way out by 1957 and that Teds were accepting a compromise. Velvet collars became popular in the mid-to-late 1950s. They were rare in the early days since they pushed the price up and would have been ruined by the Brylcreem on the hair. However, velvet roll collars became popular with the Teddy Boy revival in the 1970s.

For Teds without much money, hire purchase was often the answer. Tailors were blamed for selling the suits on the 'never never', thereby allowing teenagers to become gangsters overnight. Youth clubs in Liverpool complained that membership was falling because lads were using their subs money to buy suits. Liverpool youth leader Stan Morris explained: 'The "never never" is a mode of life around here. On a Monday you can see the "knock knock men" going to practically every door down the street.' A sixteen-year-old Liverpool Ted called Robert landed his parents in debt for his fancy suits; his father threatened to burn his next pair of drainpipe trousers. When two Liverpool Teddy Boys were arrested, one admitted, 'I can't pay any fines. I've got the suit to pay for.' His mate was even more annoyed: 'OK Jack, don't crease the suit,' he told the arresting officer.

Teddy Boys were sometimes called 'Mississippi Gamblers', since their long jackets were similar to the frock-coats of American Wild West gunfighters. For some the look was further enhanced by the wearing of bootlace ties, sometimes held together by a medallion depicting symbols such as a death's head, cross-bones or cow's skull. Some wore a western bow tie, also known as a 'Maverick' tie after the Western TV show of the same name featuring James Garner. The look conjured images of the American outlaw and gambler popularised in countless Western films. Like many Teds, these characters were lawless outsiders who lived by their wits. Their look was therefore borrowed from both Western styles and aristocratic Edwardian tailoring. However, bootlace ties belong more to the late 1950s. Slim-Jim narrow ties were probably more popular.

Shirts were mostly white. One popular kind was called a 'Billy Eckstein shirt', after the sharply dressed American singer and bandleader, adorned with a long fly-over collar (also known as a 'Mr B collar'). Some Teds also wore waistcoats. These were usually plain, though the more flashy lads boasted flowery or brocade showpieces.

Not everyone could afford to wear the full outfit, but all of them had at least one of these elements. Narrow trousers, called 'strides', were a mandatory feature. Boys would coax their mothers to unpick the seams of their old trousers and sew them up again as narrow as sixteen-inch. Although not exactly drainpipe, they were a contrast to the usual baggy look popular in the 1940s. One fifteen-year-old aspiring Ted took the trousers from his first suit down to the dry cleaners to have them narrowed, or 'drainpiped', at his own expense. Such alterations led to friction in some households. One Glasgow father, after refusing to let his son have his trousers narrowed, was kneed in the stomach and poked in the eye. The son admitted relations between them had become strained since his father forbade him to dress as a Ted.

As trouser widths became narrower, taking them off became more difficult. Liverpool MP Bessie Braddock once saw some Teddy Boys sporting the tightest strides imaginable. She asked, 'How do you get into them pants?' 'Dead easy,' came the reply. 'We grease our boots.' This may not have been a joke. Ray Gosling claims to have rubbed Vaseline on his ankles to remove his trousers. Alan Endersby, an ex-Ted from Catford, South East London, revealed that he first had to remove his socks. Trousers were worn slightly too short, or with a guardsman's fall, in order to show a little bit of the sock.

In 1956 a seventeen-year-old called Michael Jackson appeared in court in Edwardian dress complete with pink socks. He was accused of being part of gang that had tried to force its way into the Regal Cinema, Hammersmith. Some lads favoured yellow or pale blue socks, although diagonal patterns and hooped stripes were also popular. Most, however, wore white socks. Fluorescent hosiery was a much later development.

The original footwear of choice was a plain black Oxford shoe. This gradually gave way to the wearing of heavy-soled brogues. Thick soles could be achieved by adding a further layer of leather at the cobblers. Also popular were crepe-soled shoes, called the Eaton 'Clubman' and Eaton 'Chukka Boot'. They were known as 'brothel creepers' or 'beetle crushers' due to their thick flat soles. The crepe soles kept them from slipping when jiving, although in the rain they would eventually become waterlogged and squelch with each step. The brushed-suede shoe with a crepe sole, which was otherwise known as the chukka desert boot, was originally worn by British soldiers in the North African desert. The soles were usually an inch thick, chunkier soles being a 1970s invention.

Pop and cultural critic Nik Cohn maintains that after 1956, creepers began to be replaced by black 'winkle-pickers' – Italian-style shoes with pointed toes – and that these, worn with blue jeans, became the basic teenage look of the late 1950s and early 1960s, particularly in the north. Winkle-pickers, however, were essentially an early 1960s fashion. Most Teds would not wear them and preferred creepers.

* * *

As the fashion spread geographically and over time, it became more diluted and diverse. Individuals modified the look. Few outside London boasted the entire Teddy Boy uniform, wearing only the items that they could afford (or that their parents would let them get away with). Indeed, some later Teds contented themselves with a pair of tight blue jeans and a DA hairstyle. Most parents didn't want their children becoming Teds, especially in the north where it was seen as an effeminate southern craze. 'Darlington was a very conservative place in the 1950s, where fathers ruled the roost,' claimed Ray Pratt. He wanted to be a Teddy Boy but was scared of his father's reaction, fearing that he would be thrown out of the house. He bought his suit in bits and pieces but never dared wear it at home, keeping it at a friend's house to change into before a night out. The father of singer Billy Fury also disapproved of his drainpipe jeans. The teenage Fury hid them in the outdoor lavatory. He would go out in his baggy flannels, turn the corner and re-enter the back yard by climbing over the wall to retrieve his beloved drainpipes.

It tended to be Teddy Boys who belonged to gangs who sported the whole regalia. Gang identity was often expressed by a particular item, such as sock colour. Suit colour was also important. Members of Fulham's Walham Green Gang opted for a shimmering silver herringbone material. A Liverpool tailor reported that he was occasionally invaded by gangs of

Teds: the leader would choose a suit and his followers would order exactly the same. Some gangs also customised their uniforms by adding, for example, green velvet collars.

Despite vivid modern representations of the drape suit, early Teddy boys did not wear bright, primary-colours. Suits were originally in dark, conservative shades such as grey, brown and black. On being arrested, one Liverpool lad was alarmed to hear the policeman describe the colour of his drape jacket as 'black'. 'No mister, not black, midnight blue,' was his more accurate description. These sombre colours did eventually give way to vivid hues of green or powder blue and by the end of the 1950s came the odd pillar-box-red drape.

Styles became more exaggerated over time, possibly as a defiant response to the negative publicity in the press. In 1957 a Ted in Dundee was seen parading the city square on a Sunday night wearing gold-coloured chains around his black-suede-covered insteps. Young Sheffield men sported coloured shirts, particularly bright scarlet or striped green and black or maroon and black, worn perhaps as a reaction to the drabness and dreariness of the industrial landscape around them. A Deptford tailor revealed that Teds would come in and describe something they had seen in town. Some favoured a mix and match ethic. A Ted from Brockley, South London, designed his own suit from the pages of the magazine *Man About Town*, choosing a coat from one page and a waistcoat from another before adding his own trimmings.

Just as the public began to regard the Teds as a threat, the fashion started changing. As early as 1954, Superintendent Fabian felt that the zoot suits and Edwardian fashions were already 'fading' among the capital's hooligan element. Young gangsters now preferred dark suits with pleated hacking slits, fancy waistcoats, knitted ties and thick-soled shoes embroidered with leather strips. **A year later a report of the Senior Detention Centre at Blantyre House, Kent, claimed that there were signs that the 'Edwardian craze was dying'. In 1954 the prominent inmates of the centre had been Teddy Boys but by the following year it was motor car and motorbike offenders**

who predominated. It was believed that the lads were benefiting from the shock treatment imposed. New Teddy Boy inmates were considered provincial or 'fruity', meaning that they hadn't realised that the Teds were out of date.

By 1958, especially in London and southern England, youths began flirting with the smart, slimline 'Italian' or 'college boy' look that would herald the 1960s 'Mod' style. While some Teds started wearing longer drapes below the knee, in a reverse trend youths began to replace the draped jacket with the short, box-like 'bum freezers'. Indeed, by the time of the Notting Hill disturbances in 1958, the heyday of the Teddy Boy was virtually over except in provincial cities such as Sheffield, Manchester and Liverpool. The original Teds had by this time begun to get married and settle down. Some turned to leather jackets and motorbikes to become 'ton-up boys', the precursors of the Rockers.

By 1959 the old-style Teds were a minority group, although still strong in more remote places. Jazz singer and writer George Melly found that in small Yorkshire mining communities it was still possible to find Edwardian suits as late as 1960. Dave Douglass also recalls a tense encounter with a group of pit village Teds in mid-1960s Tyneside. Wearing his quasi-mod jacket with high collar and ankle-swingers proudly displaying his Cuban heels, he was at once identified as a 'toonie' (or more precisely a 'soft shite'). The Teds, on the other hand, were 'Neolithic and terrifying' in their drapes, oiled-back hair, black crepe shoes, luminous socks and big studded belts.

When Teddy Boy Dave Milward was released from borstal in 1965, he persuaded the institution's tailor to alter his discharge suit so that he had an extra-long jacket and tapered trousers. By then, however, the look was dead and buried. The course of this chapter, a journey from bespoke tailors to custodial institutions, very much follows the story of the Edwardian suit: in less than a decade, what began as a youthful expression of sartorial innovation and creativity had become a symbol of destruction, disorder and criminality.

5

DELINQUENTS IN DRAPE JACKETS

'The new dress heralded a new kind of crime and a new kind of social problem for anybody who was anxious for the stability of society.'

(Jeff Nuttall, writer)

A Canvey Island holiday resort in 1954 crowned a greengrocer's assistant as winner of its competition for 'Best Dressed Teddy Boy' – a sure sign that the style was becoming more acceptable to the general public. Further endorsement came from Sir Edward Boyle, of the Ministry of Education, who thought that such an interest in clothing led to greatly increased standards of personal tidiness and cleanliness. For fashion writer Pearl Binder there was a sense of national pride and social climbing in the handsomely dressed Teds. By rejecting American influences, and cultivating the gravity and aloofness of the Regency dandy, they aspired to be English gents and to help Englishmen regain a sense of importance in the world. Youth worker Elizabeth Stucley also defended Edwardian garb. She felt that if the Swiss and Belgians could enjoy wearing national costume, why shouldn't young Cockneys invent their own uniform, adding that the brilliant waistcoats, crazy ties and dazzling socks added a dash of colour to Britain's dreary streets.

It was acknowledged that the teenage desire to dress up was healthy and normal. The educationalist Dr Josephine Macalister Brew offered an interesting explanation for the emergence of the Teddy Boy. It seems that for the first time in generations, the number of young men was about equal to that of young women. After the carnage of the First World War there was a large surplus of women and so they had to dress up to attract the remaining eligible males. By the 1950s the situation was beginning to reverse. When there were more boys than girls, the girls could pick and choose who they wanted and felt less pressure to make themselves look attractive. For the boys, however, there was fierce competition to attract an available female and so the Teds more than ever needed to adopt their 'fine plumage'.

It was certainly a look that attracted female attention. In a radio programme broadcast in 1956, a young woman from West Ham, in East London, described the ideal attire for her man. This included thick crepe soles, drainpipe trousers, 'spivvy socks' and a cheese cutter cap. For George Melly, the adoption of an upper-class fashion, conveying messages of class privilege and sexual licence, corresponded to the Teds' own promiscuity. A Birmingham youth leader blamed the Welfare State for breeding a race of early-maturing young people. He was horrified that the Teddy Boy movement, by sanctioning sexual freedom, encouraged boys of fifteen to become sexually active. Even young Teds aged thirteen and fourteen boasted of their sexual conquests and the youth leader did not doubt their word: 'Once they don Teddy boy clothing, the breakaway from conventional morality is complete.'

For writer Nik Cohn the preening Teds had made clothes sexual again, particularly with the emphasis on the tightness of the trousers at the thigh. Since the war had destroyed a sense of family and tradition, of cherished values being handed down from one generation to another, young people no longer wished to dress like their parents: they wanted to look the opposite. 'Their clothes said three things: *I am different; I am tough; I fuck.*'

* * *

If the suit was about sexual attraction, it was also a means of signalling a sense of separation and aloofness from the rest of society. For child expert Donald Ford, the Teddy Boy had 'chosen to symbolise his apartness from society by the way he dresses'. Their clothing involved two levels of rebellion: youth against the older generation, and the lower classes against the upper classes. Sociologist David Lowson, writing in 1960, noted how the Teddy Boys sought prestige in embracing a set of opposing standards. For example, while the short-back-and-sides remained the national haircut for men, the Teds wore their hair long. While dressing up to be different might seem harmless, the problem for Lowson was that the Teds' desire for action often exhibited itself in destructive and violent behaviour. Similarly, for journalist Hugh Latimer the adoption of such clothing visibly asserted the separateness of young people and consequently intensified their tendency to clash with the rest of society.

Sensing this rift, C. Geoffrey How, the Rector of Bethnal Green, a man aware of his responsibilities for the spiritual lives of the Teddy Boys in his district, spoke of the need for more adults to offer interest and friendship to lost young people. Others also sensed a need for adults to reach out to youth. In May 1958 a *Times* reader complained that the 'Teddy Boys versus the rest' attitude came from a refusal to integrate them into society. However, the writer also acknowledges that while some Teds resented this, others thrived on the distinction.

It wasn't so much that adults were failing to connect with young people, but that the Teds were actively rejecting adult society. To be more precise, they were rejecting anybody who did not dress like them. Their eccentricities of fashion helped raise their sense of solidarity and reliance upon each other. As George Melly points out, what might look to outsiders like 'eccentric individualism' was actually a sense of group conformity. Wearing Teddy Boy clothes was both an act of rebellion against authority and compliance with peer-group pressure.

Some boys just wanted to look like their mates. In certain areas youths were told by older Teds that it would be just as well that they purchase a Teddy suit. One youth splashed out but then decided that he no longer wanted to wear it and went back to his sports jacket and flannel trousers. On his way home from the youth club he was waylaid by the local Teds, who grabbed him by his arms and legs and threw him head-first through the bay window of a nearby house. Donald Ford claims that this type of terrorism was used in certain areas and, worryingly, no prosecutions seemed to follow.

At Elizabeth Stucley's youth club one boy, called Des, suddenly altered his appearance. As well as adopting the clothing, his behaviour became nastier. Stucley wondered whether the boy had joined a gang because he was flattered by being noticed by older boys, or whether it was out of self-preservation. The power of conformity is demonstrated in the tragic tale of fourteen-year-old Peter Winchester, an aspiring Teddy Boy from Stockwell, South London. The cricket-loving boy from a respectable and religious family came under the influence of Teds at school. As well as wearing the gear, he began to carry a flick-knife and knuckle-duster. In a desperate effort to stop their son turning wayward his parents burned his drainpipes and threw his jacket into the bin. The lad ran away from home for two days but secretly returned to the empty house to rescue his jacket. Putting it on, along with another pair of narrow trousers from a converted suit, he turned on the gas oven and put his head inside. His distraught parents found his body on their return.

The case was not unique. In Lambeth, also in South London, a fifteen-year-old Teddy Girl tried to gas herself after her father ripped up her Edwardian coat. He felt that she had been 'getting a bit spivvy lately'. The girl was found with the pipe of the bathroom water heater in her mouth. A court judged her to be in need of care and protection and she was remanded.

* * *

For some, the uniform had undertones not only of delinquency but of sexual deviancy. As part of the backlash against the flamboyantly dressed Teds, their very masculinity was brought into question. In the post-war period, a time when homosexual acts between men were illegal, dressiness was largely confined to gay men, the outrageousness of the clothes serving as a badge of their marginality as social and sexual outsiders. By 1949, in London, the grandiose Edwardian look, with half-collars of velvet on long jackets, had been adopted and camped up by some ex-Guards officers and interior decorators. At the time, both groups were associated with homosexuality. However, by 1954 butch Teddy Boys had made the style so notorious that even gay men were embarrassed to wear it.

Nevertheless, links were still made between Teddy Boys and homosexuality. In her study of a Liverpool street in the 1950s, Madeline Kerr noticed that many of the most prolific lawbreakers were effeminate looking, deceptively gentle mannered and took great care over their appearance, particularly their hair. In spring 1955 the Teddy Boy craze hit the streets and was avidly taken up by the effeminate boys.

Reg Millbank, one of the teenage Teds in the 1959 novel *Cosh Boy*, is another effeminate and clothes-obsessed youth. Nicknamed 'Millie', he is treated cruelly by his family and the rest of the community for his homosexuality. He therefore takes revenge on society through acts of criminality. After discovering the Edwardian style in a copy of *Tailor and Cutter* magazine, he kits himself out as a Ted, reasoning that since he is already viewed by society as a criminal, he might as well become a well-dressed one.

For some people, an excessive interest in fashion and homosexuality amounted to the same thing. London Ted Tony Reuter was conscious of the accusations:

> A lot of folk think we dress up in Teddy suits because we're pansies. Don't you believe it. We do it to be in a sort of uniform so that we can get together and act big. Funny thing is we don't realise that when we start. We just dress up to be smart – and so as the girls will notice us.

Many parents in the 1950s were alarmed by what they took to be any trace of effeminacy in their sons. A youthful interest in patterns, fashions and materials was seen as perverse and Edwardian clothing, viewed as either degenerate or delinquent, could tear families apart. One father's objection to his son's clothes led to the breakdown of an Essex couple's thirty-year marriage. The mother sided with her son, who had grown his hair long and bought a leather belt with a swivel-ring and dagger.

In traditional working-class neighbourhoods there is great emphasis on toughness and manliness, qualities essential for survival. It seems appropriate that a gritty Northern town such as Wigan reported no serious Teddy Boy problem. It seems that young men preferred rugby and thought that the Teds were 'cissies'. Some Northerners certainly ridiculed the clothes as effeminate. In 1954 a young Middlesbrough plumber called Terry Farnham heard workmates describe Teddy Boys as criminals. To prove them wrong he decided to become a Ted. For six weeks he grew his hair long and had it permed. After kitting himself out in Edwardian clothing his mates began giving him the 'come-on' whistle, while his boss adopted a lisp and started calling him 'Cecil'.

Others also questioned the sexuality of the Teds. An Irish observer, who had knocked around with the Teds for some time, claimed that if you picked any 100 Teds, especially from those who had been to prison, 75 would have had some homosexual experience: some for cash, some out of curiosity, most out of 'sheer boredom'. He added that even if they weren't all 'effeminate' (by which he meant homosexual), even though at least some of them were, the point was that the Teds felt a need to outshine the way the girls were dressed. For the so-called Teddy girls were already aping elements of the male fashion, such as wearing jeans and adopting stylistic touches such as velvet collars on long jackets.

T.R. Fyvel suggests that the male obsession with fashion, combined with a fascination with violence, betrayed in some a sexual insecurity. He pondered whether the Teds' nightly prowl for girls (or prostitutes even) was the outward sign of a need to assert their threatened sense of masculinity. Rev. Griffiths also claimed that the Teds paid so much attention to their looks that they half-consciously feared that they were not men. They made up for it, however, by carrying knives and razors.

It was also felt that putting on the uniform changed the wearer's personality. Liverpool probation officer John Woolfenden felt that the clothes served to compensate for an inferiority complex: 'The exaggerated clothes they wear proclaim their basic self-sufficiency. The shoes often have inch-thick soles and raised heels to flatter stunted height ... The whole attitude shouts: "If I can't attract attention, my suit can. If I can't fight, my suit can".' The clothes presented a puzzling, contradictory set of messages, highlighted by *Observer* journalist Cyril Dunn who viewed Edwardian dress as feminine but without making its wearers look effeminate. It was the brooding sense of masculine aggression that prevented the look becoming wholly feminine.

Yet if the clothing was worn aggressively as a sort of weapon (and it must be remembered that some Teds hid bicycle chains inside their collars), it could also be a means of defence. For journalist Hilde Marchant, the clothing was both a shield against the world and a screen to conceal inner vulnerability. In Ernest Ryman's 1958 novel *Teddy Boy*, teen thug Jimmy Alban buys himself an Edwardian suit, which he puts on as if donning armour, feeling like a powerful knight riding into battle. Elsewhere, a psychiatrist declared: 'The clothes we wear are our armour. The Teddy Boy flaunts his fantastic uniform as a protection against society.' The (Liverpool) *Evening Express* agreed: 'Their dress is only a suit of armour.' More damningly, the uniform was 'a prop to sagging personalities and a sop to mentalities starved of worthwhile impulses'.

* * *

According to Irishman James O' Connor, writing in 1963, the Teddy Boy was 'something more than just a youth in

Edwardian costume'. He represented a certain 'anti-social behaviour, an attitude of rebellion and viciousness, tending towards violence'. O'Connor acknowledged that not all boys who dressed in Edwardian clothes were Teddy Boys, since some merely adopted the style just to show off before their friends or because the uniform was fashionable in their area. However, there was the danger that these boys, having adopted the costume, would go on to acquire their habits.

The clothes and the delinquency certainly became inseparable. When a fourteen-year-old 'bully', who used a knife to threaten people, appeared in court his headmaster explained: 'He shows a desire to dress as a Teddy Boy'. In 1956 the Mayor of Harrogate pondered a chicken-and-egg dilemma. He was unsure whether the fashion created the hooligan or the hooligan created the fashion. 'Is it the outfitter who provides the style, or the hooligans who make the demand on the outfitter?' The clothing was so bound up with criminality that in 1954, days after one highly publicised gang battle, senior Scotland Yard officers called for reports of any incidents in which the dreaded Edwardian uniform appeared.

The clothes certainly had an adverse effect on people. In court, the clothing of the accused, not simply their alleged crimes, needed to be defended. In a court in Penge, South East London, the defence solicitor asked the magistrate to ignore the dress and hairstyle of his client, arguing that too much was heard about Teddy Boys. Prosecution witnesses sometimes appeared to be more aware of the dress than the deeds of the young defendants. One magistrate, at least, was aware of the implication of simply labelling youths as Teds so as to denigrate them. At the trial of three men accused of robbing a postmaster, a witness claimed that he saw 'four Teddy boys' enter the post office in West London. The magistrate interrupted: 'Just call them young men. It does not signify anything referring to them like that.' A solicitor defending a Ted in Kettering, Northamptonshire, told the court, 'I must protest against the words "Edwardian clothes" being used ... It is apt to bring prejudice to the minds of the magistrates.' He spoke after a police Superintendent described the defendant's uniform.

Certainly Teds in the dock felt that the uniform marked them out. After being convicted of being part of a mass brawl against twenty policemen at Bankfoot, Bradford, one aggrieved Ted complained to the judge: 'You take the officer's word for it because he was in uniform and I was wearing Teddy boy clothing, as you call it.' When Philip Barsby of Taunton, Somerset, appeared in court in 1958 charged with assaulting two police officers during an outbreak of gang disorder, he wore a powder-blue, knee-length drape and drainpipe trousers. He denied the charges and claimed, 'I think they picked on me because I had the longest coat.' During a public protest against heavy-handed policing in Portsmouth, Hampshire, Rex Evans was arrested for allegedly throwing handbills in the street. In court he was referred to by a police solicitor as a 'Teddy Boy'. Evans was not happy and declared that the way he dressed was not on trial. After the case was adjourned for a week he next turned up for court in a hired suit of top hat and tails to see if the court had a better opinion of him.

The uniform soon came under attack from all sides. When a Ted assaulted a young woman on a train, the *Sunday Chronicle* declared that the Edwardian suit 'was mortally wounded'. The Chairman at Dartford Magistrates Court was horrified that a sixteen-year-old Ted convicted of robbing a woman of £20 had used the money to buy an Edwardian suit – he considered such clothing to be ridiculous in the eyes of ordinary people, being flashy, cheap and nasty, stamping the wearer as a particularly undesirable type. It was the suit as much as the behaviour that caused offence. 'In Teddy Boys Clothes' was the headline in the *Somerset County Herald* describing the trial of four youths accused of smashing windows. It was as if the clothes were on trial.

An editorial in *The Star* pointed out that 'no doubt dozens of young men who like to wear drainpipe trousers and boot-lace ties are law abiding but their uniform has been disgraced. They should either discard it or share the disgrace'. An elderly

Christian member of Bristol's Dockland Settlement felt that the Teddy Boy suit was 'the Devil's garb'. A youth counsellor in Southend, Essex, called the Teddy Boy suit 'an ugly badge of violence', while a colleague warned that 'these trouble-makers are now recognisable and club leaders know who to guard against'. Because of such negative reporting, clothes dealers reported that increasing numbers of such suits were being sold to them for give-away prices because they had become 'the emblem of the spiv and the cosh boy'.

Some did warn against stigmatising the clothing. One Liverpudlian objected to the demonization of Teds and pointed out that many were not criminals: 'It is not the clothes that matter: it is the person wearing them.' He added that it was as if hooliganism had never existed in the first half of the century. Some newspapers agreed. 'There is a danger that people will see in the Edwardians some new strange and evil social phenomenon,' ran a *Star* editorial. 'By any other dress, this is still the old problem of juvenile delinquents. They are still naughty boys whether they are Teddy Boys or Teddy Bears.'

Links between the dress code and criminality continued to lead to anyone wearing the clothes being judged unfavourably. In 1954, an article on the 'typical' Ted in the *Daily Sketch* featured a lad called William Prendergast. Aged eighteen, he was unemployed and living with his parents in Battersea Park Road, south of the River Thames. After leaving school at fifteen, Prendergast had had eight jobs but now felt discriminated against because of his clothes. Nobody was bothered if a proper gentleman wore tight-bottomed trousers, he explained, yet when a young man wore them he was sneered at. It was this type of reaction that provoked trouble. Prendergast was sick of being insulted in the street, claiming that this was why his colleagues went around in crowds, seven- or eight-handed. He went on to claim that he was often refused admission to dance halls and cinemas and moved on from street corners by the police, all because he dared to wear a suit that labelled him a hooligan and troublemaker.

Their peers could also be critical. In Edward Blishen's 1955 novel of schoolboy life, *Roaring Boys*, a teacher asks a class of thirteen-year-olds what they think about the Teddy Boys. Their ungrammatical, badly spelt essays show that they are largely against the phenomenon. 'Nearly evry day you hear of them killing peple smaler than them selfs,' writes one boy, adding, 'you migt as well paint your legs black than were drainpip trousers.' Blishen's fictional observation about drainpipe trousers had a factual basis; in an essay also written in 1955, a pupil from a school in King's Norton, Birmingham, wrote of the Teds: 'They are a disgrace to the country with their tight trousers.' Indeed, Donald Chapman, Labour MP for Northfield, suggested giving final-year schoolchildren lessons in sartorial taste in order to warn them off such clothing.

* * *

As it passed from black to white, from America to Britain, the drape style changed its meaning. Originally a symbol of racial resistance, it became, through its adoption by white American youths, a mark of youthful rebellion against adult society. By 1948 the fashion had entered the British mainstream but had also acquired new delinquent associations when it became the uniform of the spiv and would-be gangster. By the time the Teds took up the Edwardian look, the drape jacket was already viewed as the uniform of the criminal classes.

Teds further used the style as a means of adopting swagger and provoking confrontation. Yet if the Teds employed fashion to assert their right to be noticed, they also scorned the attention. 'Look at me,' the clothes shouted. 'Who are you looking at?' the wearer would then add. In a sense the Teds simultaneously flaunted and resented their social alienation. For T.R. Fyvel, the early Teds were lads holding a grudge against society and an urge to assert themselves. That element of assertion was not confined to the wearing of a flashy uniform but often extended to the carrying of some sort of weapon.

6

WEAPONS

'Can you turn the other cheek to a Teddy Boy and hope that it will not be slashed by a razor, cut by a chain, or bruised by a knuckle duster?'

([Liverpool] *Evening Express*, 1955)

An essential accessory to the Teddy Boy uniform was a weapon – often anything that they could get their hands on. In 1957, fearing that a gang fight was about to break out, two detectives forced seventy-five young customers in a coffee bar in Wallington, Surrey, to stand with their hands above their heads. Body searches uncovered two heavy belts, a weighted chain, a sheath knife, two flick-knives, a penknife, three lengths of chain (two attached to handles), two bottles and a stiletto knife.

A London probation officer revealed that it was not unusual for youths to carry a weapon to give them status in the gang. Superintendent Fabian claimed that boys carried weapons not only to make themselves 'feel important' but because they knew that their weaponry could instil fear in adults. Looking back to this mythical golden age, Fabian recalls that in the past a member of the public could deal with a couple of badly behaved teenagers by giving them a clout. By the early 1950s, however, citizens risked being confronted by a dozen armed gangsters seeking revenge.

The Labour MP for Kensington North, George Rogers, wondered what we had done to deserve the kind of youth that was being produced. No doubt referring to the recent racial disturbances in Notting Hill and Nottingham, Rogers reported in 1958 that lads were wandering around armed with knives, knuckle-dusters and sharpened bicycle chains. Incidents had broken out that had resulted in horrific injuries, although the assaults often went unreported. The constant threat of violence on the streets made it difficult for law-abiding citizens to go about their business. Rogers felt that there should be a much stricter application of the law regarding the carrying of offensive weapons. He argued that since Teddy Boys and hooligans were easily recognisable they should be regularly subjected to police searches in the street. Rogers reasoned that since these lads were cowards hunting in packs, they would not want to take part in disturbances if they were unarmed. Confiscating their weapons, whether it was a knife or a milk bottle, would do much to prevent further outbreaks of street violence.

Empty milk bottles were a handy missile and could be found in great numbers on almost every doorstep late at night awaiting collection by the milkman in the morning. At Withy Grove, Manchester, Teds beat up a man before throwing milk bottles at people chasing them. In 1954 four members of Liverpool's Midnight Blue Gang, so called because of the colour of their suits, used a broken bottle to assault a lad walking a girl home from a dance. The sadistic attack left the victim needing fifteen stitches to a face wound. In 1956 the Chief Constable of nearby Bootle reported that incidents in which bottles and belt buckles were used as weapons had increased from six to twenty-two during the previous year. Two years later more than sixty London Teds threw bottles at each other near Alexandra Palace. In Banbury, Oxfordshire, following a fight between Teds and local youths, a lad was jabbed in the face with a broken bottle. He required thirty-nine stitches.

* * *

Although jagged glass could cause serious injury, bottles were usually spur-of-the- moment weapons. The possession of a knife, on the other hand, was a more deliberate act. Home Secretary Sir David Maxwell Fyfe announced that during the first six months of 1952, twenty-seven cases of stabbing were known to the Metropolitan Police. In most cases a knife or a dagger was used, although one incident involved a bayonet. Blades became known as the silent killer.

After the Clapham Common murder of 1953, Teds were regularly identified as savages routinely armed with flick-knives. Teddy Boys and knife crime became almost synonymous. In 1954, in Wigan, a child was randomly stabbed shortly before another youngster was murdered. Police worked on various theories, including one that the attacker was a Teddy Boy eager to show off with a knife to his mates; in fact, the murderer turned out to have no links to the Teds.

One of Michael Davies' colleagues revealed that lads from Clapham would carry large knives wrapped in folded newspapers that were placed in the side pockets of their coats. It was claimed that they carried the knives mainly to show off but they were there if needed. The lad further explained that during the fight on Clapham Common, when someone shouted 'Get the knives out', the words were used defensively rather than aggressively. If lads were fighting a larger gang the shout would go up to pull out the weapons to let the others know that they were armed. It was a means of scaring off opponents, particularly when the smaller group was outnumbered and looked as if it was going to be on the receiving end of a beating. Members of the dominant group didn't need to yell the words. The implication was that the words had actually been shouted by the boys being beaten up in the Clapham case.

One Newcastle Ted confirmed in an interview that his gang liked to carry flick-knives as it made them feel 'secure'. Others clearly carried them as aggressors. In the summer of 1954, teenage gang members from London and various south coast towns began travelling to Brighton looking for fights. Trouble came to a head that November when three young men were stabbed and slashed in the town's Regent Dance Hall. The youths, all innocent bystanders who did not know each other, were attacked with what appeared to be shoemakers' knives, sharpened to a razor's edge. One victim needed thirteen stitches in his face. The disturbance erupted for no apparent reason when a group of youths in Edwardian uniform entered the venue and began throwing chairs about. They then scarpered just before the police arrived.

It wasn't only youngsters who got caught up in the violence. In 1955, a 65-year-old London shopkeeper was stabbed to death during a robbery. Nineteen-year-old Donald Brown, wearing a duffle coat over his velvet-collared Teddy Boy suit, walked into the shop in Willesden and invited Herbert 'Buster' Blades for a drink. As the tobacconist, who was an old friend, turned to wash his hands, Brown stabbed him repeatedly in the back with a bowie knife. 'Goodbye Buster,' he said. The killer took £40 out of a tin hidden behind the counter and calmly walked out of the shop. Brown then took a friend to the cinema where he kissed the knife and put it under the seat. He confided his deed to his friend who then told the police. Meanwhile, Brown bought new clothes to replace his Teddy Boy suit, had a haircut and took a coach to Folkestone, Kent, where he watched a play. Afterwards he took some aspirins and sat on a cliff. Brown, who had spent an unhappy childhood in foster care and institutions, was caught and sentenced to death but later reprieved owing to his mental state.

A group of Leicester Teds proudly admitted that they carried spring-clip knives. One stated, 'We've never used our knives ... We just carry them in case we get mixed up in gang warfare.' After easily buying such a knife in a shop in 1955, a journalist wrote an article that led to questions being asked in Parliament. Barnett Janner, MP for Leicester, found it unbelievable that such weapons were on sale when hooliganism by Teds was rife. Around the same time Gilbert Harding, the radio and television personality, demonstrated the use of a flick-knife on his programme and urged that they be banned. He later received anonymous letters threatening to cut him up.

In South West London, Fulham police took to warning youths not to buy flick-knives as they would be confiscated. The blades, said to vary in length from four to twelve inches, were hidden inside the handle and sprung out when a button was pressed. The compactness of such knives made them a popular accessory. A 1957 Metropolitan Police report estimated that more than half the Teds who roamed the streets after dark carried knives, ranging from flick-knives and pistol-type blades to stilettos and daggers.

In 1958, at a Stockport Town Council meeting, the Chairman of the Watch Committee revealed that cases of wounding had increased from thirty to forty-four over the past year. Of particular concern was the use of flick-knives by Teddy Boys. The apparent widespread use of such weapons, together with the eagerness with which some young people employed them, was perceived as another sign that something was going badly wrong with the younger generation. An ex-Ted detected some changes when he came out of the Navy in 1958. In particular he noticed that flick-knives had become fashionable, although most youths carried them only out of bravado. Lord Morris revealed that a cinema manager had told him that he had confiscated flick-knives from children at Saturday morning matinees. Older Teds also used them to slash the seats.

By 1959 a Private Member's Bill to outlaw flick-knives was given a surprise reading in the House of Commons. It was the beginning of the end. Throughout March and April the *Daily Mirror* highlighted the problem of knife use among the young, running a national campaign to alert and educate parents and backing an amnesty for the voluntary surrender of flick-knives, coshes, bicycle chains and knuckle-dusters. After a week, the newspaper had received hundreds of weapons. It had taken four years but on 4 June 1959 the importation, sale, hire or lending of flick-knives and 'gravity knives' was banned under an 'anti-Teddy-Boy' piece of legislation called The Restriction of Offensive Weapons Act.

When a journalist suggested to some gang members that stiletto knives should be banned, one scornfully replied that they made their own weapons. A boys' club leader, who held an armoury of confiscated weaponry, confirmed the practice.

'Shivs' were made from a block of wood with two razors slotted in and were apparently used for slashing clothes.

* * *

In the days before disposable razors, the old-fashioned cut-throat razor could be found in most homes. In 1955, a Birkenhead lad was attacked on his way to the youth club to play basketball; as he turned into a dark street, four razor-wielding Teds ambushed him and slashed him about the head. In the same year a Dumfries Ted, described as the 'best razor slasher' in town, was fined 10 shillings. In Wythenshawe, Manchester, in an unprovoked attack, a fourteen-year-old was slashed across the face by a razor-wielding Ted. At a hostel in Harlesden, North West London, thirty Teds walked in shouting and making a disturbance. A man felt a blow and then discovered that his ear had been sliced. In 1958 a Ted slashed a fifteen-year-old girl in the leg when she refused to go for a walk with him; her wound required twelve stitches. During a Christmas night brawl at a small village called Mattersey Thorpe, four Nottingham youths were slashed by a razor-wielding Ted. Derek Foster, aged twenty-two, from Yorkshire, allegedly told the police: 'Yes, I had a razor but I used it to protect myself. They were in a semi-circle round me. I promised the razor to the first to start. When they began to come in thick and fast, I slashed out with the razor and my fist.' He pleaded not guilty to wounding with intent and was cleared.

In the Welsh seaside resort of Rhyl a Teddy Boy who had been refused admission to a dance hall, pulled out a cut-throat razor and threatened to fight his way inside. The razor had been ground down to half its normal size. In Bootle, near Liverpool, five Teddy Boy members of the Hot Cross Gang attacked and robbed a seventeen-year-old called John Peachment. One used a razor to play noughts and crosses on his face while others held his arms. The lad suffered thirty slash wounds. In Berkshire, outside Slough Public Library, a Ted slashed a man's face so badly it needed twenty-five stitches to close. When the casualty saw his bloodied face in the mirror, he collapsed in shock. A victim of Birmingham's Holloway Head Gang claimed that one of his attackers had razor-blades stuck in the crepe soles of his shoes.

Following the theme quite bizarrely, in 1958 a tattooist from St Leonards on Sea, East Sussex, had requests from Teds to have razor slashes tattooed on their faces. He refused.

* * *

Aggressive young men didn't need knives and razors to behave sadistically, of course. In 1957 a thirteen-year-old boy from the East End borough of Clapton was held down by a pair who then ignited a firework inside his shirt and hung around to watch it burn his chest and stomach. In Bolton, Lancashire, another thirteen-year-old, innocently watching a bonfire, was grabbed by four Teds and held face down while his trousers were pulled down. Having heated an iron bar, they branded him four times on the buttocks and hips.

The anarchic atmosphere of Bonfire Night seemed to bring out the very worst behaviour. Twenty miles down the road in Stockport, in 1962, three Teds approached an eight-year-old boy dressed as Guy Fawkes, complete with mask and cowboy hat, and said, 'Let's stick the guy' before stabbing the young boy in the face. The victim's thirteen-year-old brother ran after them and told them that there was a boy under the mask but they didn't seem to care. The boy needed stitches to a wound in his cheek. A seventeen-year-old was later acquitted after explaining to the court that he thought the guy was made of straw. In 1954 gangs of Teds armed with broken bottles attacked London firemen extinguishing dangerous and over-size bonfires in Paddington. With the police on their way, Teds drew knives and slashed the hoses. One witness claimed, 'These boys in long jackets and drainpipe trousers were really vicious.' On the same night Teds were also active in Trafalgar Square having firework battles with a large body of students. A Liverpool shopkeeper told a tale of a youngster running crying into his shop after being robbed of his 'penny for the

Guy' coppers by some Teds. Because the boy had refused to hand them over they had beaten him up, broken his nose and blackened his eye.

Indeed the Teds harked back to the Victorian age in their use of improvised weapons. Makeshift coshes included socks filled with sand or broken bricks and steel rods encased in lengths of rubber hose. One Liverpool tailor would automatically include a 'special cosh pocket' in all suits made for teenagers. Brass rings were worn on several fingers, both for ornament and smashing opponents' teeth. In one affray a youth club lavatory had its chain pulled off to be used as a weapon. The boardroom at the Blackpool Tower ballroom housed a museum of weapons confiscated from Teds, including knuckle-dusters, razors, coshes, bicycle chains and garrotters. In Great Barr, Birmingham, warring Teds armed themselves with brass-ended chimney sweep rods. One Manchester Ted went into battle wielding a shovel. In Glasgow Teds clashed with road forks. In East London seven Teds refused to allow two boys to continue walking along Barking Road. One of the pair, a policeman's son, was then slashed across the face with a razor embedded in a potato.

In his memoirs of police life in London in the early 1950s, Superintendent Fabian describes the armour and weaponry of two fifteen-year-old members of the Eagle Gang. In addition to a spiked knuckle-duster, an embossed ring with a sharpened hook and a flick-knife, the boys had aluminium shields running from wrist to elbow, concealed under the arms of their shirts. One boy also had half a dozen fish-hooks sewn into his right-hand jacket sleeve near the cuff buttons. Fabian's colleague recalled that an innocent young girl had recently had half her cheek ripped off by fish-hooks after becoming caught up in a milk-bar gang fight.

Bicycle chains were another Ted favourite. In Suffolk, two brothers appeared before Lowestoft magistrates accused of a breach of the peace; one was further accused of being in possession of an offensive weapon: a bike chain. He denied that it was a weapon, defiantly explaining, 'If it had been intended as a weapon, the constable would have had a couple of scars on his face by now.' If bicycle chains proved inadequate, Teds could improvise with something a bit bigger. During a clash between rival Welsh gangs from Nantyglo and Abergavenny, in the Market Square of Brynmawr, each side wielded a nine-foot length of spiked chain weighing 7lb, ripped from the ornamental enclosure around the square. One bystander heard shouts of 'Kill him' and 'Do him in'. Another claimed it was 'like the battlefield at Waterloo'.

Seven Teds in the Lancashire mill town of Oldham blocked the pavement, forcing pedestrians to leave the footpath; one had placed pennies between his fingers and covered them with a handkerchief to make a knuckle-duster. Down the road in the Manchester suburb of Northenden, three youths were chased and beaten by eight Teds. Weapons found abandoned at the scene included bicycle chains, a knife and a glove with five steel studs clipped to the knuckles.

Throughout the 1950s knuckle-dusters lent themselves to a great deal of modification and sadistic ingenuity. A trawl through the court reports in the newspapers reveals a frightening variety. There are heavy ornamental rings, spiked knuckle-dusters, leather straps with protruding nails that were wrapped around the fist, chains likewise fixed to leather straps and – in one instance – a bicycle cogwheel was used as a knuckle-duster. One Yorkshire Ted, from Morley, wore a particularly elaborate knuckle-duster in the form of a glove adorned with a leather strap with bent nails, brooches, pins and heavy chain links sewn into it.

Although not officially classed as an offensive weapon, the belt that held up their trousers could cause plenty of damage when swung with force and especially if the belt had been modified. In 1955 a nineteen-year-old Teddy Boy was jailed for three years after striking an innocent bus passenger in the face with the sharpened metal buckle of a belt. The victim's wound needed nineteen stitches. In Brentwood, Essex, a Ted stopped by police was found to be carrying an Army webbing belt adorned with boot studs and loaded with lead hammered onto one end. One seized after a running battle between Teds in Stourport, Worcestershire, contained seventy-eight studs. A Wolverhampton policeman confiscated another adorned with twenty-six nuts and bolts. He asked its wearer what it was for. 'To keep my trousers up!' was the flippant reply. This was untrue as the Ted had another normal belt underneath. One Ted from Moston, Manchester, had a metal-studded belt with a one-inch nail driven through one end.

A Detective Inspector Bonner revealed in 1954 that Liverpool police had recently dealt with a case in which ice skates were used as a weapon. Two years later the city's Teddy Boy gangs were said to have adopted 'jungle law' by arming themselves with knives, bayonets, loaded coshes, bicycle chains, heavily studded belts and even axes, to attack rival gangs, the police and the public. Elsewhere, a Ted boasted of being permanently tooled up: 'I'd have a bicycle chain and fish-hooks behind my lapels so that if somebody grabbed hold of me they'd get stuck and I could bang them. That never happened with me, but it could get nasty.'

* * *

Weapons were not confined to older youths. In 1954, a thirteen-year-old appeared at West London Juvenile Court accused of heading a protection racket in school, forcing terrified pupils to hand over their dinner money; some hadn't eaten lunch for months. The boy even used a knife to slice the initials TB (Teddy Boy) onto the arms of four classmates. Dressed in a bright blue suit with yellow striped socks, he burst into tears when told he would be sent to an approved school.

In 1956, teachers at three Yorkshire schools found gashes on the backs of the hands of nearly 200 pupils, aged between seven and twelve. The wounds were caused by finger nails, zip fasteners and pen nibs; it seems that the children had been playing a new game called 'Chinese torture'. 'It's all the rage,' claimed one child. In one published account, a teacher revealed the 'blackboard jungle' state of Britain's classrooms: there were disturbing tales of youngsters being tortured by older boys in the lavatories and having cigarettes stubbed on their foreheads if they refused to sing, while weapons confiscated included spiked knuckle-dusters and bicycle chains. The fourteen- to fifteen-year olds were said to be the worst, since it was the age when they apparently became hooligans. In response to such negative press reporting, particularly allegations that young Teds were terrorising their teachers and classmates, the National Union of Teachers (NUT) conducted a survey of 346 schools in 1956. The report found that there was no evidence of a 'jungle schoolroom'.

However, fifty schools did admit that weapons were being brought into class, although in only five were they considered serious. Flick-knives were reported in two boys' schools, and one school in a slum area reported finds of open razors, devices for firing darning needles, knives made from files, coshes, and knuckle-dusters. Nine boys at one school were found to be carrying razor-blades in their trouser turn-ups, while three from another stole phosphorus and prepared home-made bombs to throw at a teacher's house. During a national tour of selected schools in difficult areas, including London and Liverpool, Fred Jarvis, assistant secretary of the NUT, found only 'a poor collection of weapons' including a potato laced with razor-blades. The 'jungle' was, according to Jarvis, 'no more than a weedy undergrowth'. It was, of course, the 1955 film *Blackboard Jungle*, a serious social drama about a liberal teacher's attempts to gain the respect of his unruly pupils at a New York slum school, that inspired the Teds to further mayhem in the cinemas.

Despite the NUT's assurances, some children undoubtedly carried knives, which were even given as Christmas and birthday presents by parents. Elizabeth Stucley ran a youth club at a time when some were drifting towards the Teddy Boy movement. During one camping trip fight, after one lad stabbed another, Stucley immediately lined up the boys and demanded their weapons. A frightening collection of knives and daggers were promptly surrendered without much protest.

She then frisked the boys for coshes and bicycle chains. From then on a new rule was introduced to the club: on future expeditions, all arms were to be surrendered.

Perhaps the most visible weapon that the Teddy Boy possessed was his very presence. Even the way he walked was meant to inspire fear: a kind of exaggerated swagger, with the roll of the shoulders said to be typical of habitual drunkards. In extreme cases the head was also said to roll from side to side and the customary sneer further distorted into a snarl. The delinquent associations of the clothing, the weapons, and the sneering arrogance, were a cocktail that led to anti-social behaviour, criminality and ultimately to gang-related murder.

7

GANGS

> *'There is no harm in wearing eccentric clothes and adopting weird hair styles, but there is a suspicion that, with many Teddy Boys, the exhibitionism is extended to indulge in mass violence.'*
>
> (*Somerset County Herald*, 1958)

'What is a gang?' asks Superintendent Langton in Julian Symons' novel *The Progress of a Crime* (1961), the tale of a murder committed by a group of Teds. For Langton, 'gangs' is hardly the right word to describe the local suspects who would gather in the cafes, listening to records and drinking coffee with their girls after dances. Langton's question is one that has been hotly disputed by countless commentators from the 1950s to the present day.

In 1956, having returned from a tour of America, London magistrate Basil Henriques told the Manchester Luncheon Club that crime among young people in Britain was not as bad as that in America, where gangs could be 150-strong and armed with guns. In comparison, the British Teds were 'harmless little rabbits'. Elsewhere, Henriques explained that Teddy Boys had no real leadership and did not go around 'armed to the teeth and ready to shoot people'. This is not quite true; there were a few isolated firearms incidents. A sixteen-year-old from Brislington, Bristol, was shot in the mouth by Teds. A London girl was also shot in the eye. A Ted once pulled a revolver on the foreman of the Morley Street Picture House in Bradford. In 1958, a plain-clothed policeman was beaten and threatened with an air pistol as he fought a mob of Teds in the West End of London.

However, even in 1956, when the movement was at its peak, with reputedly up to 30,000 Teds in Greater London alone, organised delinquent gangs were rare in Britain.[1] Unlike American gangs, which were bound together by ethnic and racial factors, most British gangs were merely groups of mates who came together temporarily for a punch-up or a particular incident. Criminologist David Downes studied delinquency in London's East End in the late 1950s and early 1960s. He defined a 'gang proper' as having a leader, definite membership, a den or headquarters, some form of initiation ceremony and criminal objectives. He concluded that such qualities were unusual in Britain and that delinquent gangs were merely loose street-corner groups without the American sense of structure.

Police in North London confirmed that gangs were little more than social gatherings of bored youths in dance halls and cafes located in each area. They had no organisation or even name, being known simply as 'the mob from Highbury' or 'the mob from the Angel'. Similarly, in Birmingham, Teds were also characterised by territory. There was the 'Bradshaw Street Mob', the 'Balsall Heath Boys', the 'Quinton Lot' and 'the Teds from the new flats'. There were no permanent leaders or defined positions. Nor were these gangs as unified, focused or devoted to violence as they were popularly portrayed in the press. One of the Plough Boys explained that people referred to 'gangs' as if they really existed but such groups were never organised. There were no elections or membership cards. What people took for gangs were merely lads hanging around with their mates. If they were spotted off their own manor people would call them 'the Plough Boys'. It was as if the name created the gang.

On the other hand, a report in the *Sunday Graphic* claimed that Teddy Boy gang leaders were usually aged from eighteen to twenty-five and surrounded themselves with a nucleus of

1. Downes believes that this figure is based on conjecture and states that there is no way of knowing what proportion of that number operated as gangs, mobs, cliques or pairs. See *The Delinquent Solution*, p. 120.

six chosen lieutenants. They would pick a back-street cafe or billiard hall as their headquarters, telling the owner to 'keep your trap shut'. Hilde Marchant felt that the boy with the worst criminal record was looked up to as the natural Teddy leader. A Huddersfield solicitor claimed that there were Teddy Boy gang bosses operating in the town. They would persuade boys to commit crimes and then take a cut of the proceeds. According to T.R. Fyvel, at least some of the London gang leaders were called 'governors', with their local subordinates acting as 'assistant governors'. It was a point of honour for the governor to be able to call out a ragtag army of 100 youths for what sometimes amounted to a 'mock battle', although it could also turn into a real one.

Superintendent Fabian tells a different story. He claims that London gang membership was in fact gained through initiation ceremonies. A potential recruit might have to demonstrate his foolhardy courage and viciousness by, for example, stealing a car, fighting or throwing a brick at a policeman. Teds in Bristol invented a new sport based on the car dare game featured in the film *Rebel Without a Cause* (1955), starring James Dean, where the last driver to jump from the vehicle before it goes over a cliff is the winner. To join one gang youths had to stand in the road in front of heavy traffic and defy drivers to knock them down. The gang shouted 'Za-Za', meaning yellow, if a lad jumped too early.

By the mid 1950s magistrates, senior policemen and newspapers often referred to Teddy Boys in terms of gangs. Fashion uniformity was interpreted as social uniformity, giving some a sense of solidarity, organisation and structure that they perhaps lacked in reality. Increasingly, Teds were referred to as 'gang members' even though there was no evidence to suggest that they were all organised into gangs. In 1958, Somerset's Chief Constable claimed that young thugs were appearing in the provinces, copying the ideas of criminal gangs in the more squalid parts of London and other big cities. The Dean of Manchester, Rev. H. A. Jones, noticed that in one quiet, unnamed West Country town he had seen more Teds per square mile than in Moss Side, Manchester. Even if a few individual Teds appeared in an area it was feared that gang activity had spread to that district. This was particularly true of more remote and genteel locations where residents were ever-vigilant of Teddy Boy invasions. A plan to convert a smithy in the village of Ickwell, Bedfordshire into a teashop was met by protests and petitions. Lady of the Manor Mary Wells, who owned the village green, complained, 'I am appalled at the idea of ice-cream papers and juke boxes. Then there will be teddy boys in the village.' Her instincts were probably correct. In 1957, the Easter Fair at Daisy Nook, near Manchester, saw more than the usual number of Teddy Boy visitors, attracted by the rock 'n' roll music blasting out of the funfair roundabout. A child psychiatrist argued that 'the fact that these Edwardian "creepers" are appearing in small country towns should surely convince us it is time to take this phenomenon seriously'.

* * *

Some Teds certainly banded together to use their sheer number to intimidate and terrorise. In the harsh words of one Liverpool journalist: 'When out in force, each bolstering the others piffling and miserable ego, they overawe decent folk and drive them away like a bad smell.' Probation officer John Woolfenden fumed, 'They are thorough cowards. Have you ever heard of a lone Teddy Boy making an attack? Of course not. They are creatures of the degenerate gang.' Indeed, an ex-prisoner related with some contempt how they were tough in numbers but helpless on their own in prison, adding he once saw a Ted crying in his cell.

There was certainly strength in numbers and their actions were sometimes deliberately stage-managed. About forty Teds marched in single file into an amusement arcade in New Brighton, Cheshire, a deliberate manoeuvre designed to make their presence felt. After leaving the Corn Exchange dance hall at Wisbech in 1955, where they had already beaten and kicked unconscious the attendant, five Teds were said to have marched in a line down the Cambridgeshire street like a band of Nazi *Gauleiters*, ready to beat up the first person to cross their path; on meeting an American serviceman they kicked and bit him. In 1957 twenty-three Oxford Teds walked shoulder to shoulder to force pedestrians off the pavement.

Despite these shows of defiance, some young people banded together not for reasons of aggression but for defence. One member of the Plough Boys explained the mentality of the gangs: they could not be seen to be weak. If a group of lads was walking down the street and by chance came across some others who looked in any way threatening, one of them would immediately confront the biggest and offer to fight him and the others one by one. Shocked, the other group would most likely back down by trying to calm the aggressive one. In this way, hard-man reputations were dramatically forged without any blood being shed.

In various reports and conferences, experts offered various reasons for youths joining gangs. Some pointed out the psychological deficiencies that drove lads to band together. For one *Manchester Guardian* journalist, gang membership was a means of compensating for an unconscious inferiority complex. For youths lacking educational or career opportunities, joining a gang offered an alternative source of self-esteem. Dr J. Stephen-Spinks expressed the view that Teddy Boys were hapless creatures lacking a proper place in society. Instead, boys found a false society in gangs where they idolised the leader. He felt that boys at his remand home had no proper role models.

A 1961 report by the Bristol Social Project revealed that gang members saw themselves as failures, first at school and then at work where they usually had the worst jobs. They behaved badly partly out of a sense of inferiority and partly as a rejection of a society that valued success and condemned them to a life of failure. It was suggested that their behaviour would not change if their sense of worthlessness continued to be aggravated by public disapproval. Worryingly, a perverse sense of their own importance was only fed by public panic at their antisocial behaviour.

For some youths it was pride rather than a sense of worthlessness that bound them together. In 1959, Karel Reisz made the film *We Are the Lambeth Boys*, a landmark documentary about Alford House, a youth club in central London. The club contained some who could be described as Teds, and in one scene the boys sing:

We are the Lambeth Boys,
We know our manners.
We spend our tanners.
We are respected wherever we go.

The boys are being ironic. They hope to be respected for their fighting ability rather than their good etiquette.

Perhaps the most common reason why such groups form is that members live in the same clearly defined neighbourhood. Then, as today, the need to defend territorial space was vitally important. Superintendent Fabian claims that London youths sometimes acted in gangs 100-strong. Territory was carved up between rival groups. A milk-bar on one side of the street could 'belong' to one gang, while a soft-drinks bar further up the road could be considered the territory of another. Incursions by either side into rival space could result in a skirmish needing the force of several car-loads of policemen to break it up.

In the packed urban spaces of the capital, territorial possessions led to ongoing simmering tensions. Around 1953 a bus conductor revealed that on Saturday nights, near a certain public house at the end of his route, he could see huddled groups from different gangs watching each other like cats. They didn't have far to go for a fight. As George Melly points out, the hardcore Teds were largely confined to their own 'manors', unable to travel far as a mob. Speaking of the Clapham Common gang, a policeman said that if the lads were told to go to Shepherd's Bush they would not have a clue how to get there. Forays outside their own area were dependent on the vagaries of bus or train timetables. Unlike their American counterparts, or the later Mods and Rockers, it was unusual for pre-1960 British teenagers to own a motorbike, never mind a car.

Nevertheless, in the latter half of the 1950s there were a few isolated incidents involving more mobile Teds. In 1957, Teds in cars fought a battle on Richmond Bridge, South West London; police received 'kidnap' warnings after one of the injured youths was seen being bundled into one of the cars. Months later in East London, six Teds threw bricks through a public house window in Poplar before jumping in a motor and driving away. The licensee was struck on the head.

* * *

Despite their insularity, some Teds did invade other areas in search of girls and entertainment. Disputes over women were a common cause of aggravation. 'Nine times out of ten the trouble started over a girl,' said Mick Johns, from Tunbridge Wells. 'You get two gangs of Teds at a dance and somebody would fancy somebody else's girlfriend.' Malcolm 'Curly' Philips was the sixteen-year-old leader of a gang in the West Riding town of Heckmondwike. In 1957, he beat up a love rival outside a cafe. Philips was unrepentant: 'It serves him right. I'd do it again if I had the chance. He should not go out with my girl.' A gang in East London was said to be able to summon 150 members within an hour to repel groups from other boroughs raiding their women.

In late-night cafes, youths would sit and brood over insults from other groups. Night after night the resentment would grow until tempers were sufficiently excited. Telephone calls would be made and the lads would tool up ready for a retaliatory expedition into rival territory. One ex-Ted spoke of these cafe-based war summits where future skirmishes were planned. He claimed that knives were rare: lads usually armed themselves with lumps of wood or bottles. A London probation officer suggested that the frequenting of such cafes inspired younger boys to join gangs. Youths would get caught up in criminality after being attracted to romantic notions of gang membership, particularly after listening to older lads boasting about their criminal exploits.

The Teds also stuck together as a defiant response to the social upheaval and fragmentation of their run-down neighbourhoods, not helped by the capital's post-war housing redevelopment. During the war one and a half million Londoners found themselves homeless and over eight million people were forced to leave their neighbourhoods, many never to return. As the builders and developers further began to demolish what was left of their physical and cultural spaces, some youths tried stubbornly to hold on to their sense of community. Loyalty to each other became a means of resistance. In Nottingham, and the Notting Hill district of West London, there were also socio-economic threats from what seemed like invading immigrants. Teds feared that other nationalities, particularly the black pimps and landlords, were becoming financially successful at their expense. Sensitive to their own lowly social status, and feeling economically threatened, the Teds responded in the only way they knew how – with gang violence.

Gang fights also became something of a sport, similar to the regular 'scuttles' involving Victorian youths from Manchester and Salford. In South East London, Alan Endersby, one of the Catford Boys, admitted to tooling up with coshes, rocks, iron bars and bicycle chains to fight pitched battles with neighbouring gangs on the local recreation ground. He likened the skirmishes to matches between public schools. Such battles were often ritualised and pre-arranged and, although they were not meant to affect innocent bystanders, the general public could still be caught in the crossfire, as they were during the Mods and Rockers seaside riot at Clacton-on-Sea, Essex, in Easter 1964. Indeed, seaside battles were nothing new: as already mentioned, the Teds had been visiting coastal towns looking for trouble ever since the first recorded inter-gang battle at a Brighton dance hall eleven years earlier. The Teddy Boy wars had already begun.

8
PITCHED BATTLES

'Something must be done to stop this wave of violence before it gets out of hand.'

(MP for Brighton Kemptown, 1954)

The Teddy Boy battleground of Brighton saw a major clash in March 1954, when rival gangs from Southsea, Portsmouth and Croydon fought on the seafront with stones and bottles, causing holidaymakers to scatter. It began when the Southsea Teds argued with local youths over two girls. The Southsea lads got the worst of it but announced that they would be back with reinforcements on Easter Sunday. Police were put on standby.

Revenge missions were a common motivation for gang disorder. Also in 1954 rival groups started a fight at a village hall dance at Blucher, Northumberland. The brawl spread along half a mile of the main West Road and into neighbouring fields. Trouble began when a gang from Scotswood, Newcastle, arrived at the venue to avenge an incident against one of their members the previous week. Fearing that they would be outnumbered, the Blucher lads sent a message to colleagues at a dance in Westhope requesting reinforcements. There was chaos in the hall as youths ran amok, punching anyone in sight. One lad was assaulted while being held by a policeman. He claimed that if the officer had not had hold of his hands he would have killed his assailant. A chain and a blood-stained fence post embedded with nails were later found at the scene. Twelve lads appeared in court, including the fifteen-year-old ringleader of one gang, dressed in drape jackets with tuxedo lapels. They were sentenced to prison and remand homes.

Brighton might have been the first scene of gang fights, but it was the Battle of St Mary Cray, near Orpington in Kent, on 24 April 1954 that marked the true arrival of the Teds as a force for large-scale public violence. The headline in *The Orpington & Kentish Times* ran, '"Gang Battle" at Railway Station: Edwardian Youths in Half-Hour Fight: Wooden Stakes, Sand-Filled Socks as Weapons'. The catalyst was a feud between rival gangs from Downham and nearby St Paul's Cray. Trouble began when a rowdy group of Teds and a few girls from the Downham Estate arrived at a dance at St Paul's Cray Community Centre. Inside the venue a member of the group responded to being jostled by drawing a knife. During a fierce exchange of words a man also had a glass of orange juice thrown in his face. The MC was confronted with a difficult situation: 'I warned the crowd police were standing by and also took the precaution of having the band play only calming music – no quicksteps. Several older people felt there might be trouble and left. I felt the few of us responsible for keeping order were in a precarious position, and I breathed a sigh of relief when 11 o'clock came.'

The crowd dispersed peacefully until it reached the nearby railway station, where all hell broke loose. Teds tore up spiked wooden fence posts and jousted with shunting poles and fire-buckets until the police arrived and managed to lock them all in the booking hall. Fifty-five youths were arrested and questioned by the police, although no charges were ever brought. When the police returned to inspect the damage in daylight they found abandoned weapons including jagged glass, a clasp-knife, a knuckle-duster; also drawings of automatic pistols. A worrying message had also been scrawled on a fire-bucket: 'It is time St Mary Cray was woken up'. The event did, indeed, rouse not just St Mary Cray but the entire nation to the threat from the Teddy Boys. From now they were public enemy number one. In response to the gang problem, three days later lads in Edwardian dress, for the first time, were refused entry to cinemas and dance halls.

Dance halls provided the venue for many battles. In the same year, members of Liverpool's Swallow Gang, aged fifteen and sixteen, fought with rivals outside a dance hall in Marmaduke Street. When a policeman tried to separate them, one explained, 'They started the "nark" in the dance and got us thrown out.' An associate added, 'Our mates got nicked through them and we're going to settle them.' One lad was arrested for swinging a leather belt above his head. He told the officer, 'I'll get back in and lace [beat] those two fingers [informers].' In court, the boys showed the magistrate the swallow tattoos on the backs of their hands, near the thumb and forefinger.

* * *

The year 1955 saw several major clashes as the contagion of gang-brawling spread. Two mobs of up to fifty Teds fought a Saturday-night battle with twenty policemen on leaving the Ideal Ballroom in Bankfoot, Bradford. Traffic on the main road was held up for forty minutes as the fighting raged. Police helmets were knocked off and three girls suffered stab wounds. Threats were made to release lads already detained in police vans. The dance hall owner had been warned in an anonymous phone call that there would be trouble between rival gangs from outside the area. Police were waiting in a van. Three youths were later sent to prison and fourteen fined.

Fifty Teds, banned from Brighton dance halls, invaded Shoreham-by-Sea seven miles along the coast. The gang, many of them carrying walking sticks and wearing cravats and knee-length drapes, visited a local dance before making a tour of the public houses. A group of about twenty-five entered the Swiss Cottage Inn where the licensee, Mr Brookes, refused to serve them because of their behaviour. In response three local youths were set upon, one of them knocked unconscious with a blow from a stick. Mr Brookes explained, 'It was an ugly situation, but I refused to serve them ... I think this is the way in which all the town's licensees should deal with these Teddy boy hooligans.'

In Coventry, Scottish and Irish Teds were involved in a street fight that resulted in one lad being jabbed in the neck with a broken bottle. Up to fifty Glasgow Teds also swaggered through a Pollok housing scheme waving sticks and shouting 'We are the Bingo Boys'. They then attacked a Scout hall hosting a dance. Every window was smashed, showering the terrified dancers cowering inside. One girl collapsed after being hit on the head with a stone.

Glasgow had a long-standing gang problem, and the arrival of the Teds served to exacerbate it. In 1956, two rival Bridgeton gangs, the Stick It Boys and the Nuneaton Boys, staged a four-hour on and off running street battle. Hundreds of residents watched the skirmishes from their tenement windows. There was also a pitched battle between Teds in a Clydebank dance hall. The feud then spilled onto the street where fifteen policemen, with batons drawn, tried to control up to 200 teenagers. Bottles were thrown at the officers as screaming teenage girls egged on their boyfriends. One local witness stated that it was like a riot and the first real problem they'd had with Teddy Boys. It was claimed the trouble was started by invading Glasgow Teds.

In Smethwick a twenty-minute street battle broke out between up to forty rival Midlands Teds who hurled beer bottles and swiped at each other with bicycle chains. Four lads were taken to hospital and many more received minor injuries. In the North East, a seventy-strong gang of Teds turned a Hebburn dance hall into a battlefield. Trouble began when members of the Daisy Hill Flower Gang from Wallsend sought revenge after one of their members had been assaulted at a previous dance. At the end of the night over 200 Teds and their girls were milling about the streets waiting for further trouble.

Ten miles up the road from Hebburn, Easter visitors to Whitley Bay were shocked by outbreaks of disorder, a foretaste of a violent summer. Rival gangs of up to thirty youths would loiter menacingly on the pavements during the evening. The Spanish City funfair was a focal point. Officials and staff held an emergency conference to discuss how best to protect their property from hooliganism. On the Good Friday, a Ted had been beaten up after trouble broke out on one of the roundabouts. Then on Easter Sunday about 300 Teds gathered looking for revenge and refused to disperse until the police arrived. Between Good Friday and Easter Monday up to 1,000 Teds and their female followers had invaded the seaside town from both side of the Tyne. The train back to Newcastle was known as the 'Teddy Special'.

A running fight outside Burton's Dance Hall in Bootle involved 300 Teds. 'Come on, get stuck into them,' some shouted as they fought. Even as police moved in to make arrests, one lad yelled, 'Never mind the flat feet, get stuck into them.' In Southport, Teds staged a midnight battle in Lord Street; the trouble began outside a cafe when two started fighting. In another Lord Street battle, a young girl and a lad had their faces gashed; witnesses said that a razor and broken bottle were used. The incident started when a gang of twenty Teds walking along the street met some similarly dressed locals and decided to fight over two Teddy Girls who had emerged from a shop door.

In June, a man claiming to be the leader of the Wythenshawe gang rang the *Manchester Evening News* to declare that if the Moss Side Gang came looking for more trouble in Wythenshawe, the locals would be ready for them. Two weeks later, a thirty-strong gang of Salford Teds planned to visit Longford Park, Stretford, to meet the Moss Side Teds who had beaten up one of their gang in Old Trafford. A Wythenshawe cafe owner admitted that he never got much trouble from the local Teds, even though there were some 'bad 'uns' among them. It was other gangs, particularly the Moss Siders, who caused the nuisance. The following month Wythenshawe Park hosted the latest battle in the long-running feud between Wythenshawe and Moss Side; about forty young men were involved. 'They seemed to be fighting and screaming all over the place,' said a resident. 'Some were using bicycle chains and lead piping.' Another witness said, 'They ran about the park like a pack of Red Indians on the warpath.'

Gang fights were not restricted to the densely populated urban slums of the major cities. Neighbouring towns and villages were also at odds. Inter-town feuds could be intense. Alan Wright, a member of the Rebels from the Midlands town of Warwick, claimed that his gang was feared as far away as Birmingham. In 1956 a team of *Manchester Evening News* reporters visited various outlying areas to research the Teds. They discovered that in Newton-le-Willows, disturbances were caused by visiting Teds from St Helens, Warrington and Wigan. Warrington blamed its troubles on Teds from Chester, while in Derbyshire, trouble in Glossop was blamed on Teds from Hyde, Ashton-under-Lyne and Sheffield.

Mary Blandy ran a youth club in an ancient market town near Kingston on Thames which had, over time, become surrounded by industrial and slum districts. Teddy Boys from the nearby dockland area began to migrate, partly in search of amusement and partly driven on by the police from each new area in which they tried to settle. Local youths in Blandy's home town resented the intruders and began a series of evening brawls. The locals were descendants of Irish costermongers and among them were a few fighters. Dressed in leather jackets and jeans, they wore heavy brass-buckled and studded belts, together with metal-tipped shoes for 'putting in the leather' (kicking an opponent when he was down). Coffee bars were smashed and cinemas inevitably banned teenagers. Eventually, police reinforcements drove the Teds elsewhere.

Other relatively quiet areas also suffered gang violence. In 1957, on a carnival night in the sleepy village of Sandiacre in Derbyshire, twenty-seven Nottingham Teds travelled eight miles just to terrorise the locals. From the bus station they paraded through the village swinging chains and heavily studded belts above their heads. Stopped by the police, one of them shouted, 'Mind your own business.' Watched by an eventual crowd of 2,000, the lads then set off for neighbouring Stapleford, marching along the main road still swinging their belts and sending people fleeing down the side streets. They then returned to Sandiacre and took control of the traffic island in the centre of the village where they challenged the police to a fight.

After three hours the lads tried to commandeer a bus heading back to Nottingham. Violently pushing other passengers out of the way they then banged on the roof and sides with fists and belts. The ringleader appeared to be Charles O'Leary, who stood at the top of the stairs kicking out as the police moved in to arrest him. He shouted to officers that they would 'have their hearts cut out'. O'Leary was nevertheless snatched from the bus and the driver ordered to drive straight to the police station, where the rest of the mob was arrested by a waiting posse of policemen. A search of the vehicle revealed three knuckle-dusters, a broken bottle on a string, a knife and a spiked bottle opener. This was in addition to sixteen leather belts that had been hastily removed and discarded. O'Leary claimed that they were on a revenge mission after one of his boys had been attacked by locals from Sandiacre the previous week.

One of the biggest battles broke out n London in 1957. Shortly before midnight, in pouring rain, the two gangs, each 100-strong, clashed outside the Cypriot-owned Domino Club in Euston. Girls fought side by side with their boyfriends as they hacked and slashed at one another with knives, razors and broken bottles; one youth brandished an axe. People watching the battle from their bedroom windows said that before the police arrived some of the wounded had been carried off by their supporters. One witness claimed that the gutters were running with blood.

* * *

Police intervention did prevent some battles. Seventeen youths from Walton-on-Thames, in Surrey, were arrested in Shepperton as they waited for their opponents to turn up. One of the lads explained, 'This Shepperton mob has been coming over to Walton and beating us up. We got fed up with it and decided to come over that night in force and beat them up.' Around the same time in South London, a large group of Battersea youths were seen marching down a street near Tooting Bec Common like 'Hitler's Brownshirts', forcing people off the pavement. Thirty-eight arrests were made. One of the youths explained, 'About fifty of us met at the Belleville Club at Battersea and came to Tooting to see the blokes that did one of our blokes last week.' A year later, twenty-two Teds were arrested near Wallington Town Hall in Surrey as they waited for their rivals – among their weapons were a weighted cane, a stiletto-knife, two flick-knives, two chains, two belts and two bottles. A policeman had overheard one of the youths complaining, 'They are a long time, the windy —.' Another lad asked, 'Where's the Rosehill Mob? They must be milky.'

Police in Staffordshire discovered up to forty Teds assembled in groups in Holyhead Road, Smethwick, in an incident the following year. Although they ran away, five were caught and arrested. Weapons seized included a razor, spiked knuckle-dusters, weighted belts and a paper-knife that had been strapped to a lad's wrist. The area had been plagued by gang battles involving youths from Birmingham and surrounding towns. One of those arrested explained, 'Snyder's Gang from West Bromwich was going to do my cousin so I came here for them.' Another added, 'There was going to be a fight with the Hockley paddies. We challenged them but they didn't turn up.'

Since police officers were employed to put a stop to gang warfare, they became a popular target for attack. Some youths were fearless. A St Albans officer who tried to arrest a group of five lads was told, 'Get lost, copper, the Teddy Boys are taking over the town.' A fundraising dance at the Jubilee Hall, Breward, turned into chaos after Wolverhampton Teds paid a visit and started fighting; a policeman trying to evict the youths was kicked in the testicles by the seventeen-year-old leader of the gang. In London, two West End policemen were knocked unconscious by a gang of Teds resisting the arrest of a friend, while in Vauxhall a policeman had his skull fractured as a result of being coshed by four Teds; he had simply asked them to move on after a disturbance outside a public house. In

Glossop, Derbyshire, three policemen tried to break up a Teddy Boy gang fight watched by 200 spectators. As an officer tried to make an arrest, a youth attacked him with a belt. The crowd began chanting, 'Kill that copper.'

A crowd of drunken Teds from Huyton, on the oustkirts of Liverpool, caused a disturbance in nearby Prescot in 1954. As police tried to arrest two of the lads, one of them threatened to 'bring their mobs down on them'. The constables had to draw truncheons to stave off the rest of the hostile rabble. And at Liverpool's Wavertree funfair, a gang of Teds attacked a policeman who tried to stop them fighting. 'This is a showdown no copper can stop,' shouted one. He then hit the officer with the leather belt wrapped around his fist before jumping on his back.

A year later, Liverpool police cautioned a gang of twenty youths causing trouble in Wavertree. Most heeded the warning and moved on but a sixteen-year-old shouted, 'Don't go. We will get them. We are the Swallow Gang.' He then lashed out at a constable with his fist, around which was wrapped an Army belt. In court, he denied being a member of the gang until asked to show his hands to the magistrate. The swallow tattoos put an end to his argument and he was found guilty. In Bootle, near Liverpool, a twenty-strong mob stood outside a dance hall and defied the police. One lad shouted, '— cops. We'll throw them over the — canal bridge.' In 1956, as he tried to stop a fight between rival gangs in Edge Hill, a Liverpool police sergeant was stabbed in the thigh with a bayonet. The attacker, who had the scabbard attached to his belt, was about to use the weapon against another lad when he attacked the officer instead.

After leaving a dance at Willenhall, Staffordshire, a group of seventeen-year-old Teddy Boys and Girls attacked police officers in an attempt to rescue a comrade who had been arrested. At the police station one of the lads ran fearlessly through the corridors into the charge office, still determined to release his friend. In a similar incident in 1960, about 300 teenagers, including Teds and their girlfriends, battled with police for more than an hour outside York's central police headquarters, in a bid to rescue eleven youths from the cells.

The mob attempted to overturn a police car that had come to help. They succeeded in tearing off its aerial and wing mirrors and ripping tyres. Trouble had flared after officers broke up a fight at a rock 'n' roll dance.

Nothing could unite rival gangs more than the sight of a policeman. In Hertfordshire several officers were injured trying to stop a fight involving bottle-wielding Teds outside a Watford dance hall. Their attackers knocked them down, tore uniforms, blackened eyes and cut faces. Some were even kicked as they lay helpless on the floor. It took four officers to arrest one Ted who was biting and kicking them.

In 1960, up to fifty Teds jumped out of a furniture-van in Midsomer Norton, Somerset, and tried to enter a public house. After being refused admission they threatened the publican and started misbehaving outside. Traffic was halted while bricks and beer glasses were thrown and things escalated until police reinforcements were called from nearby Frome and Keynsham. During a two-hour battle attempts were made to overturn a patrol car and officers were forced to draw their truncheons. 'The street was like a battlefield,' claimed one witness.

One policeman managed to handcuff a culprit to his wrist but was then subjected to a savage attack by the howling mob. 'Break his — arm,' they shouted. 'Let's get him away and we will do the copper,' was another cry. The PC managed to drag the youth into the patrol car and, on the arrival of more officers, the lads retired to another pub where they barricaded themselves in, pelting the police with bottles, glasses and stones from a nearby rockery. It was a terrific struggle to make arrests. Seven lads from Bristol later appeared in court and were variously fined or imprisoned for up to six months. Sheath knives, studded belts, bicycle chains and a cut-throat razor were exhibited in court.

In Somerset assaults on the police, together with outbreaks of hooliganism and a general rise in the crime figures, were becoming a cause for concern. Asked whether he thought alcohol was to blame, the Chief Constable explained, 'Some Teddy boys seem to be able to do it on coffee.'

* * *

The year 1958 would see yet another increase in Teddy Boy violence, beginning with a couple of dance-hall stabbings and culminating in the Nottingham and Notting Hill racial disturbances (see chapters 15 and 16). In February, in the quiet Cornish village of Calstock, a new coffee bar began to attract Plymouth Teds on their way to a dance at the nearby village hall. Numerous weekly incidents of disorder culminated in an invasion of twenty Teds swinging chains and flashing flick-knives. The proprietor's husband had to fire his shotgun to scare them off. Eight policemen also arrived to drive the gang away. As they left by train, one shouted out of the window, 'Don't worry, we'll be back.' The terrified cafe owner decided to cut her losses and close down.

In Liverpool two gangs of up to fifty Teds and girls fought on the forecourt of a tenement block called Myrtle House. Police reinforcements arrived in Jeeps, only to have one of their windows smashed. With truncheons drawn the police chased some of the youths back into the flats. In another incident, seventy Teds from South Liverpool, armed with spanners, coshes and sawn-off axe handles, marched into Runcorn to do battle with their Widnes rivals. The marauding army wrecked a cafe. Around the same time, 100 Teds from rival gangs brought traffic to a standstill as they fought it out on Stanley Road, Bootle.

Further south a twenty-strong gang comprising Sutton Coldfield and Kingstanding Teds, armed with chains, studded belts and conduit piping, visited Tamworth 'to teach the local lads a lesson'. In the village of Ratby, near Leicester, a public house and cinema were attacked as the streets were overrun for two hours by twenty shrieking Teds. At Weston-super-Mare, Somerset, sixty Teddy Boys and Girls, belonging to rival gangs, fought at an amusement arcade. Police managed to break up the fight only to be turned upon themselves. Later, a large crowd gathered outside the police station to jeer at the officers as they returned.

The year 1958 ended with a particularly tragic incident. On 14 December a London policeman was stabbed to death outside Gray's Dancing Academy in Seven Sisters Road, Holloway. The area had been terrorised for months by rival gangs of Teds, among them the Budd Mob, led by Johnny Budd, and the Dean Mob led by Peter Dean, both aged nineteen. The train of events that led to the murder began with a trivial incident at Barry's Dancing Academy a few days earlier when a lad flicked a screwed-up piece of paper at Budd. Feeling disrespected, Budd gathered some friends and attacked the culprit. Dean joined in on the side of the paper-flicker but got the worst of it. Threatening revenge, he called Budd a 'flash —', the words echoing those that had sparked the Clapham Common killing five years earlier.

Ronald Marwood got involved in the feud after meeting some of Budd's gang in a public house. Five years their senior, Marwood was married and earning good wages as a scaffolder. With no police record he was perhaps too old to be knocking around with gangs of youths. However, he was a local hard man who carried a knife. That night he was celebrating his wedding anniversary but rather than spend the evening at home with his wife, who wanted to watch TV, Marwood went out with his mates. Ironically, his wife watched a programme called *Dangerous World*, about a riot in a British Colony in Africa which resulted in a policeman being killed. Four miles away, on the 'jungle' of Seven Sisters Road, similar events were about to unfold.

Marwood, who had already drunk ten pints of brown ale, was told that the lads were off on a straightener to fix Dean. He joined them in three cars on the trip to the dance hall, where 200 teenagers were enjoying themselves. Budd's mob were suitably tooled up with six axes, or 'choppers', hidden inside their coats, as well as weighted coshes, knives, a plasterer's hammer, a bayonet, air pistols and various chisels. Dean was inside the venue when he heard that there was a gang waiting outside. He went out to confront Budd but was dragged back inside by a colleague.

As various youths left the building, scuffles broke out and a brief but violent affray erupted on the pavement. One sixteen-year-old witness recalled an axe-wielding youth approaching him and asking, 'Which side would you like your hair parted?' A six-foot-four-inch bobby called PC Raymond Henry Summers waded into the fray and grabbed the tallest lad, Mick Bloom, who had been best man at Marwood's wedding. As Bloom was led away, Marwood ran after the policeman and stabbed him in the back with a thin, ten-inch-long diver's knife. The weapon pierced five layers of clothing and punctured Summers' body to a depth of four inches, fatally severing his aorta. The victim, who was engaged and saving up to be married, was dying before he hit the floor.

Twenty minutes later, Marwood and a colleague were picked up by the police and taken in for questioning. Asked about the blood and cuts on his fingers Marwood claimed that he had been involved in a fight at a hotel in Finsbury Park. He was released on bail but went into hiding at a flat in Edgware provided by notorious gangster Reggie Kray. Six weeks later, after attempting to dye his hair ginger and grow a moustache, Marwood walked into a police station, accompanied by his father. He initially admitted stabbing the policeman but at his trial withdrew his statement. The jury nevertheless found him guilty and he was sentenced to hang, although the decision aroused a wave of protest for various reasons: the verdict rested solely on Marwood's initial confession; he had a clean police record and he was drunk at the time. Petitions and appeals for his reprieve, together with motions in the House of Commons, were raised to no avail.

On the evening before the execution at Pentonville Prison, there were disturbances among the inmates. Screaming prisoners smashed crockery and set fire to material before pushing it out of cell windows. At the hour of his execution, on the morning of 8 May 1959, there was also trouble outside the prison. Inside the jail a senior officer was beaten over the head by a prisoner armed with a bucket. Budd received fifteen months' imprisonment for his part in the affray while Dean was handed three months in a detention centre. Ten months after the murder of PC Summers, his fiancée Sheila McKenzie, aged twenty-one, died of an asthma attack. They were buried in the same grave.

* * *

Although the waves of destruction and violence began to ebb after the Notting Hill disturbances, isolated incidents still broke out to remind the public that the threat of gang warfare had not completely subsided. At the beginning of 1959, Teddy Boy fights took on a new turn as some youths jumped on motorbikes to become 'ton-up boys'. The Woodward Hall Community Centre, in quiet suburban East Barking, Essex, was used for dances and concerts and Tuesday evenings were set aside for rock 'n' roll sessions. During 1959 these evenings were invaded by youths belonging to motorised gangs from Dagenham and Canning Town. A Dagenham gang had already made its mark: in January, a sixteen-year-old was stabbed in the shoulder and two other boys and a girl taken to hospital after a gang of Dagenham Teds, armed with sticks, belts and knives, forced their way into a club dance at Rainham, Essex.

As if anticipating trouble, the management at Woodward Hall appointed seven stewards to keep order. On the evening of 24 February there were around 200 revellers on the dance floor when a group of menacing-looking youths entered: it was the Dagenham boys, out for revenge against their Canning Town rivals. Most were unarmed and only fancied a punch-up but one nineteen-year-old was carrying a sheath-knife he had bought earlier that day for 1s. The Dagenham boys toured the hall asking each male dancer where he came from. Anyone confessing to be from Canning Town was attacked.

Ex-sailor Alan Johnson was one of the first dancers to be asked. Admitting that he lived in nearby Stratford, he was smacked in the face. As he fought back he was stabbed in the stomach and fell bleeding to the floor. Before the stewards could intervene the place erupted. Women ran screaming from the hall as chairs were thrown and bottles wielded. While the dance organiser rang the police, the fight spilled onto the street where about fifty youths from Dagenham and Canning Town had it out using broken chair legs and bottles as weapons and dustbin lids as shields. Residents living in Woodward Road watched in horror until the police arrived. The fighters dispersed into the night leaving Johnson's life to ebb away before the ambulance arrived. He had suffered three stab wounds, including one through the heart.

The next day a Dagenham youth called Terence Cooney handed himself in to the police. Other youths were charged with common affray and given various prison sentences. The culprit's defence, in what became known as the 'Rock 'n' Roll Murder', was that he thought Johnson might also have been carrying a knife. In June 1959, at the Old Bailey, the nineteen-year-old was sentenced to life imprisonment.

Elsewhere, up to fifty youths belonging to rival gangs of Teds from Bury and Rawtenstall met up in Ramsbottom to sort out their differences after trouble at a dance the previous week. One gang marched three to four abreast down the road until police intervened. The fight nevertheless broke out outside the police station and spilled into the nearby churchyard where nail-studded sticks, stones and broken bottles were used. Some lads even climbed onto the police station roof to throw stones. 'It was absolute pandemonium,' said a police sergeant.

A gang of Moss Side Teds paid a visit to confront their rivals at a dance being held at Levenshulme Public Baths. Two doormen were stabbed as they tried to stop them entering the venue and as the Moss Side gang steamed in, fights broke out and girls ran screaming from the building. The brawl then spilled outside with milk bottles used as missiles, forcing residents to cower in their homes and passers-by to take refuge in neighbouring gardens. Police reinforcements eventually regained control and made sixteen arrests. Two youths were taken to hospital with head injuries and stomach wounds.

Rival gangs from Smethwick and Blackheath also had a pitched battle in Stourport, Worcestershire. One youth had swum across the River Severn to escape his pursuers. Two girl supporters of the opposing gangs had their own fight, with one striking the other with her pointed shoe. Also in Stourport, on the Easter Monday, fifty Teds and their girls, armed with wooden palings, studded belts and bicycle chains, engaged in another running fight. In the July a potential battle in Hadley Wood, North London, between twenty Tottenham Teds and their East Barnet rivals, was thwarted when police raided the area. They all scattered, dropping weapons as they ran.

In August a gang of around sixty Edinburgh Teds split into small groups in order to quietly infiltrate Musselburgh, six miles east. They then regrouped and headed for a dance at the Miners' Institute in nearby Wallyford, where they hoped to meet their rivals to continue a week-old feud. But there had been a tip-off, and waiting for them was a special police riot squad, dressed as workmen and civilians, which sprang out of cars and broke up the bicycle-chain-swinging mob.

Mention has already been made of a group of Birmingham Teds called the Holloway Head Gang. Armed with knives and broken bottles, they would loiter on the streets, intimidating and assaulting people visiting restaurants and bars. After knocking down and kicking two young Handsworth men, one of the gang declared, 'This part of Birmingham belongs to us, and anyone who comes down here without our permission does so at his own risk.'

Although by the 1960s Teddy Boy gang warfare was virtually over, one case acted as a reminder that it was not yet dead. The Finchley affair of 1962 has been described as 'almost a microcosm of the dynamics of the Teddy Boy movement'. On 4 April, fifteen members of a gang from Muswell Hill trekked to St Barnabas Church Hall in North Finchley on a revenge mission after one of their members had been assaulted. The incident that sparked the mission happened in the packed Dugout Cafe in Golders Green, North London, where eighteen-year-old Vic Green took offence at a remark made by a younger boy called Tommy Chamberlin. Green hit Chamberlin and split his lip, a wound that needed six stitches. Chamberlin told his friend Ronald Fletcher, a plumber with nine previous convictions, who decided to muster a posse of friends and associates, aged between fifteen and nineteen, to teach their Finchley rivals a lesson.

Fletcher and the so-called 'Mussies' tracked Green down. They knew that the Finchley Mob attended the Wednesday night dance at the church hall and at 10 p.m. the gang, armed with bottles, knives and iron bars, burst into the hall, knocking over the middle-aged club chairman before going on the rampage. Lads were cracked over the head and six of them were stabbed, some several times. One of the most badly hurt was Green, whose own brother Michael had been stabbed to death after leaving a cinema six years earlier.

The fight was reported in the press as a feud between the 'Mussies' and the 'Finchley Mob'. During the eleven-day trial, fifteen youths stood in the dock at the Old Bailey with numbered placards hung with pink string around their necks. Number one was Fletcher, aged twenty, who was alleged to be the ringleader. The jury took two hours twenty minutes to find the gang guilty of various charges. Sentences ranged from three months in a detention centre to the five years' imprisonment handed down to Fletcher. The judge declared, 'All of you have behaved in a way that would bring discredit on a pack of wolves.'

It could be argued that by 1962 the activities of so-called Teddy Boy gangs were totally unrelated to the original Edwardian trend-setters. The feuds were merely outbursts of violence by youths who had latched on to the movement, usually by sporting particular items of Teddy fashion. It did not help that the newspapers continued to fan the flames by indiscriminately applying the label 'Teddy Boy' to any incidents involving youths and violence.

Another media device was to refer to a gang leader as the 'King of the Teds', awarding him a sense of gangland status and giving the groups a sense of structure and hierarchy which, in reality, was probably lacking. Not all honours were media inventions: sometimes the title was self-conferred; sometimes it was hard-earned in the dance halls and on the tough inner-city streets.

9

KINGS OF THE TEDS

Born on a roof top in Battersea,
Joined the Teds when he was only three,
Coshed a cop when he was only four
And now he's in Dartmoor for evermore.
Davy, Davy Crockett, King of the Teddy boys.

Standing on the corner, swinging his chain,
Along came a policeman and took his name;
He pulled out the razor and he slit the copper's throat,
Now he's wiping up the blood with his Teddy boy's coat.
Davy, Davy Crockett, King of the Teddy boys.

(Variations of a playground folksong, 1956–57)

The honorary title 'King of the Teds' was a local rather than national one. There were a number of ways that Teds could become 'kings' of their neighbourhoods. Newspapers would sometimes refer to a particular Ted as the King merely because he was the leader or prominent member of a respectable 'Teddy Boy Club'. These were simply youth clubs, usually run by churchmen, where Teds met to play records and socialise. Bradford and London both had such clubs. An entirely different type of King would be crowned after fighting his way to the top. Other lads looked up to and feared such characters. Sometimes a contender to the throne would beat up a reigning King and snatch his title. Occasionally lads appointed themselves King as a means of striking terror into opponents or victims. There were no formal ceremonies, special uniforms or duties. Kings simply had to be tougher than the rest.

Perhaps the first was Ronald Coleman, the so-called 'King of the Common' who instigated the trouble on Clapham Common that led to the murder of John Beckley. The title King of the Teds had not yet been coined but the fifteen-year-old must also rank as one of the youngest. Pat Munion, of Fife's Valleyfield Gang, was another King, while Tommy Limond, originally from Glasgow, was King of Aberdeen's Teds. In 1956 he appeared in the *Sunday Mail* in an attempt to contact his mother; the twenty-three-year-old hadn't seen her for ten years after being sent to an industrial school, an establishment for children in need of care and protection that taught them a trade in the hope that they would not turn to crime. Unfortunately there is no record of him finding her.

Northampton was said to have a King called John Facer. In Penge, South London, 26-year-old Johnny Smith was acknowledged as King, although he had his work cut out defending his throne; in 1953 a magistrate had claimed that Penge had some of the toughest boys south of the Thames. Three years later, Smith complained to *The Crystal Palace and Norwood Advertiser* that the magistrate's words had only encouraged rival gangs from other areas to seek out the Penge Teds and beat them up.

Bristol's King was nineteen-year-old Alan Chaffey. Questioned as part of a magazine exposé, he told a *Picture Post* journalist that visits to the Palais de Danse were welcome relief from his job at the nearby Pensford Colliery. Acknowledging that his reign was destined to be short, he explained that in a year or two he expected to be married and busy organising his home. John Avey, the self-styled King of Dudley's Teds, was less industrious. When jailed for theft in 1957, the 24-year-old was described by a Detective Inspector as a lazy type who refused to work. Avey was the source of many local disturbances, particularly in cafes. He was also a bad influence on others, particularly his young companions, some of whom were on probation and easily led astray. In 1958 Avey was jailed for another twelve months for housebreaking. Even his two accomplices were said to be scared of him.

In his memoirs, Kray twins henchman Albert Donoghue awards the title to 'Curly' King, who led a large East London gang of smart dressers. Donoghue claims to have confronted and 'faced down' King after he found him bullying an ex-serviceman. However, the fighting abilities of King and his gang have been called into question by Brian McDonald, the author of a book called *Elephant Boys*, an account of the London underworld. Eddie Richardson, one half of the notorious South London gangster brothers, also had some claim to the title after knocking out reigning King Tony Rolands.

In court it was alleged that the King of Newcastle-under-Lyme Teds was a 21-year-old named Hugh Rennie, from Porthill. In 1955, Rennie and a colleague were accused of beating up a lad standing at a bus stop. Rennie was said to have told Bernard Cavanagh to 'Look the other way'. When Cavanagh said that he didn't like being spoken to like that, he was butted in the face, kneed in the stomach, and kicked in the head while on the ground. The victim alleged that Rennie later told him, 'In street fighting anything goes.'

In 1957, after a dance at Trent Vale, Rennie, along with Harold Lewis and another lad, beat up a man. The trio then turned on a stranger who hadn't even been to the dance, leaving him unconscious with a broken nose and other injuries. Rennie was imprisoned for three years and Lewis bound over for the same period. The third youth received probation. With Rennie dethroned, the crown passed to Lewis. In 1958 the nineteen-year-old bricklayer-cum-King of the Teds was jailed for a year after he joined others in beating up two men in a public house. It was the fifth time that he had appeared in court for eleven offences, five of them involving violence. Lewis was also jailed for eighteen months for breaching his order, the sentence to run concurrently.

Peter Sharp was King of the Medway Teds in Kent. In 1957, after being sentenced for driving while disqualified, the twenty-four-year-old escaped from a police car while on his way to Canterbury Prison; he was later recaptured at a house in Rochester. It was his fourth sentence in three years. His criminal career began at the age of ten. The following year he was at it again, this time escaping from a police van outside Chatham Court where he was due to appear on a charge of conspiring to rob a Gillingham woman. Sharp, who had exceptionally small hands, simply slipped his cuffs while bound to another prisoner. Both ran for it but were recaptured five hours later in Gillingham, over a mile away. In 1992, the 59-year-old Sharp was jailed for life for murdering Joy Taylor, his former partner of ten years. After waging a hate campaign against her, he blasted her in the head with a shotgun at point-blank range. He also turned his gun on her new husband, seriously injuring him.

The King of the Teds in Barry, South Wales, was Thomas Kelly, aged twenty-one. In 1958 he was sent to prison for three months for attacking a Swedish seaman. A police inspector said of his gang: 'They are the hard core of a local gang of Teddy Boy ruffians of which Kelly, a lazy and low-class bully, is the leader ... They hunt in a pack and over weekends take a delight in terrorising law abiding people.'

In 1959, at Leamington Borough Magistrates Court, twenty-one-year-old Haydn Jones denied that he was the self-styled King of the Teds. He was one of five youths arrested after a Sunday night disturbance, involving thirty Teds, near a café in the town's Oxford Street. The chairman of the magistrates thought that there was at least one good thing about Jones, since he had the decency to apologise for his actions.

One lad who did not deny his sovereignty was nineteen-year-old Michael Banks. In 1959, Banks and Trevor Webber, who both lived in the Hartcliffe district of Bristol, launched an unprovoked attack on a lad called John Waite. Full of bravado, Banks approached his victim in the street and announced, 'They call me Rocky, king of the Teddy Boys.' Waite was then punched and hit on the head with a piece of wood before being kicked unconscious. Banks was sentenced to two months' imprisonment while Webber was fined.

Some kingships were official appointments and represented the acceptable, non-violent face of the movement. One such

King was 21-year-old Tom Gauntlet, leader of the National Association of Teddy Boys, the NATB (see chapter 23). In 1959 he visited the West Midlands town of Wednesbury on a 'peace mission' to stop rioting in the streets. Armed with a petition containing 200 signatures, Gauntlet had to battle his way through a crowd of jeering teenagers to attend a meeting at the Conservative Hall. Although extra policemen were on duty to stop any trouble, the worst that Gauntlet faced was the cold shoulder. Perhaps the rougher element among the Teds did not feel that Gauntlet represented them. A Ted called Tommy questioned what Gauntlet was up to and asked, 'Who is he anyway? He's no-one.' Tommy's mate, known as 'Tiger', was equally dismissive, adding that Gauntlet was 'causing a fuss about nothing'.

Another respectable King was Keith Robinson, the eighteen-year-old secretary of the Bradford Teddy Boy Club. In 1956 Rev. Maurice Barnett, superintendent of the local Methodist mission, tried to evict two young Teds for misbehaving. During a scuffle, Robinson helped him eject the boys but they later came back with six friends, leaving Robinson with a black eye. Robinson claimed that there were only ten true Teds in Bradford; the others he called 'Creeps'. These wore longish coats called 'drapes' that were not in the Edwardian style and trousers that were not so tight. Robinson also claimed that real Teds did not seek trouble and wanted to be left alone.

Robinson was awarded his title by the local newspaper, but the self-elected leader of Bradford's Teds was 22-year-old Jack Binns, a young man with a completely different agenda. In 1956 the builder's labourer appeared in court with four others accused of robbery with violence. One of the gang allegedly told a passing youth that he had better get out of the Manningham Lane area as 'there were only Teddy Boys in that district'. The victim, on home leave from the RAF, was then beaten up and robbed. Binns pleaded guilty to an assault charge.

A year later Binns was also found guilty of head-butting the manager of the Roxy Cinema, which Teds had been banned from visiting for two years. In Binns' account of the incident it was the manager who started the trouble. He was said to be drunk and threatening, claiming that he was a judo expert and wrestler and able to take them all on. Binns alleged that he was assaulted as he went to walk away and only retaliated in self-defence. A cross-summons taken out by Binns against the manager was dismissed. In 1958, Binns was jailed after taking part in a gang attack on two youths in which the Assistant Chief Constable was also assaulted.

As leaders were gaoled and taken off the streets others were ready to step into their blue-suede shoes. Seventeen-year-old Michael Parker was yet another to be labelled 'King' of Bradford's Teds. He was one of fourteen youths who engaged in the 1959 'Battle of Thornton Road', which was watched by 100 spectators. The trouble began inside the Gaumont Dance Hall, and Parker armed himself with a tyre lever outside. He then challenged a 21-year-old soldier called Arthur Murray to a fight. When Murray declined, Parker stated that he dropped his weapon and walked down the road. He claimed that Murray, along with a scaffolder called John Bond, then ran after him and hit him with a belt. According to a policeman, Bond pointed at Parker and said, 'He's King of the Teds and he's going to get us.' The three were arrested. In court, Murray denied using the belt and maintained that Parker was still armed with the tyre lever when the fight started. All three pleaded guilty to causing a breach of the peace and were fined. Parker appeared in court with sticking plaster over his nose and left eye.

Trouble at the cinema was the undoing of another King in 1956. When the musical film *Rock Around The Clock* was banned in Reading, through fear of the disorder which was erupting in cinemas nationwide, local King of the Teds, Desmond Turrell, and some mates decided to travel the nineteen miles to High Wycombe instead. Trouble broke out when his twenty-three-strong gang visited a pub afterwards. It was alleged that Turrell punched a police inspector in the eye after being told to move. He was found guilty and sentenced to six months' imprisonment. After his sentence a local cinema manager claimed that he relied on Turrell to keep other Teds under control. Turrell's girlfriend also warned that there would now be trouble over who would take over his leadership role.

A month earlier Turrell had been fined for assaulting a youth at a dance. Barred from most cinemas and dance halls in Reading, the charmer once issued the following threat to a cinema usherette: 'Your face and figure won't look so good by the time I've finished with you.' A Chief Inspector described Turrell's usual tactic as egging on his mates while keeping a safe distance from the trouble.

Some kings were purely media inventions, like the one crowned at the Leyton British Legion fete in 1957. After winning through the heats of its 'Best Dressed Teddy Boy' competition, local East London Teds failed to turn up for the final. With the event threatening to become a damp squib, the organisers encouraged audience members to participate and nine youths stepped forward – including a thirteen-year-old, suitably called Ted Evans, who borrowed his uncle's grey drape jacket to complement his red check shirt, blue jeans and heavy black brogues. After being handed the winning cup, and perhaps wondering what his father would say when he found out, the lad embarrassingly explained that he wasn't really a Ted, just a schoolboy. For the local newspaper, however, he was 'King of the Teds'.

Likewise the King of Wolverhampton's Teds turned out to be an imposter who was forced to abdicate shortly after his coronation. In 1958 a group of Teds and their girlfriends stormed into the office of the *Wolverhampton Chronicle* clutching an edition of the newspaper that stated that eighteen-year-old David Langley-Forest was their King of the Teds; he had been photographed and interviewed for an article on Saturday night entertainment. The irate youths handed in a letter protesting that the lad, who was actually sixteen, was not the King and that his 'tribe' consisted of boys aged ten and eleven. The letter suggested that if the newspaper wanted to find the 'real king' they should contact somebody over the age of sixteen. Langley-Forest went along to the office later to deny all claims to kingship.

Along with Ronald Coleman, Michael Field from London must rank as one of the youngest to be a 'King of the Teds'. An orphan, Field was brought up in local authority care and at fifteen was already the leader of a Teddy Boy gang. He began his criminal career with a raid on a sweet shop in Fulham, South West London. From then on he was in and out of approved schools, absconding nine times. The skills he learnt while escaping led him to become an expert cat burglar. He then formed a gang based in an underground chamber of a disused hospital in Fulham Palace Road. From a motley group of kids he formed a well-dressed and disciplined gang, specialising in jewellery and cash robberies. His orders were 'No rough stuff'.

Throughout 1957, while on the run from police, Field's gang of four (who were all older than himself) terrorised Hammersmith and Kensington, raiding shops, factories, homes and offices. His criminality netted a total profit of £1,000, at a time when the average wage was about £8 a week and the average house cost £2,000. Gang members were paid weekly wages. Field spent his money on 20-guinea suits, numerous shirts and frequent visits to the cinema. While waiting in the queue to see a Western, Field was spotted by a policeman and arrested. Despite being unable to read and write he was said to have the mentality of a man in his mid-twenties. A probation officer warned that a spell in a detention centre would be futile, partly perhaps because he would simply escape and partly because he was so hardened in crime and incapable of rehabilitation. Field was instead jailed for a year with the option of a transfer to borstal. Field was so small that he could barely see over the dock rail.

* * *

The most controversial King of the Teds was Tony Reuter, who terrorised the streets of London's Peckham Rye and Old Kent Road. A hard case from inner-city Walworth, Reuter once struck a policeman with a bottle after a disturbance at a coffee stall. The officer was hit so hard that he developed a stammer and had to resign from the force. Twelve days later, Reuter punched two girls as they walked home from a dance; one was also kicked as she lay on the floor and suffered a broken nose and eye damage. When her friend said that she would call the police, Reuter replied, 'You wouldn't if you knew who I was.' She was also assaulted.

Some argued that the self-styled King of the Teddy Boys wasn't even a real Ted but a member of the Elephant Mob, a tough gang from the Elephant and Castle area. In reality, he was said to despise Teds. Indeed, he was considered a bit too old and his Edwardian suit was rumoured to be hired. According to hard man Frederick 'Nosher' Powell, an actor and stuntman, it was Reuter's younger brother Peter who was actually the local King of the Teds. In his autobiography, Powell recounts the time his own brother, 'Dinny', got the better of Tony Reuter in a street fight. He nevertheless confirms that both Reuters wore Teddy Boy clothing. With his fearsome reputation, Reuter was as entitled to the title as anyone else.

While on the run after his attack on the constable, Reuter was spotted by two policemen. In the pursuit, it was alleged that he threw an Army 'thunder flash' at the officers, yelling 'It's a bomb. I'll blow you up!' He escaped and while still on the run was asked by *The People* Sunday newspaper to attend a Billy Graham evangelist meeting at Wembley Stadium. Under the headline 'A Teddy Boy Confesses', his photo and story appeared in a series of articles where he claimed to have been converted. However, when he went to the newspaper office to collect his fee, reputed to be £500 (about £12,000 today), he was promptly arrested by the police. Jailing him for five years, the judge called him a coward and a bully, although his defence denied that he ever wore a Teddy Boy suit; Reuter's father also played down the link. On another occasion Reuter was jailed for ten years after using a car to attack a girl.

In his serialised memoirs, Reuter, then aged 24, describes the tough upbringing that led him to become a hard man and a Ted. As a wartime child he was evacuated from London's

Elephant and Castle but begged to return home as he didn't like the quiet streets. Despite the bombing, Reuter felt at home in the city. Hating school, he refused to comply and ended up being caned. After forging absence notes from his mother he then started to play truant. At an early age he was viewed as trouble. With a group of other kids he began to run wild among the capital's bombed-out buildings. With nobody at home to stop him (his dad was in the Royal Air Force and his mother was out working to make ends meet) he soon grew too big for his grandmother to chastise and did whatever he liked.

Reuter portrays himself as a victim who grew up fast to stand up for himself. As a young child he developed a lisp and was teased and laughed at by other boys. With a German surname, Reuter was also bullied by kids who called him a Nazi and threw stones at him. At first he cried and let them hit him, but soon he was retaliating. Because his tormentors were often bigger than him, he started using his feet and knees as well as his fists to gain the upper hand.

Reuter first got into trouble with the law in 1943. Aged eleven, he tried to rescue a stray cat from a bombed-out building. He started a fire in order to smoke out the animal but panicked and ran away. A policeman tracked him down and gave him a warning. After leaving school at fourteen the burly Reuter worked for an engineering firm but refused to undergo the traditional initiation ceremony in which new staff were ritually humiliated by other employees. In some factories apprentices would be stripped naked, mocked and jeered as they were paraded through the factory. Remembering the bullying about his lisp, he beat up the foreman who tried to force him into the ceremony. He was promptly sacked.

His next job – with a friend at a toy stall – ended in the same way but he was soon attracted to the Edwardian look being worn around the area. Buying himself a drape jacket and loud tie he began hanging around the amusement arcades, cinemas and dance halls. His lisp still made him shy with the opposite sex, but by the age of seventeen, thanks to his Teddy Boy suit, he gained some confidence and met a girl. He took her to a dance at Manor Place Baths but, unable to dance, sat with his girl watching the others. He noticed that a member of the Walworth Road mob, from Southwark, kept kicking his girl's ankle every time he passed. Reuter was unaware that the girl herself had provoked the assaults by earlier making comments about the other lad while she was dancing. Reuter's girl asked him what he was going to do about it. He told the boy to stop but it seems that the lad was something of a fighter and simply laughed in his face, so Reuter responded by hitting him. The police were called and both lads ran away.

On his way home Reuter was warned by a friend that his rival's gang would be waiting for him. The friend then rounded up a thirty-strong army of Elephant & Castle boys who found the Walworth gang kicking in the windows of his parents' basement flat. Reuter and his boys gave the leader a kicking while the rest of his boys ran away.

That night Reuter's reputation was made, particularly with the girls. He also realised that carrying a weapon was essential to ward off rivals. Reuter began throwing his weight around and getting into trouble with the law. After being carried in a stolen car he was put on probation which only made him even more of a hero. After trouble at the local youth club, sparked by girls playing off two groups of lads, Reuter and his boys broke down the doors, smashed every window in the place, wrecked bicycles and tossed the billiards table out of the window.

Although he was looking forward to the adventure of a two-year spell of National Service, Reuter was reminded by his pals that he wouldn't like being bossed around by military superiors. They advised him to pretend that he was a lunatic and the trick worked. When he was given a medical he grabbed a fire extinguisher off the wall and squirted it all over the doctors. He later found that he was being excused service because of ear trouble.

Reuter was soon in more trouble. After knocking over a glass at a pub on the Walworth Road, he and his friends were warned by the publican that they would be thrown out if it happened again. Seeing this more as a challenge than a threat they deliberately dropped a bottle. As the man tried to remove the lads they turned on him and beat him up. Despite escaping, Reuter was later caught and sent to prison for twenty-one months. Rather than curbing his behaviour, the experience gave him an even greater reputation. At the age of twenty, Reuter was actually looking forward to a spell in prison and felt it was an experience every self-respecting Teddy Boy should have.

Ignoring his own violent streak and love of a good punch-up, Reuter blamed the Teds' destructiveness on the influence of girls who had picked up ideas from watching movies – they incited and provoked the boys into starting trouble, he felt. The girls, however, were more than capable of starting their own trouble. A new generation of assertive young women was being raised among the wartime ruins, some of them armed, and they could match the boys in viciousness and aggression. Named after the fierce leader of the ancient British Iceni tribe, they were known as the 'Bombsite Boudiccas', or the Teddy Girls.

10

'BOMBSITE BOUDICCAS': THE RISE OF THE TEDDY GIRL

'Young girls are today too often the evil geniuses behind teenage gangs.'

(*Empire News*, 1959)

'Are there no cosh *girls*?' asked Belfast MP Colonel Montgomery Hyde in February 1953. His question was provoked by the use of the word 'him' in a Government Bill aimed at curbing the carrying of weapons. Hyde knew of a girl who had armed herself with a knitting needle, which she used to jab a lad in his genitals when he tried to snatch her bag. Hyde wondered whether the carrying of knitting needles would be covered by the Bill. The answer to his question was 'no', since coshing people over the head and robbing them seemed to be the exclusive pursuit of young males.

Teddy Girls did exist, however, and they were set to make their mark. The originals hailed from London: feisty, financially independent young working-class women who were determined to use fashion to create their own identity. In 1955 the *Picture Post* carried an illustrated feature on Teddy Girl fashions. Unlike the men's style they were not based on what women wore during the Edwardian era but were simply an adaptation of the male Teddy Boy uniform. Teddy Girls wore high-necked, elaborately embroidered blouses with turned-down collars and cameo brooches, loose-fitting, many-pocketed jackets and 'mannish' waistcoats. There was a preference for black and white. They also wore lace-up Grecian sandals and coolie hats or striped boaters. Accessories included long umbrellas and long, flat handbags.

Another early description of Teddy Girls claimed that they dressed in grey, fitted short jackets worn over tight, high-necked black sweaters. This was accompanied by a tight black skirt, nylon stockings and high-heeled shoes. It is more likely that girls from different districts sported their own stylistic touches and interpretations. In London some girls dressed in rolled-up jeans, flat shoes, tailored jackets with velvet collars, scarves tied high on the neck, coolie hats and long, elegant clutch bags. When an eighteen-year-old appeared before Wallasey magistrates charged with possessing a sheath knife, she wore drainpipe trousers and blue suede shoes. It seems her trouble began six months earlier when she bought a pair of 'drainees'.

In Glasgow, Teddy Girls wore ballet or 'bumper' shoes, fingertip-length jackets and pencil skirts with a six-inch split at the back, which they sometimes opened up even higher – anything up to twelve inches. Some wore tight black bullfighter-style breeches with mother-of-pearl buttons at the knees. The look was completed by a bootlace bow tie, long chunky earrings, wrist bracelets carrying their boyfriend's name and ankle bracelets. Some would match their hair with their boyfriend's: the Tony Curtis style was particularly popular. Those without boyfriends sported ponytails. The girls aspired to own at least one complete all-black outfit, leading to the nickname 'Black Widows'. Appearing before a court in Kirkcaldy, Scotland, accused of a breach of the peace at the Regal cinema, twenty-year-old girl Margaret Turner wore a blue and white headscarf, royal blue coat, black drainpipe trousers, a red jumper and bright green socks. The prosecutor stated that it was 'quite improper that anyone should appear dressed up like that in a court of law'.

The clothes were the chief attraction for many aspiring Teddy Girls. Young women would normally have worn blouses, modest calf-length skirts or two-piece suits. Southend teenager Margaret Richardson explained, 'I'm not a gang girl, not a hooligan's moll, just a girl who believes the Edwardian fashion is the smartest rig-out of all.' It wasn't within everyone's price range, however. One Warwick schoolgirl stole £23 so that she could buy fancy clothes and dress like a Teddy Girl. She admitted that she was jealous of those who had fine clothes and plenty of spending money. In Lichfield, Staffordshire, a young girl was caught stealing a pension book in order to indulge her passion for the new look. Aware that many girls could not afford the latest fashions, Howards fashion store in Newcastle advertised a nine-month payment plan, 'when you dress to be a Teddy Girl'.

This growing love of fashion was seen by some as a problem. A psychiatrist explained that some parents now liked to see their daughters mature quickly, particularly by allowing them to wear adult clothes when they became teenagers. Perhaps parents wished to see their daughters married so that they were no longer responsible for them. Nevertheless, the psychiatrist believed that early maturity led to a loosening of morals. The clothing certainly gave these young women a sense of status and self-confidence. In Shropshire a girl was brought before the courts in Shrewsbury for 'being in need of care and protection'. She told a policewoman, 'I expect it is because I want to be a bit of a Teddy Girl that I act like I do ... I like to dress in tight skirts and I like folks to think I'm tough.'

Status was also gained by acts of daring. A Birmingham girl called Jean explained her lifestyle: 'I get fed up with sitting in front of the telly at home. So I go out with the gang. Then someone dares you and you do something to show that you're not custard.' The girls generally did nothing more than break milk bottles but one night Jean threw a shoe through a shop window. 'It made a grand bang,' she boasted. Rev. Griffiths claimed that the female followers of the Teds had all the fun but none of the danger that came with gang membership. Perhaps he felt that girls, unlike boys, could enjoy the excitement and prestige of gang membership without the risk of violence from inter-gang warfare. Being the girlfriend of a Teddy Boy must also have offered a sense of protection.

* * *

Becoming a Teddy Girl was part and parcel of being attracted to Teddy Boys. In 1954, girls in the Dagenham area of East London were sporting the initials of their boyfriends cut into their arms with razor-blades or penknives, or burnt by cigarettes. Some would rub paraffin into the wounds to make them permanent. Aged around fifteen, the girls claimed to do it for a dare, although they didn't want their parents to know. Another craze was for girls to have an eagle, the American army emblem, tattooed on their legs; one fifteen-year-old, wearing a pencil skirt, showed her tattoo at Leicester City Juvenile Court and was judged to be beyond her parents' control. In Liverpool, fifteen-year-old girls underwent initiation ceremonies in which they allowed male members of the Swallow Gang to use a pin and dye to tattoo their inner thighs or shoulder with a blue swallow.

Wolverhampton's Chief Constable explained that some girls aspired to date bad boys and were lured by the Teddy Boy lifestyle. One sixteen-year-old Teddy Girl from Birmingham explained: 'In a gang like ours, all the girls go for the big kid. We call him Big Jim. He's really tough and he could have any of the girls. There's five of us – five girls, that is – in our lot. My boyfriend is tough all right, but he's not as tough as Big Jim.' One Ted also explained the attraction: it seems that women considered a Teddy boyfriend as a 'big hound', putting them one up on other girls.

The trouble with bad boys was that they were only after one thing. Another Birmingham girl scanned the titles of songs on the jukebox: 'See all these records – love, love, love. But a Ted don't know anything about love. Just sex, sex, sex.' Some girls did very much want the same thing. During a disturbance at a dance in Hainault, North East London, a group of fifteen-year-old girls began chanting 'We want sex, we want sex'. The dance ended in chaos as fireworks were let off.

'Girls Blamed for "Edwardian" Gang Fights' was one headline in the *South London Advertiser*. The sexual chemistry between Teddy Boys and Teddy Girls often inspired anti-social behaviour and criminality. In 1955 Rev. Griffiths noted that the girls hung around the gangs in larger numbers than ever before and made dates with members of two or more gangs to get a kick out of being fought over. Over in Harrow, North West London, a magistrate warned a gang of seven Teds and three Teddy Girls, 'This is Harrow, not Chicago.' The magistrate's wife explained that the girls were using their sex to incite lads to compete with each other. After banning Teds from the Alhambra Theatre in Openshaw, Manchester, the manager received numerous threats. He declared that some Teddy Girls were worse than the boys they egged on. No doubt for the same reason, the Wicker Cinema in Sheffield banned gum-chewing Teddy Girls from accompanying their boyfriends.

According to child expert Donald Ford, Teddy Girls were a bad influence since lads often boasted about and exaggerated their bad behaviour to impress them. The girls, in turn, incited the boys to carry out their dares and the boys would do so in order not to lose face in front of them. One Teddy Boy admitted that trouble in pubs came from rival gangs who tried to out-drink each other to impress their girlfriends. The *Banbury Guardian* also pinpointed the girls' harmful influence: 'Young Teddy Girls, some still at school, both local and imported, take their full share of the blame. They specialise in provoking fights between rival gangs. And not to be outdone, those gentle examples of the fair sex have a go themselves on occasions.'

* * *

Since they were unlikely to be searched by policemen, some Teddy Girls acted as weapon-carriers for the boys. Their large frock pockets could conceal anything from a flick-knife to a bicycle chain. One of Michael Davies' colleagues claimed that girls in Clapham, South West London, often carried small knives in their handbags. They would use them for doing their nails, although they were probably borrowed by their boyfriends for more sinister purposes. In the capital's Elephant & Castle district a girl told a journalist that she had heard rumours that young women were carrying knives for protection. They were said to believe that they were more glamorous than film stars and needed weapons to fight off their admirers. In 1954 two sixteen-year-old Teddy Girls wearing drape coats carried cut-throat razors tucked into the waistbands of their pencil skirts. As they were kissing two Teds outside a public house in Kingston-on-Thames, South West London, a passer-by saw one of the razors fall to the ground and called the police. One girl explained that they carried the razors to frighten any lads that got 'fresh' with them.

While some carried knives for self-defence, others were armed for more menacing purposes. In 1956 members of the ballroom security staff at the Winter Gardens in Blackpool were warned about Teddy Girls carrying small knives concealed in garters and specially made suspenders. In Liverpool's Everton district, vigilantes formed to curb the activities of Teddy Girls. Locals also appealed for police protection against gangs of girls carrying knuckle-dusters, bicycle chains and flick-knives.

In 1953 local magistrates were expressing concern about aggressive girls from Durham, Sunderland and Newcastle who were terrorising other youths with knives and high-heeled shoes. A year later in Hampshire, a fifteen-year-old appeared before Portsmouth Children's Court accused of attacking two older girls who had called her 'a Teddy Girl'. At the time she was wearing a sweater, tight trousers and brightly coloured socks. One of the victims received several stab wounds to her head, face and hands. When searched, the young girl was found to be carrying a flick-knife. 'It looks big to carry this around,' she admitted before bursting into tears. Not long afterwards, another Portsmouth Teddy Girl, aged seventeen, repeatedly stabbed a girl. In Suffolk in 1957 a 21-year-old Ipswich Teddy Girl appeared in court after brandishing an open razor during an altercation in the street. The razor was concealed in a hidden pocket inside the lining of her coat.

A Welsh Teddy Girl from Porth also went around armed with a knife 'because one of these days I'm going to knife my grandfather'. She further explained, 'My grandfather does not like rock 'n' roll music or any of the clothes I wear. I wear black tight skirts and black tight sweaters when I am on duty as a Teddy Girl ... I also wear chunky jewellery, which he doesn't like.' The sixteen-year-old, who also carried a cosh, appeared before the juvenile court, where a psychiatrist's report was sought.

Some South London Teddy Girls took to wearing four-inch knives in broad leather belts slung low on one side, aping Western gunslingers. Witnesses observed the girls swaggering off a train in one south coast resort, elbowing their way through the holiday crowds. Police were determined to stamp out the craze before it spread. In 1959, Arthur Pegg, of Somerset County Remand Home, claimed that girls and boys were showing an increasing tendency to violence. He had heard 'blood curdling' tales about girls and their use of flick-knives.

Some young women, nicknamed Black Angels, aimed to dress completely in black, including their hair ribbons. Around 1954 the girls, usually the sisters of Teds, would turn up in groups of ten or twelve to cause trouble in various Tyneside dance halls. One manager searching a girl's handbag discovered a comb with the teeth filed to sharp points, 'for protection'. Newcastle dance hall manager Alf Sheppard claimed that the Teddy Girls were 'vicious'. A member of staff at a Newcastle dance hall reckoned the girls were out to rival the Teddy Boys.

* * *

Teddy Girls were certainly not afraid of joining in battles. During a disturbance outside a Reading dance hall, involving Teds and servicemen, several Berkshire police officers were knocked to the ground and even struck by handbags wielded by angry Teddy Girls, egged on by their boyfriends. In 1955, at a Brighouse juvenile court, a seventeen-year-old Heckmondwike girl was found guilty of wounding a sixteen-year-old inside the Astoria ballroom. She explained, 'One girl got nasty with me, so I got nasty with her.' And in another area of West Yorkshire, the Spen Valley and Dewsbury districts were also becoming blighted with Teddy Girls. One group was known as the Galleon Gang. Doorman Vincent Collins told a magistrate that many of the girls in the groups wore 'Teddy Girl outfits, tight black skirts and large earrings'. The magistrate declared, 'It was a deplorable thing in the life of this town that young girls were going about in large gangs visiting dance halls, and fighting with each other.'

Sexual rivalry was a common cause of female violence. Trouble at the Pavilion Dance Hall, Bath, in May 1955, was sparked by two rival Teddy Girls pouncing on each other in the corner of the dance floor. As they clawed and scratched at each other, the lads joined in, leading to a riot that was quelled only by the intervention of twenty policemen. Three months later, in a cafe in South London, a jealous Teddy Girl took care of a rival who had flirted with her man by kicking her in the face with her high heels, knocking her teeth out. They would usually parade in pairs between Charlmont Road and Tooting Broadway, waiting to be picked up by Teds and taken to the Common.

Pontypridd was once labelled 'The Teddy Boy town of South Wales,' after vicious clashes between gangs. The violence culminated in 1956 when sixty youths ran amok through the town. Trouble started at the Graigwen Social Club after a Cardiff boy had the audacity to dance with a Pontypridd girl. The furious locals went for the Cardiff contingent with chairs. After the dance was stopped the scrap continued outside. The Cardiff Teds, armed with knives, were outnumbered but managed to fight their way to the station. The local boys, wielding chains, continued to battle until the train arrived. As the carriage transporting the Cardiff Teds pulled out of the station, a Teddy Girl, clutching a large knife, was heard shouting at the police, 'I'll carve you up boyo.'

Some mouthy girls had little respect for the police or magistrates. When a policeman in Runcorn, Cheshire, tried to stop a group of Widnes girls from singing in the street he was warned that the Teddy Girls would be set upon him. At Weston-super-Mare, sixteen-year-old Roberta Dike appeared before a juvenile court in the Somerset resort accused of being part of a mixed gang who had gone looking for rivals. Dike grinned through most of her trial but when sentenced to a spell in an approved school shouted, 'I won't go.' She then struggled with a policeman and attacked two female officers as they tried to remove her from the dock. A young woman from Halifax told a magistrate to 'drop dead'. She had been arrested for carrying a knife and knuckle-duster with the aim of stabbing her older sister after an argument. When the arresting officer asked her why she had the knife, she replied that it wasn't for cutting bread. A Glasgow policeman was shocked at the behaviour of two Teddy Girls arrested for shoplifting. Six times they gave the wrong names and addresses. They sat at ease in the cell, singing rock 'n' roll songs and laughed when they were being questioned.

* * *

Teddy Girls were guilty of some merciless and often unprovoked assaults. In Brentford, West London, in 1958, eighteen-year-old Doreen Riches had just finished work when she was pounced upon by four Teddy Girls. Two held her arms while one secured her legs; the fourth slashed her arms and legs repeatedly with a razor. 'It was like a nightmare,' said the victim. 'It all happened so suddenly. One minute I was being slashed, the next I was left lying on the pavement feeling giddy.' She had not seen her attackers before. In Hampshire in the same year, two Teddy Girls waylaid and injured a young woman in a Southampton shopping centre. The attackers lashed at their victim with studded belts. A thirteen-year-old girl suffered a broken nose after being beaten up by two Teddy girls in Tooting High Street, in South London. The victim's mother claimed that 'These Teddy girls seem far worse than the boys. They're more like animals than girls.' When two Lancashire schoolgirls told off some Teddy Girls for throwing stones at horses, they were beaten up and one had a flick-knife held to her throat.

North of the border, at a Dundee cinema in 1959 a gang of Teddy Girls attacked an usherette after she asked them to leave for misbehaving. They broke her arm with a cosh. A senior police officer was aghast: 'Things looked bad enough when Teddy Boys started carrying razors and coshes … But we are coming to a pretty pass if girls started arming themselves too … You don't need much knowledge of psychology to visualise that this will only spur street corner louts on to greater violence to impress girls who can already match their present standards.' During a showing of the film *The Tommy Steele Story* at the Regal Cinema, Stowmarket, four Suffolk Teddy Girls were also ejected, but not before one of them hit an usherette in the face, knocking her out.

Like police officers and park wardens, usherettes represented authority and were easily identified by their uniform. It was this combination of uniform and authority that also riled the Teddy Boys and led to ongoing battles with soldiers, airmen and Royal Navy personnel – in fact anyone in a uniform.

11

TEDS VERSUS THE MILITARY

'Every manifestation of any form of authority is a threat to them as individuals – this is a measure of their basic insecurity.'

(Child expert Donald Ford on the Teds, 1957)

Perhaps because of their dislike of compulsory National Service, and by extension all military life, Teds seemed to consider soldiers, seamen and airmen as their common enemy (see chapter 20). The sight of one of these uniforms was like a red rag to a bull. It prompted a group of servicemen to write to the *Daily Mirror* in 1954, complaining that when visiting London they found it difficult to walk along the pavement without being molested by gangs. Scotland suffered the same problem; a gang of Teds was reported to be responsible for two attacks on National Servicemen near the Cowglen Military Hospital. In the first incident two soldiers returning to base had bottles thrown at them but managed to escape. Hours later another pair were not so lucky when the gang ambushed them and wrestled one to the floor before thrusting a broken bottle in his face.

A year later, Private P.J. McMullan was found lying in the road with stab wounds to his chest and stomach following an argument with a group of Teds outside the Bridging Camp near Rochester in Kent. And when a funfair at Bootle's North Park attracted the usual crowd of Teddy Boys, a younger bunch started some trouble with a soldier and a sailor before calling for reinforcements. Older Teds then pounced, using their belts to crack heads. One of the men was left with several smashed teeth after he was kicked in the face. His friend sustained a fractured skull and was left with a gaping wound in his forehead that exposed the bone. He was then thrown head-first into the paddling pool. After members of the gang were found guilty, the victims received anonymous letters threatening to 'do them in'.

The most extraordinary incident came in 1956, when more than 500 Teddy Boys from various districts travelled to Dunfermline to battle with a common enemy: the Royal Navy Artificer Apprentices from nearby Rosyth, known as the 'Tiffies'. The trouble was blamed on a shortage of young women in the area. It seems that the Navy lads were seen as a more attractive catch for the girls, which led to jealousy. In one incident, 200 Tiffies marched into a dance hall, fought with some Teds and then marched back to their ship. The next day, in retaliation, a lone Tiffy was beaten up by some Teds. Pat Munion, one of the local Valleyfield Gang leaders, maintained that the trouble started because the 'Tiffies' treated them and their girlfriends 'like dirt'. He added, 'They also get off with all the good-looking girls ... and they rub it in until it hurts.'

Referring to a previous feud he then declared, 'We're not putting up with Sunday's beating up of our boys. The "Tiffies" outnumbered us ten to one. If they want trouble we can give it to them.' Reinforcements from Alloa, Kirkcaldy, Oakley, Cowdenbeath and Blairhall were mustered for a revenge mission, even though many of the gangs were natural enemies. The mob also included a 'special guest' appearance of over thirty Glasgow toughs, who travelled in a private hired bus and intended staying overnight in West Fife. A worried petty officer at the base said, 'I don't like this at all, I am afraid to take my wife into Dunfermline now if I'm wearing my uniform. It's not safe out late at night.'

He was right to be concerned. In one incident twenty Teds chased a group of Tiffies into a hotel where they had to be rescued by the police. The Teds promised that they would break every bone in their bodies. Subsequently about 100 Tiffies descended on Dunfermline to answer the challenge.

Terrified women cried in the streets and anxious householders called the police as the Tiffies went searching for their prey. Those Teds roaming the streets soon scarpered, leaving the Tiffies singing 'Oh why are we waiting'. Police patrolled the area looking for signs of trouble while Navy reinforcements waited at base ready to give assistance.

There was another non-show in Manchester's Levenshulme area in February 1956, as B Company of the 1st Cadet Battalion, Manchester Regiment, prepared for a counter-attack by local Teds. It was rumoured that up to sixty lads were going to pounce in response to a defeat the previous week. Trouble began when four Teds waylaid two cadets before the arrival of a third cadet prompted them to run off. The sergeant major was also followed by a gang, who threatened him with bottles. One of the Teds was captured and taken to the Battalion's headquarters for a telling off. He simply swore revenge. The following week, after parade, the cadets were ready for action but nothing happened.

In Liverpool, Speke's Sea Cadets became the target of Teds who would gather outside their headquarters to jeer at them as they paraded. Later, in the dark, the Teds would hide behind hedges to ambush the cadets on their way home. Some were beaten and had their uniforms torn; one had a belt pulled around his throat. An officer promised to give the Teds a taste of their own medicine. In London that same year, 1956, there was a ten-minute brawl in a King's Road public house between Teds and Scots Guardsmen; the Guards won. The Hampshire resort of Southsea saw a group of Teds beat up two Marines; one suffered concussion while the other had part of his ear bitten off. A year later, 400 members of the 1st Battalion of the King's Regiment, stationed in Essex, were confined to barracks to prevent clashes with Teds. Trouble began after the lads began provoking the soldiers. In 1958, on a Southport to Liverpool train, three soldier cadets were attacked by ten Teds wearing cowboy hats. One of the victims was thrashed with a belt and left covered in blood on the carriage floor.

One of the most spectacular battles erupted when fifty

Essex Teds took on an equal number of soldiers from the King's Regiment in 1958. The soldiers were ambushed near their barracks by two coach loads of Teds armed with belts, chains, knives and bottles. The King's men were unarmed until the plate glass window of an ironmonger's store was smashed, enabling them to grab makeshift weapons. The Battle of Brentwood lasted half an hour and caused damage estimated at £450. The squaddies, from Liverpool and Manchester, were given an unofficial 'well done' by their Commanding Officer for winning the skirmish. A few weeks later, Brentwood police stopped a seventeen-year-old for possessing a knife and belt. He explained that he carried them to protect himself from the troops. When told that the King's men had left town two weeks earlier he replied, 'Well, the East Anglians are here now.' In Newcastle-upon-Tyne, sailor Philip Kane was arrested for carrying a chain knuckle-duster wrapped around his fist; he explained to the officer that it was for protection against the Gosforth Teds.

Sometimes Teds did take the side of soldiers – but only, it seems, if a squaddy was one of their own. In 1955, a soldier prisoner dressed in Teddy Boy uniform was being escorted to Paddington train station when he suddenly assaulted his two military guards and broke free. As he made a run for it a flower-seller stopped him, only for three passing Teddy Boys to intervene and set him free once again. A year later in North London, in Stoke Newington High Street, a Ted leaped from a taxi into a stationary Army truck where he coshed a military policeman who was guarding a soldier prisoner called George Dam. The two escaped through the maze of streets. The Ted had ordered the taxi driver to tail the Army vehicle to rescue his friend.

* * *

Like their British counterparts, American servicemen were a prime target for attacks. The Teds' animosity perhaps stemmed from sexual jealousy, particularly because US servicemen were able to win girls by showering them with gifts such as nylons. The Teds might also have realised that their culture, rooted as it was in American films and rock 'n' roll music, was but a pale imitation of the real thing. Jealousy, prejudice, hostility and cultural inferiority could lead only to one thing – violence.

Four Glasgow youths attacked an American airman called Edward Newberger in 1954 as he was leaving his girlfriend's home. He was held against a wall and punched and kicked until he collapsed unconscious. The lads walked away singing. At Monckton, also in Scotland, a group of US airmen out for a drink were pestered for cigarettes by local Teds. The airmen were then beaten up, one of them ending up in the local infirmary. In West London, at an Uxbridge cinema in 1955, a message flashed up on the screen: 'Get back to base.' The warning was aimed at American servicemen, after police had been told to expect trouble between the soldiers and local Teds. Several miles across the capital at Colindale, a gang of Teds beat up a group of airmen from the Royal Air Force base at Hendon.

A year later in central London, police drew truncheons as twelve Teds in two cars fought with American servicemen in Mayfair. The Teds, armed with broken milk bottles and car starting handles, had pulled up alongside the Americans before attacking them. While police took statements from the victims, another carload of Teds roared past Savile Row police station and threw milk bottles at the wall. Seven Teds also attacked two American torpedo crewmen, part of a US flotilla anchored off Greenwich, South East London. United States Navy shore patrols and police were also forced to guard Edinburgh's Fountainbridge area to prevent trouble between Teds and American sailors from a visiting aircraft carrier. Outside a dance hall in Wethersfield, Essex, an airman was pounced upon, beaten and bitten by Teds. When he arrived back at his base he was unrecognisable.

Another was attacked at the Casino Ballroom in Warrington, when Teds fought with Americans from the nearby RAF

Burtonwood base. The airman claimed that he had only had one dance when a Ted approached him and cracked him over the head with a broken bottle, badly cutting his ear. In retaliation some Teds were thrown down a flight of stairs. One of them warned, 'We are leaving this town now but next week we will be back with the mob.' The airmen chased after them and another fight broke out in the street. Nine Chester Teds and two airmen later appeared in court. The victim claimed that he had also been attacked by Teds in Liverpool. Warrington Teds saw the Americans as a handy target for attacks. In 1957 two airmen were jumped by four Teds in the subway of Warrington railway station. The men had just put their girlfriends on a Liverpool-bound train when they were attacked. One victim claimed to have been 'slugged' (hit over the head) before being kicked and beaten.

In 1958, at Braintree, Teds went out in sorties looking for servicemen to attack. Essex police stopped a potential pitched battle between American servicemen and 200 Teds, drawing upon reinforcements from Bardfield, Colchester, Sudbury, Southend and Chelmsford. Nine Teds were arrested. A year later American airmen, stationed in Bruntingthorpe, Leicestershire, agreed to fight some local Teds. After finding a suitable venue they set to battle. However, five Teds ended up giving two airmen a kicking, leaving them unconscious. One Ted was heard to shout, 'Give him the knife.' The two victims, along with three Teds, were subsequently jailed although the airmen later had their sentences quashed and were fined instead.

In 1960, more than fifty Teds fought with a dozen American airmen in a car park at Braintree, Essex, and as late as 1962, a gang of about fifteen young men, described by one victim as 'Teddy boys', beat up six members of the Somerset Army Cadet Force. The incident happened after trouble between members of the gang and some regular soldiers. It seems that the innocent cadets were singled out for a revenge attack.

* * *

It wasn't only military personnel who were targeted by the Teds. Uniformed civilians wielding any form of authority provided a suitable replacement. Bus conductors working alone, particularly late at night when drunken Teds made their way home, were particularly vulnerable. A conductor called Jim Fell was on duty during the final night journey in London from Camberwell Green to Chingford when he asked four Teds to move along from the platform. He was severely beaten and kicked and had to spend two months in hospital. The doctors battled to save the sight in one of his eyes.

It wasn't only the capital's male conductors who were under threat. In 1954 a Teddy Boy just managed to catch a bus at Gipsy Hill in Upper Norwood, London but complained to the female conductor that his mate hadn't managed to get on board. The lad began fighting with the woman and the driver had to come to her aid. A year later, on a Prescot-bound bus travelling from Liverpool, four Teddy Girls assaulted a conductress after being asked to make less noise. In Dundee it was proposed that conductresses receive judo training if Teddy Boy attacks on late-night buses continued.

In 1955 two Teds beat up a bus conductor in Lambeth, South London. Across the Thames in North London, a conductor in Golders Green was also injured after a scuffle with two Teds who were arguing about their fare. Six Teds also stole a bus from a terminus in Harlesden, driving it a mile through the streets while shouting insults at people waiting at bus stops. In Liverpool, as a bus travelled along Scotland Road, a group of Teds threw lit fireworks through the open window of the driver's cab, causing him to crash. Seventy Nottingham Teddy Boys, singing, shouting and swinging bicycle chains, boarded a Derbyshire double-decker and ordered the driver 'to get a move on'. And that he did – straight to Sandiacre police station, where officers were waiting as part of a pre-arranged plan. The police had been awaiting their chance to break up this rowdy city gang who had been causing trouble every weekend.

One ex-Ted from London revealed that when a mob jumped on a bus they would play around with the conductor, each claiming that someone else was paying the fares. Sometimes, however, bus conductors let their prejudices against Teds affect their judgement. One lad boarded the last bus home, paid his fare but then gave his seat to a lady. The conductor then told him to get off the bus as there were too many passengers standing. When the lad asked for a refund of his ticket money he was called a 'Teddy Boy' and a rebel.

In 1957, at Oldham, sixteen Teds held up traffic as they marched in front of a bus on a main road, ignoring the driver's horn. They then surrounded a policeman who tried to stop them, tugging at his clothes. When more police arrived they charged down the street, scattering queues and knocking people into doorways. The following year, in nearby Salford, a gang of Teds tried a similar trick by lining up across the road to force a bus to slow down. Two lads then jumped aboard, one of them kicking the conductor. The man fell and bashed his head, leaving him with impaired eyesight. Conservative Minister of Pensions and National Insurance, John Boyd-Carpenter, later referred to the case. He pointed out that the statutory authorities found that, though the incident was clearly in the course of the conductor's employment, it was a risk common to anybody who might be in that street and, therefore, did not arise out of his employment. The unfortunate man was refused compensation.

Attacks on transport staff continued. By 1962 it was reported that railway workers who had been assaulted by furious passengers, including Teddy Boys, were to receive a special allowance if they were forced to stay off work due to their injuries. The payments, brokered by the National Union of Railwaymen and the British Transport Commission, were to last six months. One of the incidents cited involved a Lancashire porter who was beaten up by Teds while locking up a station late at night.

Teddy Boy assaults were not only directed at those in charge of the buses; passengers were at risk too. One evening in the summer of 1955, a Ted sat on a bus next to a woman and pinched her legs and stroked her bosom. Fearing that she would be slashed with a razor if she complained to the conductor, she jumped off the bus and got on the next one. Around the same time, in Kilmarnock, a gang of rowdy Scottish Teds boarded a bus and tried to force some Air Training Corps cadets to sing along with them. A man intervened but was beaten up.

The same year some Teddy Boys piled onto the top deck of a bus as it stopped in Wavertree, Liverpool. Two men and their partners were sitting quietly and objected to the lads' bad language. One of the men remonstrated with them but was punched and beaten. When his girlfriend tried to stop the assault, a youth stood on the seat and booted her in the face. The police later took the women to a local dance hall where they were able to identify the attackers.

Because of such incidents, many members of the public came to fear the Teds. Yet it was a fear that was often reciprocated.

12

'LONG JACKETS AND SHORT TEMPERS'

'How much longer will decent, law-abiding citizens have to fear a sudden onslaught by these bullying louts who dress like Edwardians and act like Chicago gangsters?'

(*The Smethwick Telephone*, 1958)

In the beginning the Teds, wherever they lived, stood out. This made many feel vulnerable. It took courage for the first pioneers to strut through their working-class neighbourhoods dressed like upper-class dandies, while most other youths were wore their dads' uniform of 'demob' suits or baggy flannel trousers. Not untypical was the experience of a young Londoner in Edwardian clothing in 1954. He was queuing in a Hammersmith shop when he heard someone making fun of his clothes. Three men then assaulted him, only to run away when a witness shouted 'Police'. Unluckily the Teddy Boy later met the men in the street; the was again attacked and stabbed three times in the back. His wounds needed seventy-one stitches.

Another Ted told the author T.R. Fyvel that he felt a sense of victimisation that could be alleviated only by retaliatory violence. He blamed the public for causing the trouble, claiming that even if a group of 'normal' lads entered a cafe they'd be called Teddy Boys and told that they were barred to prevent any trouble. He hated it when people stared and laughed at him. He warned that nobody was going to laugh at the boys and get away with it.

Two Staffordshire Teds admitted to Tamworth magistrates that they committed assaults because they objected to being 'stared at'. In Edinburgh a drunken sixteen-year-old stabbed an older lad who teased him about being a Ted. A youth in West Earlham, Norfolk, assaulted two men at Thorpe Station because they stared at his clothes. The Chairman of Norwich magistrates pointed out, 'If you dress in unusual clothes you must expect to be stared at, and even if you are stared at you have no right to assault anyone.'

Teds were extremely touchy with insults, real or imagined, about their appearance. Denying that they picked on members of the public, a Birmingham Ted admitted: 'A square only gets done if he grins at a Ted or tries to pinch his screamer [girlfriend].' Norman Shrapnel, a journalist from the *Manchester Guardian*, claimed that if you criticised a Ted's clothes, the effect was to make him strengthen his look by adding a few inches to his hair, jacket and cuffs. He warned that the situation might become dangerous if people continued to call them names. What seem to be quite trivial insults, or even innocent remarks, which belittled the Teds were swiftly and brutally avenged. In Liverpool a Ted butted another youth in the face. 'He made fun of my Teddy Boy trousers,' was his explanation to the police. At Workington bus station in Cumberland (now Cumbria), one of four youths made a remark to an Edwardian-clad soldier: 'Dig that crazy jacket.' After an argument the Ted knocked down one of the lads, breaking his leg, but was later cleared in court, most likely after claiming self-defence.

Tragically remarks sometimes led to fatal attacks. In 1955, eighteen-year-old Cypriot Michael Xinaris, an alleged Teddy Boy gang leader, was sentenced to death at the Old Bailey for the murder of a National Serviceman called James Robinson. The soldier, on home leave after bandit-hunting in Malaya, had been sitting in an Islington cafe and was supposed to have sneered at the clothes worn by members of the Angel Gang. He was stabbed three times, beaten and kicked. The Home Secretary later recommended a reprieve for Xinaris.

Teds seem to have adopted defensive-aggressive strategies to cope with any unfavourable comments from the public. In one case, some lads were larking about when a man passed them minding his own business. A Ted asked him if he was swearing at them. Being friendly, the man addressed the youth as 'cocky' (a friendly term meaning 'cock') and explained that he hadn't said anything. 'Call me "mate", not cocky,' was the Ted's response. The gang then jumped on the unfortunate man and beat him almost unconscious before throwing him through a plate glass window. Elsewhere, one eighteen-year-old Nottingham Teddy Boy reacted to being called 'Sonny' by beating and kicking a man in the face.

It's true to say that some almost wished to be stared at in order to seek retaliation. Ray Gosling recalls hanging around a Northampton bus station with his mates; they would file their nails with long metal nail-files while leering at people and daring them to return the stare. If they did, he recalls, you were supposed to confront them and ask who they were looking at. If you were a tougher type of Ted you might also add, as the victim scurried away, a warning to the 'waphead' that he'd better not be looking or the boys would come and give him a pasting. Gosling admits to not being quite tough enough to add the second sentence.

* * *

It was through such aggression and belligerence that Teds soon became widely feared. Teds and violence became synonymous as the result of some appalling cases of entirely unprovoked and over-the-top savagery. One Ted gloated that he had seen his colleagues heave a stranger through a plate-glass window. Shockingly, he couldn't stop laughing. In Newcastle, seven Teds knocked over a one-armed man. Those who came to the victim's assistance were also attacked, including one man who was 'kicked in the nuts'.

When a blind man entered the toilets at the Locarno Dance Hall in Nottingham, one of a group of Teds followed him and attacked him. The victim was kneed in the groin, punched in the stomach and butted in the face before having his head banged against the wall. In court the attacker claimed that the blind man had called him 'a Ted' and offered to fight him. He was jailed for three months.

In 1955, sixteen-year-old Frank Beer was stabbed in the back on Hampstead Heath, North London. The son of a policeman, he was walking home from a funfair with three mates when he was challenged to a fight by three Teds. His mother said that there had been a lot of trouble in the area with Teds. 'It is not safe for decent youngsters to be out at night,' she reported. A year later, at Gateshead, eight drunken Teddy Boys attacked four innocent lads who were knocked unconscious and kicked as they lay on the ground. In court, with brutal candour, the Teds explained their actions: 'We went looking for a fight ... The lads we attacked mean nothing to us.' Tragically, one of the victims had travelled to the North East from New Zealand to see a specialist about eye trouble. He was left with loss of sensation on one side of his face. In another gratuitous attack, four young men were beaten up by a dozen Teds as they stepped off the bus at Middleton, north of Manchester. One, a promising cricketer, had his bowling hand stamped on and the fingertip almost severed.

In London, more than a dozen Battersea Teds beat up three brothers in 1956. One was slashed in the eye and his left wrist so badly sliced that he nearly bled to death. He subsequently lost the use of his injured hand. In the same year six Leicester youths were attacked on a train by a large gang of Teds who were returning from Nottingham Goose Fair. The lads were beaten with bicycle chains and pieces of metal. One explained, 'They just swarmed into the compartment and beat us up.' To escape, the victims pulled the communication cord and jumped from the train.

Two years later an inoffensive 52-year-old man was sitting in a pub in Harrow Road, North West London, enjoying a drink, when three Teds, led by Mike Collins, burst in and smashed a glass on the counter before jabbing it into his face.

A chunk of his nose was sliced off and a large flap of flesh left hanging down his cheek. When the victim fell to the floor he was also kicked. The gang, who had terrorised the neighbourhood for months, was so wild that even other Teds were terrified of them.

Liverpool suffered several incidents where the victims were hopelessly outnumbered. In August 1954, ten Teddy Boys set upon two youths in Aintree, kicking one unconscious. The following month a gang ambushed three boys in the South End of the city; one was butted in the face and booted while on the ground. Another youth was attacked at the Pier Head and repeatedly kicked while he lay on the floor; at the same place, two lads walking with their girlfriends were left battered. In another incident a gang of about twenty Teds beat unconscious eighteen-year-old Geoffrey Wilkie before throwing him into the road, where he was hit by a car, suffering a broken leg and crushed ribs. In all 100 detectives were assigned to the case to search local dance halls for the culprits. Undercover women officers even put on their best frocks to partner local Teds in the hope of gleaning information.

In the space of one weekend in September 1957 there were two stabbings in Liverpool: an American serviceman was knifed in the stomach after he went to investigate noise from a gang of youths outside his home, and a seventeen-year-old was kicked, punched and stabbed in the back by three lads in the street. Police visited local cafes looking for Teddy Boys. Later in the year, in the Toxteth district, Teds set upon two young men, stabbing one of them in the back. The *Manchester Guardian* once awarded Liverpool the honour of having the toughest Teddy Boys in the country. Judging by the previous examples, the city also boasted some of the most cowardly.

In many incidents the victims presented no threat; the attacks were simply sadistic bullying. At Chippenham, Wiltshire, two Teds, part of a rowdy group of youths on a train, followed a slightly built bespectacled youth onto the platform and punched him six times in the stomach for 'some fun'. In another unprovoked incident a seventeen-year-old leaving a

London dance hall was jumped on by sixteen Teds who tore off his spectacles, threw pepper in his eyes, knocked him to the pavement and kicked him in the stomach. The lad managed to run home but was seized outside his front door and stabbed. In another case a West London mother wrote to a newspaper to say that her son, who was wearing his school uniform at the time, had been beaten up by Teds brandishing flick-knives; they had promised to 'do him in'. And in 1957, five members of a Teddy Boy gang were convicted of various assaults after patrolling the streets of Loughborough, Leicestershire, and beating up anyone who crossed their path.

In a case that shocked the nation in 1960, Allan Jee, a 23-year-old apprentice engineer, had just kissed his girlfriend goodnight and was walking home near allotments in Isleworth, near Hounslow, West London, when he was attacked. He died in hospital with a fractured skull without ever regaining consciousness. The police suspected that Jee had been waylaid by Teds. Every Ted with a criminal record for violence living within three miles of the murder was watched by the police. Four suspects were later arrested, charged and found guilty. After a last-minute reprieve failed, two were hanged: eighteen-year-old Francis 'Floss' Forsyth and Norman Harris, aged twenty-three.

Supporters argued that both men had not intended to kill their victim. Forsyth's father claimed that although his son kicked Jee it was probably the force of his fall on the concrete floor, not the kicks, that killed him. Since Forsyth had worn winkle-picker shoes the case became known as 'The Winkle Picker Murder'. A factor that might have influenced the Home Secretary in refusing a reprieve was that nine days after the killing, and before his arrest, Forsyth had been involved with other youths in a disturbance in a London airport where two policemen were attacked.

* * *

A pair of Bristol Teds once stooped so low as to set their dog on a nine-year-old girl. 'Seize her, Rover,' they ordered, leaving the child bitten, bruised and with her clothes torn. Teddy Boys were also implicated in some shocking scenes of animal cruelty. Some Nottingham Teds flung a dog into a deep rubbish pit and pelted it with bricks, while cleaners starting work at a school in Gosport, Hampshire, discovered a cat strung up by its tail on a flagpole thirty feet above the ground. The cat was rescued but later had to be put down. Police suspected that Teds were responsible.

In 1956 Liverpool suffered a spate of cat cruelty. In the area around St Andrews Gardens (known as the Bull Ring) more than fifty cats were reported missing by their owners. Apparently, Teddy Boys and their girlfriends were playing a disturbing new game called 'Throw the Cat', whereby a rope was tied around the animal's neck to swing it around before letting it go. The winner was the one who flung the poor creature the furthest distance. In back alleys and bomb-damaged sites, five cats were found with shattered skulls and ropes still attached.

When the RSPCA went to investigate, a group of Teddy Boys pelted them with bottles and bricks. Officials from the Society also received a threatening phone call: 'Call off your investigations or the boys will tear you and your place apart.' In July 1956, in the space of a fortnight, thirteen more cats were found around Bedford Street and Egypt Street, some gashed by jagged pieces of glass. An RSPCA spokesman reported that the 'game' had also spread to Yorkshire.

Occasionally Teds got their comeuppance. In Glossop, Derbyshire, in 1959, a fourteen-year-old choirboy and member of the church Scout group told off some Teds for throwing stones at the ducks in Manor Park. He claimed that they then attacked him and threw him into the brook. The choirboy responded by pulling out a knife and stabbing a seventeen-year-old Ted.

* * *

Mindless vandalism was another crime often laid at the door of the Teddy Boys. In 1954 a gang of Teds overturned a car in

Notting Hill, West London, before seizing scaffolding boards and hurling them into the basement of a house. Two years later Teds used petrol to start a fire that destroyed four acres of gorse on Ham Common, Surrey. At Colne, near Burnley, a gang of teenage Teds ransacked gardens, broke windows and smashed gates at every house in Skipton Road.

Nothing was safe. At weekends throughout 1957 a popular campsite in the village of Castleton in the Peak District was invaded by gangs of youths, including Teddy Boys. They would arrive from Sheffield, Leeds and Manchester looking for a bit of fun – which included beating up the locals and bouts of vandalism. Hedge-posts were uprooted, crops damaged, signs bent back to front and rocks thrown. One lad used his knife instead of darts in a game at the pub.

Damage to trains was a particular specialism. In 1954, on a late-night train from Southend to London, someone pulled the communication cord. The train stopped and light bulbs were smashed. A group of Teds were arrested when the train stopped at Barking. In 1956, another Southend to London train arrived two-and-a-half hours late after Teds continuously pulled the communication cord. The following year in Somerset a group of up to thirty Taunton Teddy Boys and Girls ran amok on a train from Weston-super-Mare, sprinting up and down the corridor, fighting and 'kicking up a shindig'. Two windows were smashed.

In 1958, the 5.45 a.m. Sunday 'newspaper train' delivering the early editions and travelling from London to Brighton was regularly used by Teds and other partygoers returning home after a late night out. In the June of that year, twenty policemen were waiting for them after fights broke out among the revellers. Weeks later, fourteen Teds were held in Brighton after a battle on an early morning train from London. The lads, who wore striped blazers and drainpipes, had used fire extinguishers and threw them out of the window along with cushions. They were sent back to London on another train on which it was later found that they had slashed seats and smashed light bulbs.

In 1959 Teddy Boy trouble meant that the 9.30 p.m. London to Nottingham train on Sundays no longer stopped at Kettering as Teds travelling from Kettering to Corby were smashing bulbs as they ran through the corridors. A year later in West Sussex, at Haywards Heath, an offside door, which had been ripped off, struck another train. Guards found the door-less compartment empty but for a pair of shoes and a suitcase. A confused barefoot man was also found wandering the corridor. He told the guard that his shoes and luggage had been taken while he slept. A group of Teddy Boys was blamed.

There were attempts to make sense of the Teds' destructive behaviour. A teacher from a tough London school explained: 'These boys are the Dead End Kids in our society. They have been neglected ... their homes are squalid, their education has been poor. Their behaviour is a protest against all that ... They cannot create so they destroy.' In 1958 the Dean of Manchester, Rev. H. A. Jones, was concerned about those lads in Edwardian uniform who rejected life rather than rebelled against it. Such youths acted in a destructive manner as if they wished to destroy everything within themselves.

The Teds offered their own excuses for their acts of destruction. One ex-Ted claimed that the reason lads smashed light bulbs in railway compartments was so that they could snog girls in the dark. Another, arrested for smashing greenhouse windows, explained his actions by saying, 'It's just rock 'n' roll.'

13

JUST ROCK 'N' ROLL

'Too many Teds think only of sex, drink, money and a good time.'

(Rev. Leslie Pickett, Holy Trinity Parish Church, Bury, 1958)

The popular image of Teddy Boys jiving with their girls to the wild strains of rock 'n' roll music is fixed in the nation's memory. It is difficult to imagine them without their music, or the music without the Teds. Rock 'n' roll certainly supplied the soundtrack to most of their era. But while this music, in the form of black rhythm and blues (R&B), had been around in America from the mid-1940s, it didn't make a big impression on British youths until October 1955 when Bill Haley's 'Rock Around the Clock' re-entered the charts and became a smash hit, having featured in the film *Blackboard Jungle*. Rock 'n' roll had not only arrived, it had arrived kicking and screaming in the context of a movie about juvenile delinquency. The two were to become ever more closely linked.

Haley might have kick-started a new British musical craze but teenagers had to wait until May 1956 for a fitting hero to appear in the form of Elvis Presley with his song 'Heartbreak Hotel'. While Haley was plump and in his thirties, Presley was young, good-looking and dangerous. His music was sexy, rebellious and a direct attack on parental values. It is easy to see why Teds took to the music and aspired to be like their hero. It is true that young people had always had their idols, such as Frank Sinatra and Johnnie Ray, but rock 'n' roll's stars were a similar age to their audience and sang of teenage concerns such as dating, dancing, school and the generation gap.

The charts on both sides of the Atlantic soon became littered with hits from white American rockers such as Gene Vincent, Jerry Lee Lewis and Buddy Holly. Although some of their songs were covered and made safe by white singers, black artists such as Little Richard and Fats Domino were also popular with the Teds. British singers were not slow to join the craze. Tony Crombie and his Rockets' 'Teach You to Rock' became the first British rock 'n' roll chart success in October 1956, followed just a week later by Tommy Steele's 'Rock with the Caveman'.

Over the next few years a host of home-grown talent such as Marty Wilde, Billy Fury and Cliff Richard would enjoy rock 'n' roll chart success. However, some British listeners perceived the music as inauthentic and lacking the excitement of original American rock. Some audiences were keen to show their disapproval. After an appearance in Liverpool in 1958, Wee Willie Harris found local Teds trying to overturn his coach. Teds pelted Cliff Richard and The Shadows with eggs and tomatoes during a performance at London's Lyceum Ballroom in 1959. In the same year, also in London, Vince Taylor was threatened after a show at Hammersmith. The following night a crowd of Teds shouted for the singer outside the stage door; he wisely left by the front entrance. When Terry Dene made a stage return after a disastrous spell of National Service, from which he was discharged after suffering a nervous breakdown, wags in the audience chanted, 'Left, right. Left, right.'

* * *

For the early Teds there was no rock 'n' roll. They developed their unique look and swagger to the strains of Vera Lynn, Winifred Atwell and Lita Roza's hit '(How Much is That) Doggie in the Window'. Roza was the vocalist with the Ted Heath Orchestra, arguably Britain's best swing band. Heath had chart success with 'Hot Toddy' and 'Dragnet' and even covered Bill Haley's 1953 American hit, 'Crazy Man, Crazy'. Ken Mackintosh and his orchestra was another Teddy Boy favourite. In January 1954 he had success with 'The Creep', named after the Teds' favourite dance.

According to T.R. Fyvel, the early Teds didn't dance much. If they did it was in a condescending manner, adopting a spiritless shuffle accompanied by a deadpan facial expression. What Fyvel was describing was probably the creep. Also described as crude, energy-saving and skill-evading, the creep became Britain's biggest dance craze since the Charleston. It is easy to see why it was so popular, since it did not involve any physical or mental exertion, and was ideal for those who could not be bothered to learn proper dance steps. Instead, couples simply shuffled around the dance floor.

The *Daily Mirror* published a helpful guide for beginners. Partners kept a foot apart. The boy's left hand held the girl's right arm straight out and low down so that the hands were level with the middle of their thighs. The boy placed his right wrist on the girl's left hip and let his hand dangle loosely. Both partners bent their knees and began to creep off, the boy taking two backwards steps and one to the side. In the beginning there was no special music to dance to until Mackintosh seized the moment.

* * *

It was against this background of big-band swing music, romantic crooners and novelty dances that rock 'n' roll hit Britain. Some astute listeners would already have been familiar with black American R&B artists and white country music singers such as Hank Williams – and in the late 1940s some youths were already wearing American-influenced fashions, such as wide-brimmed hats, drape jackets, brightly coloured shirts and flashy ties, and visiting dance clubs to hear up-tempo boogie-based music by the likes of Louis Jordan. Although the music played on BBC radio was aimed at a more mature and sedate audience, Radio Luxembourg, particularly on a Sunday night, already offered an alternative popular playlist that attracted young listeners. There were also tours by R&B musicians: boogie-woogie pianist and child prodigy Sugar Chile Robinson, for example, visited Britain in 1951.

In Liverpool, sailors making regular trips to America, known as the 'Cunard Yanks', would bring home records by artists long before the rest of the British public ever heard them. Liverpool singer Ted 'Kingsize' Taylor was also on the mailing lists of various independent American record labels and helped introduce rock 'n' roll to a wider audience. With no proper record sales charts until 1952 it is difficult to estimate the post-war popularity of black American R&B musicians such as Louis Jordan.

It was Haley, however, who made the first big impact. His music, constructed in the 'twelve-bar blues' form and played loud and at a lively pace, was so different and exciting compared with what was being offered by English singers like Dickie Valentine and Jimmy Young. A fusion of R&B and white country influences, the music had an insistent beat and infectious rhythm that compelled listeners to get up and dance. There was only one dance that would suffice – the jive – although the moves were actually nothing new. During the Second World War American GIs had introduced swinging dances such as the Lindy Hop, later known as the jitterbug. In Britain the dance was called the jive.

* * *

Rowntree and Lavers, who conducted the first post-war survey of British leisure, were shocked at what went on in some dance halls frequented by young people. They reported that modern ballroom dancing could easily degenerate into 'a sensuous form of entertainment', leading to unruly behaviour and sexual immorality, particularly if self-control was further weakened by alcohol. The report, published in 1951, hints at the teenage culture that was about to explode. No longer would young and old do the same dances to the same kind of music. A generation gap was opening up, resulting in special rock 'n' roll nights; certain venues became exclusively devoted to the new music.

Dance halls weren't, however immune from Teddy Boy

trouble before the advent of rock 'n' roll. In 1954, after being reprimanded for jiving at a dance at Fulham Town Hall in South West London, John Page, aged twenty, assaulted the dance steward, two policemen and another man who had come to assist. The altercation lasted fifteen minutes after Page's friends joined in to help free him. Elsewhere, John Henry was jiving at the Loretto Church Dance Hall at Musselburgh, near Edinburgh, when he bumped into another lad called John Robertson. Words were exchanged, followed by a brief scuffle, before six drape-suited colleagues of Robertson intervened. After both being ejected, the lads continued to fight outside. It was alleged that Henry brandished his knife first, only for Robertson to pull out his own sheath knife. In the struggle Henry was stabbed in the head and body. He staggered down the road but collapsed and died.

Also in Scotland in 1954, at the Caledonian Hall, Irvine, a dance-band singer grabbed the microphone and began crooning in the hope of relieving tension after the hall was invaded by up to forty Glasgow Teds. He stopped suddenly when a knife landed at his feet. Innocent dancers were punched and the police arrested one lad armed with a cut-down bayonet. At a dance at Bristol South Baths, a fight broke out between Teds, during which a tear-gas bomb exploded. Hundreds panicked as they fought to get out, and one Ted fell from a balcony to the dance floor. Police, ambulances and firemen in oxygen masks attended. In London, rival gangs from Kennington and Elephant & Castle fought at the Locarno dance hall in Streatham. Twice the brawl was quelled but flared up again until police were called. A fourth fight broke out even while police were patrolling the edge of the dance floor.

In 1955, fifty Bristol Teds travelled by train to confront their rivals at a dance at the Bath Pavilion. By the end of the night one youth had suffered a fractured leg and another had lost his front teeth. The so-called Bristol Boys threatened, 'We will be back with reinforcements.' Good to their word, a month later the gang caused more trouble as they left the building. As they started jostling and obstructing others, a Detective Inspector told them to move, only for one to reply: 'I don't care who you are. We are the Bristol Boys.' Lads in Edwardian uniform were among those arrested for disorderly behaviour and carrying weapons, including, in one case, a chain made of lead balls. The Bristol lads, finding their own city 'far too hot' for them, also began travelling to Cardiff for Saturday night dances. Police were called to break up fights involving up to 300 youths at the Sophia Gardens Pavilion.

* * *

The arrival of rock 'n' roll certainly changed the atmosphere of the dance halls. The music was seen as a dangerous and destructive force that worked the listener into a mindless frenzy. The very term 'rock 'n' roll' was black American slang for sexual intercourse. The pelvic gyrations of Elvis Presley and the suggestive lyrics of Little Richard were blatantly sexually aggressive. In an effort to understand the new music, in 1956 the *Daily Mirror* organised a rock 'n' roll party and invited an assortment of Teddy Boys, teenagers, a psychologist and an East End parson. The psychologist thought that the music offered a good outlet for youthful exuberance but found that its impact depended on the listener. He felt that boys liable to smash cinema seats could be roused to do so. The parson judged the music to be primitive but harmless and declared that it was wrong to blame it for the bad behaviour of the Teds. Elsewhere, however, a Pentecostal minister equated the music with devil worship and said it was likely to promote lawlessness, impair nervous stability and undermine the sanctity of marriage.

T.R. Fyvel witnessed a large Teddy Boy gathering at a rock 'n' roll dance in a London town hall. He observed how the crowdedness of the venue, together with the rock 'n' roll rhythm and the continuous noise, created not only excitement but a hint of mob destructiveness and even cruelty. He saw plenty of pushing and shoving, cigarettes being stubbed out on furniture and chairs kicked out of the way. These were minor infringements and Fyvel admits that the young people present were probably normally well-behaved: it was as if the music had an adverse effect on them.

Those in charge of organising rock 'n' roll dances were well aware that in such a frenzied atmosphere violence could easily erupt. Dance halls were forced to employ strong-arm tactics and a new breed of super-doormen emerged to combat any Teddy Boy disorder. Replacing the old men in bowler hats at one dance hall, seven burly young men were employed on Saturday nights. In 1955, New Brighton Tower had to double security staff from four to eight to combat Teddy Boy violence. The manager explained that if eight men were not enough he would employ more, adding, 'One of their aims will be to mark the Teddy Boys' precious suits.' As dance organiser Arthur Howes explained, to be a successful promoter you had to have your own private army. Howes was able to call on wrestlers, boxers, former policemen and ex-paratroopers.

Violent behaviour at rock 'n' roll dances at Holyoake Hall in Wavertree, Liverpool, was averted only by the presence of a high ratio of security staff to dancers. Nevertheless, promoter Wally Hill recalls the odd knife being thrown and an incident involving a docker's hook. The city's first rock 'n' roll DJ, Bob Wooler, also explained how the chairs at the Aintree Institute were stuck together in groups of four to prevent them being thrown at the stage.

The fast rhythms of rock 'n' roll music, and particularly the dance that accompanied it, were the cause of some of the trouble. If the creep involved disinterested partners, the jive was a wildly exuberant and interactive dance, where boys threw girls over their shoulders and under their legs. With the arrival of rock 'n' roll the dance became faster, sexier and more acrobatic. In Eastbourne, East Sussex, a 'jive corner' was established just for Teds. Some dance halls, with strict dress and behaviour codes, banned the moves outright.

Graham Bill, who hailed from a village in Staffordshire, was a regular at the local Saturday night hop. The hall was plastered with notices declaring 'No Jiving or Bopping'. A local hard-case nicknamed 'Rubber Belly' was employed to enforce the rule but when the music started the floor would divide into two groups, the jivers and those doing the quickstep. Bill remembers people being clouted around the head by the flailing arms of the rock 'n' rollers. The culprits would be marched out and barred. Another witness recalls going to dances where the house bands occasionally catered for the Teds by playing a rock number. If fights broke out they reverted to a foxtrot tempo while the brawlers were thrown out. Being ejected from a dance, however, was seen as no disgrace since it could make reputations.

With the full-blown arrival of rock 'n' roll in 1956, violence escalated. Police were called twice in one night to fights at a dance in a Bradford drill hall. A witness claimed that while the music was playing about fifteen Teds started punching and kicking. At the Scarborough Spa Ballroom Teds began fighting as the orchestra played the upbeat 'Love is a Many Splendored Thing'. Knives flashed and chairs were thrown during the ten-minute brawl.

In March the so-called Black Duffle Coat Gang from South London entered Orpington Civic Hall in Kent. They consisted of about twenty-three youths wearing Ted clothes except that the drape had been replaced by a duffle coat, normally associated with beatniks but cheaply bought at Army surplus stores. The lads jostled the dancers and tore girls from their dancing partners. The MC called for order but had his hat knocked off. Police were called and one of the lads shouted, 'C'mon, we'll go back in and cut 'em to pieces.' A stiletto and a carving knife were abandoned at the scene.

A pitched battle in 1957 between Huddersfield Teds and locals began in the Alligator Club in the town of Batley and continued all the way to the railway station. About 150 youths, armed with chair legs and bottles, took part in the fighting. Various witnesses described the disturbance as 'Reminiscent of Chicago's gangland during the 1920s', like a 'Western film' and resembling a 'battlefield'. Rock 'n' roll music was subsequently banned from the venue.

In 1958, 100 Teds took part in a St Patrick's night brawl outside a dance hall in Liverpool. In the melee two policemen were injured as bricks and bottles were thrown. Elsewhere, a detective told a court that the Metropolitan Police had received instructions to stamp firmly on anything that savoured of Teddy Boy rowdyism at dance halls. He was speaking at the trial of a nineteen-year-old who had struck a boy over the head with a bottle at a dance at Walthamstow, East London.

A year later, and around 20 miles south, a gang of six Croydon Teds brought terror to a nearby village dance. Four stewards were beaten up by the lads, who then escaped in cars. Police leave was cancelled until the 'Teddy Boy emergency' was dealt with. At Barnsley, a rock 'n' roll dance for teenagers took the place of the annual civic ball. It was the idea of the Lord Mayor's daughter and was intended to give the town's young people a sense of civic engagement. However, a riot erupted and a Ted dragged the Mayor to his knees by his chain of office. Police escorted eight bloodied Teds from the venue.

* * *

In addition to rock 'n' roll dances and television programmes such as *Six-Five Special* (1957) and *Oh Boy!* (1958), fairgrounds also helped popularise the music. American hits would blare out of the speakers, attracting Teds from far and wide. Disorder was never far away and fairgrounds often became battlegrounds. Blackpool's Glasgow Fair attracted Teds from Liverpool, Manchester, Birmingham and Scotland. The Scottish Teds got the blame for most of the trouble. 'They are the wildest of the lot,' claimed the town's publicity chief. Police were forced to close down the Newcastle Leazes fairground during Easter 1956 due to a disturbance involving 100 local Teds. At Scotland's Greenock fair in 1958, 400 Teds and Teddy Girls stoned the police during a fierce battle. Leicester's biggest ever Teddy Boy fight occurred at Saffron Lane fairground in 1959. Stallholders joined forces to protect their merchandise and rides as 100 Teds battled it out.

In 1955, police issued whistles to female stallholders at New Brighton fairground after Teds caused a wave of terrorism.

Strong-arm patrols also mingled with the crowds, listening for the blast of a whistle that would signal the first sign of trouble. The precautions were taken after a lady cashier was assaulted by a gang as they robbed her till. The 'Wall of Death' motorbike attraction nearly lost the day's takings after an attempted snatch. At a firing range, some Teddy Boys ignored the targets and shot all the prizes before pointing their rifles at the terrified stallholder. A ride attendant was beaten up on his way home after clashing with a gang the previous week. Teddy Boys also damaged the slot machines in an amusement arcade before clashing with staff who were trying to evict them.

The following year the gangs were back. Four Teds again approached a 'Wall of Death' rider as he stood outside his booth after closing. Two held his arms while the others butted him in the face and tried to snatch £70 takings from his inside pocket. Other stallholders intervened but the rider was left with a badly cut face. There had been earlier complaints of the bullying attitude of large gangs of Teds mingling with the holiday crowds.

In August 1957 there was a fairground battle in East London involving about 150 Teds. The trouble broke out after police closed a dance at Elm Park. Teds then jumped on a train to Becontree, four miles away. On their journey they smashed the carriage as they sang rock 'n' roll songs, terrifying the women passengers. On leaving the train the Teds marched into the fair, ten abreast, and immediately began kicking over stalls and threatening showmen and visitors. Some took over the dodgems. When police arrived the Teds ran to nearby roadworks and armed themselves with iron bars, pickaxe handles and stones. One picked up a pneumatic road pummeller and hit a policeman in the back. The ensuing battle saw eight officers injured and six Teds arrested.

* * *

For home consumption, rock 'n' roll music was available on 45rpm lightweight plastic discs, which were beginning to replace the old brittle 78rpm gramophone records. With the introduction of these more portable and hard-wearing 'singles' the music industry in Britain began to boom. Cafes and the non-alcohol-serving milk-bars were quick to latch on, installing jukeboxes so that young people could pay to listen to the latest hits. Although denounced as 'pagan altars' by a Stepney vicar, jukeboxes spread like wildfire. In 1950 there were 300 in Britain; in 1955 there were 3,000 and by 1958 there were about 13,000. Not everyone enjoyed listening to other people's choices though. One would-be entrepreneur proposed making a three-minute recording of silence for jukeboxes, so that people fed up with the cacophony could pay for some peace and quiet.

Since teenagers could not get served in pubs, and the Mecca and Locarno dance halls were aimed at an older clientele, the younger Teds with money in their pockets responded by taking over the few public spaces available to them. Milk-bars, jukebox cafes and espresso bars became ideal places to meet the rest of the gang and chat up girls. Milk-bars originated in the 1930s as alternatives to the public houses. Serving non-alcoholic drinks, they attracted teenagers. The espresso bars, which arrived from Italy in the mid-1950s, were a modern alternative to the working-class 'caffs'. By 1958 there were over 1,000 espresso bars. Espresso bars were particularly attractive to young people because they conveyed a continental glamour and sophistication related to the contemporary Italian style in clothes. The rich smell of coffee and the bright, modern interiors, with their plastic and Formica surfaces, must have seemed futuristic compared to traditional establishments, with their dowdy Victorian décor. Furthermore, the pre-war milk-bars and even the post-war self-service teashops were designed for speed of service and customer turnaround. They did not offer space to while away the hours, indulging in leisurely chat or simply looking cool. One Ted revealed that while the jukebox was playing the lads didn't have to think or talk. They could just sit there with a dazed expression.

Typical jukebox cafes and milk-bars consisted of a long room with contemporary decor and a counter for the sale of soft drinks and snacks. Tables were placed close together, leaving ample room for customers to dance to music from the jukebox.

According to contemporary accounts, the lads would sit in groups, laughing and joking, usually directing their banter at the worst dressed among them. Obsessive about their hair and the creases in their trousers, they would be more interested in each other than the girls, who generally sat separately waiting patiently to be picked up. The courting ritual usually began with long-distance playful teasing and ridicule. Strangers entering these establishments would be viewed suspiciously, for the cafes were small enough for particular groups to regard them as their own and for individuals to 'be somebody'.

On the downside, cafes that stayed open late to attract teenagers were not cost effective to run. The more successful ones were those that attracted large groups of Teddy Boys. Because there were so few late-night cafes open, young people had little choice but to frequent these rougher establishments. A London probation officer believed that when innocent youths began visiting these coffee bars they were easily sucked into a life of crime. A London journalist described the drab and seedy type of cafes frequented by Teds, where the conversation centred on sex and crime. Another probation officer condemned coffee bars as 'dark, unhealthy dungeons; dens that are breeding grounds for juvenile crime'. Tynemouth's Chief Constable refused to grant licences for jukeboxes since he believed they 'created disorder'.

It's true that many incidents of disorder centred in and outside cafes and coffee bars. In Twickenham, Middlesex, thirty Teds walked into a cafe in Richmond Road. One said 'Good evening' as they entered a back room only to trash it. In central London a gang of eight Teds smashed up the Carousel Restaurant in Paddington after a street battle with American servicemen. Two plate glass windows, along with assorted chairs and tables, were broken. One man was taken to hospital with fractures and another man and a waitress were beaten with chair legs. Three miles away in Chelsea, Polish countess Renata Ostrowska co-ran the Bongy-Bo coffee bar with her actress sister Beata. When six Teds refused to pay their bill, the plucky countess barred the door. The lads, with their two girlfriends, then beat up Renata and kicked her in the stomach before escaping. The victim described one of the girls as 'an animal'. Nevertheless, she maintained that Teds were still welcome in the coffee bar, reasoning that as individuals the Teds were fine. It was in the gangs that they were 'evil'.

Police knew some cafe owners were paying £10 per week protection money to London gangs. One revealed that he decided not to bar even the most unruly youngsters and felt confident of being able to handle any trouble. He welcomed the lads and encouraged them to use the premises as a meeting place. However, his plan didn't work. Some boys were so 'psychopathic' that they ruined the place. They refused to order anything so the business couldn't make any money. The owner changed tack but this aroused fierce resentment. When he altered the price tariff of the jukebox the gang was so infuriated that they burgled the place and stole the night's takings from the machine.

At a meeting of the Scarborough and Yorkshire Federation of Women's Licensed Trade Associations, it was claimed that half the trouble with Teddy Boys was the result of them frequenting milk-bars rather than public houses. It was argued that if the older Teds went to pubs, under the supervision of people with common sense, they would behave themselves and be treated as adults rather than children. A Midlands vicar agreed, claiming that local public houses were better for young people than jukebox cafes or street corner 'hot dog' stalls, since they were better regulated and controlled. He claimed that trouble usually started when bored Teds and their girls sat for hours over a cup of coffee, with nothing more interesting to do.

The dance halls, together with the fairgrounds and jukebox cafes, were just some of the venues where Teds were exposed to rock 'n' roll music. Cinema trips were another opportunity to hear this electrifying new sound and it was while watching *Blackboard Jungle* in 1955 that many Teds first heard Bill Haley's 'Rock Around the Clock'. The theme music was so exciting that audiences couldn't help but get up and dance. The trouble was that the seats were in the way and so had to be hastily disposed of, giving Britain its first taste of rock 'n' roll disorder.

14

CINEMA WARS

'I can't stand much more of this.'

(Rochdale cinema manager, 1956)

Cinemas in the mid-1950s relied increasingly upon teenage custom as a newly popular gadget, the television, kept their parents at home. And just as the cinemas needed young people, the young people needed the cinema. In a 1955 debate on slum housing and overcrowding, Labour MP George Isaacs explained that when people complained about Teddy Boys they had to bear in mind that young people could not take their partners home because of cramped conditions. They were therefore forced into the cinemas. For T.R. Fyvel, the picture houses supplied the Teds with basic emotional needs, offering them not only relaxation but temporary relief from the 'strain of being "somebody"'.

Even in the comfortable darkness of the cinema the Teds competed for attention. Some would chatter, laugh, heckle and make cat-calls throughout the performances. At cinemas in Huyton and Prescot, just outside Liverpool, lads would shout to each other from opposite sides during the film. The girls were often the source of the trouble, inciting and encouraging their boyfriends to act up. In South West London a Wandsworth cinema employee revealed the trouble caused by the Clapham Common crowd, later involved in the infamous murder. The boys would slip in quietly in ones and twos and once inside would move around, climbing over seats until half a dozen came together. They would then pick on a stranger before scuffling and shouting. After reprimanding Clapham gang leader Ronald

Coleman, the employee was followed on his way home by three youths and stabbed in the face with a broken cup. 'We'll know your face in future,' He was warned. Coleman denied using the weapon but admitted his involvement in the attack.

Despite the distractions, young audiences would remain silent during tense or violent scenes which gripped their interest. Sadistic scenes were a real favourite. Aspiring Teddy Boy Ray Gosling remembers that *Rebel Without a Cause*, starring the recently deceased James Dean, enthralled young people, who would 'Hush' anybody who tried to disturb others. Teds particularly loved American gangster films and movies featuring juvenile delinquents and gang fights.

Cinemas might have needed teenage custom but they didn't always get their money when Teddy Boys tried to sneak into the cinema for nothing. A group would shoulder their way roughly through the crowd, each signalling that the one behind was paying. The attendants would often be too late to notice what the lads were doing and wouldn't dare challenge them anyway. Fire-escape doors also had the habit of bursting open to let in groups of youths.

* * *

Even before the infamous rock 'n' roll riots of September 1956, there were many disturbances in cinemas, but as they were isolated incidents and did not usually involve large groups the authorities were not overly concerned. As early as 1954 there were several warnings of what was to come. At the Granada Cinema in South East London, a fight broke out between ushers and lads in Edwardian dress who objected to the showing of Walt Disney's *Snow White and the Seven Dwarfs*, while two Tyneside cinemas took to displaying notices at the pay boxes: 'Teddy Boys banned'. The action came after complaints from regular patrons about rowdiness during performances. The manager pointed out that the Teds were not interested in watching the films but arrived in groups merely to meet girls and carry on.

In London, the Eros Cinema in Catford decided to close its gallery on Sundays, the favourite evening of the week for Teddy Boy disturbances. In Surbiton, Surrey, four Teds were ejected from a cinema after setting off fireworks during the film. At the Odeon Cinema, Edgware, a gang of Teds started fighting during a James Cagney movie. They then attacked staff who told them to sit down. At the Classic Cinema in Hammersmith the manager was manhandled by Teds. Teds also knocked down and kicked the assistant manager of the Odeon in East Ham after being refused admission while the manager of the Empire Cinema, Islington, was taken to hospital after being attacked by Edwardian-clad youths. When Teds began to fight in the Forest Gate Cinema, the manager pinned one of the lads to a wall by pulling his drape over his arms like a straitjacket until he was arrested.

Trouble continued into 1955. In January, at the Rialto in Rochdale, six Teds caused a disturbance after a Sunday night performance. The trouble followed a similar scene the previous Sunday when one of the lads was ejected for waving his arms as if conducting an orchestra. In the same month, after being thrown out of the Astoria in London's Old Kent Road, nine Teds went back for revenge. The manager and his assistant were attacked and kicked to the floor. On the same night eight Teds attacked the 75-year-old commissionaire at the Brixton Astoria. In May police were called to disturbances at three London cinemas: Forest Gate, Camberwell and Richmond.

A more typical example of what was to come took place in September 1955 during a showing of *Blackboard Jungle*. Ray Gosling remembers watching the film when the Haley theme music struck up. It was as if he had been given an electric shock. There had already been reports of American teenage audiences rioting or simply dancing in the aisles and some British audiences also went wild. Londoner and ex-Ted Mim Scala recalls watching the film at the Red Hall Cinema, Fulham, when a member of the Putney Gang ran to the front and sliced the bottom of the screen with a razor. The Walham Green Gang retaliated, sparking a disturbance in which both seats and faces were slashed unmercifully. All this anti-social behaviour called for some sort of action. On Sunday evenings, in November 1955, police 'anti-Teddy Boy' patrols were introduced outside Leicester's Melbourne Cinema. The establishment's commissionaire was also instructed by police not to admit Teds.

These isolated incidents of youthful exuberance, aggression and anti-social behaviour were nothing to what happened next. Haley's theme song proved so popular that Columbia Pictures signed up the singer to star in *Rock Around the Clock* (1956), a film about the rise to fame of a rock 'n' roll band. The film showcased various Haley songs, together with performances from Freddie Bell and the Bellboys and black vocal group The Platters. The abundance of rock 'n' roll music, heard by many for the first time in Britain, proved too much for some audiences. After watching the film an excited fifteen-year-old told a journalist: 'This rhythm is the real razzle-dazzle. It gets you, man. I've been here three times this week. And I'm coming again.' A cinema manager was quoted as saying, 'It's a great rhythm. I've even danced it with the wife in the kitchen. But that's no reason why it should make people into hooligans.' Yet that is exactly what it did do to some.

The North East was the site of the very first recorded rock 'n' roll disturbance, at the Queen's Gaumont Cinema in Newcastle on 22 August 1956. Teenagers screamed constantly, stamped their feet and danced in the aisles. Five days later, at the Shepherd's Bush Gaumont, in West London, six Teds jived in the aisles. They also picked up the manager and carried him to the foyer. It was meant as a joke but the newspapers made it seem more serious. The following night the film was shown at the Prince of Wales Cinema in Paddington, the home turf of many early Teds. Youths jived in the aisles and vandalised seats. The manager needed nine stitches to a head wound after he was attacked by one of a group of Teds who had bunked in through a side door. Ten policemen were called to quell the disorder. The next night the cinema was protected by twenty men, including ex-soldiers and brawny ex-boxers, recruited from various North London cinemas. When some Teds began clapping rhythmically to the music the 'guards' moved in and the clapping stopped. Police were also strategically placed near the exits. Ironically, the film's theme is that rock 'n' roll music is unjustly criticised and is good, wholesome fun.

In early September, at Romford, North East London, Teddy Boys and their girlfriends tore fire buckets from the wall and scattered water and sand on the floor. A seat was torn from its mounting and thrown into the orchestra pit. The police were called to five cinemas in London and surrounding districts to deal with boisterous youths – making it seven times in a fortnight that police had been called out to cinemas. Incidents usually began with teenagers clapping their hands and stamping their feet to the rhythm of the music before jumping up to dance. Back at the Gaumont, Shepherd's Bush, a youngster warned the manager, 'Just wait for Friday, mate. We've got the boys from Notting Hill coming, and the boys from White City and Acton. We're gonna tear the place apart.' At the Gaumont in Chadwell Heath, Essex, thirty youths were ejected and a policeman injured, while at the Gaumont in West Ham about 120 youths jumped out of their seats. Dagenham's Gaumont saw crowds of lads and girls stand outside hissing and booing as police ejected dancing youths. After leaving the Gaumont in Twickenham, Middlesex, youths also sang and danced in the street. Ten arrests were made. It wasn't only the Haley film that inspired disorder. After a showing of *The Man in the Grey Flannel Suit*, at the Regal Cinema, Hammersmith, twenty Teds clashed with police.

On 11 September Britain experienced its first major rock 'n' roll riot during a screening of the Haley film at the Trocadero Cinema in Elephant & Castle. The district was one of the first centres of Teddy Boy activity, the home-ground of South London Teds. Tony Scullion, later fined £5 by Peckham magistrates, admitted that they didn't try to keep to their seats. He didn't think that they could have done so anyway. Upon hearing the first bars of 'See You Later Alligator' he signalled to the boys and they took to the aisles. For nearly two hours after the film had finished an estimated 1,000 teenagers sang and jived in the street. Two policemen were injured as their attempts to restore order were met by a shower of bottles and fireworks. Shop windows were also smashed. Those ejected for misbehaviour vented their anger on a tea stall outside, throwing cups and saucers about. Hundreds of youths also held up the traffic on Tower Bridge with a chorus of 'Mambo Rock'. There were nine arrests and a few fines issued. The following night police took measures to avoid a repeat performance. Up to 300 uniformed and plain-clothed officers were drafted into the Elephant & Castle to quell any trouble but this did not stop some youths from throwing bottles outside the cinema after the film had ended.

During a showing at the Gaumont in Lewisham seats were kicked and slashed as Teds again jived in the aisles. A crowd also began singing 'Nine little policemen hanging on a wall'. 'I'm getting into the groove,' exclaimed one teenager as the film began. A young soldier claimed to have seen the film five times and intended going every night that week. He boasted that the previous evening everybody was jiving. When the police tried to stop the dancers their attitude was 'OK, make me'. The defiance was part of the fun. When the audience left the cinema some shouted 'Rock Rock Rock' while others howled, 'Dig that crazy jive, man!'

At the Gaumont in Stratford, East London, over 100 teenagers were thrown out. 'Ranting and raving', they then danced on the flower gardens outside the cinema. Further south in Croydon, police cleared the Davis Theatre of jiving youngsters but during the second performance a fresh crowd stamped and shouted, 'We want rock 'n' roll! We want rock 'n' roll!' The manager was squirted with a fire extinguisher when he told youths to stop jiving in front of the screen. A few miles away, at the Grand Cinema in Camberwell, rows of seats were smashed by twenty Teds. Letters to the newspapers expressed the public's disgust at this primitive behaviour. One *News Chronicle* reader felt strongly that the cinema was a place where people went to enjoy films, not a centre for tribal dancing or the release of sexual neuroses and inhibitions.

At Stevenage, Hertfordshire, a sixteen-year-old boasted to a journalist, 'Of course I've slashed cinema seats. We all have. You're bored, so you get out your knife and tear it open. You don't always need a knife. You can do it with a cigarette. It's easy to burn them.'

Liverpudlian Colin Fletcher recalls watching *Rock Around the Clock* at the Palais. The local gangs had declared an unofficial truce to gain admittance: 'It was the first time the gang had been exposed to an animal rhythm that matched their behaviour.' Soon they were wrecking the seats. At the end of the film there were fourteen seats missing. In September a Liverpool doctor went to see what all the fuss was about and claimed to have witnessed teenagers performing 'horrid contortions all over the place' amid howls and yells and the smashing of cinema seats. In nearby Bootle 1,000 jiving Teds were escorted a mile through the town by truncheon-waving police. Only half had been in the audience – the rest had gathered outside the cinema waiting for something to happen. Four days later Liverpool Theatres and Public Entertainments Committee voted unanimously to ban the film at twenty of the city's cinemas.

At the first showings of the film at the Gaiety Theatre in Manchester, terrified girls struggled to escape as a group of fifty Teds, who had arrived in a truck, ran amok. The film was stopped. At a subsequent screening, as a safety precaution, policemen patrolled inside, supplemented by the cinema's own security staff who lined the walls to prevent the audience from dancing. Nevertheless, about thirty Teds succeeded in whipping up the viewers into a state of frenzy. Those on the balcony showered electric bulbs and lighted cigarettes on people sitting in the stalls. Perhaps alert to the fire hazard involved in such reckless behaviour, some Teds also fought a fire-hose battle and drenched those seated below. Some youths, irritated at the large police presence, shouted, 'We don't want no cops.' When some lads were ejected for misbehaving, others left in protest.

Expecting trouble from the dispersing crowds, police were stationed outside, ready to greet the mob of screaming teenagers who surged down Oxford Street causing pedestrians to scatter down side streets. An arm-linked police cordon was swept aside. The crowd started to jive and sing, beating out the rhythm on the panels of buses. One lad, still hypnotised by the primal rhythm of Haley's music, did a 'snake dance' while another jigged on the roof of a parked car. Others boogied on the platform of the Cenotaph at St Peter's Square until dispersed by the police. In Piccadilly Square some youths climbed on the shoulders of their friends to throw fireworks. Somebody shouted, 'The police can't touch us, there are too many of us.' He was wrong. Fourteen arrests were made, ten of them of juveniles. A police spokesman declared that nothing like it had ever been seen in the city. When the culprits appeared in court a magistrate told them that he would much prefer it if the police were allowed to deal with them in a way that would give them something to rock 'n' roll about.

Smaller towns did not escape the mayhem as teenagers jumped on the bandwagon. In Lancashire at the Empire, Burnley youths caused £150 worth of damage. Seats were torn, lamp bulbs swung against the wall and fire hoses again turned on the audience. The film was stopped for fifteen minutes while the manager took to the stage to appeal for calm. 'Enjoy yourselves less boisterously, or out you go,' he shouted. 'Kill him,' replied a voice from the back row. Disturbances continued the following night with lads climbing on seats and dancing in the aisles. During the day's continuous screenings about fifty youths were asked to leave. Extra staff mingled with police officers in plain clothes. On the third night the manager greeted the audience as they entered, warning likely troublemakers to behave or he would lose his licence. Some youths had travelled up to twenty miles to see the film.

One ex-Ted from Colne recalls, 'We all went a bit daft at the cinema. It was a great atmosphere and everybody was jiving in the aisles. And we started doing things we shouldn't have done. We were tearing seats off, ripping off covers and throwing them into the air. And they said that's it, everybody out and they closed the cinema down. It was just too exciting for words.' At Rochdale, where the audience smashed seats and let off fireworks, dozens of youths were ejected by police. Afterwards they demonstrated in the town centre for an hour, breaking shop windows.

* * *

In the first two weeks of September, over sixty youths appeared in courts throughout the country, charged with causing disturbances inside or outside cinemas showing *Rock Around the Clock*. In London alone, police made a total of 37 arrests on a single Saturday night. Between 1955 and 1957 riots connected with rock 'n' roll films and live performances also erupted in several European cities, including Copenhagen, Dortmund and Oslo. 'Teddy Boys Stormed the Tivoli, Eight Apprehended', screamed a headline in the Danish daily paper *The Politiken* in 1957. Another newspaper, *The Berlingske Aftenavis*, headlined with 'Children's Nurse Led Rock-Riots'.

Various experts tried to explain the cause of the disturbances. A Harley Street specialist thought that rock 'n' roll music was being used by youths as an excuse for their behaviour – he said the same lads would riot if a Mickey Mouse film was being shown. Dr Josephine Macalister Brew thought that the violence was copycat behaviour: a few rowdies had read about the disgraceful conduct of American audiences and simply followed suit. A psychologist explained that youths had caused trouble long before rock 'n' roll was invented and would continue to do so after the music had been forgotten.

Insurance experts took to estimating the value of a cinema manager's life. A Lloyd's broker proposed that for £5 a manager could take out £2,000 worth of insurance cover against being beaten up by Teds. Not surprisingly cinema managers throughout the country began to take drastic action to prevent further trouble from the destructive element among audiences. Various methods were tried. In Derby the soundtrack of the first three rock numbers was turned down to prevent any rioting but the 900-strong audience was so unhappy that they stamped, clapped and shouted, before somebody set off two fireworks that soon brought the police. As one youth was ejected, a Ted shouted, 'They are always picking on Ginger.' The audience responded by chanting in unison, 'We want Ginger, We want Ginger.'

The management at the Gaiety, Manchester, took the precaution of vetting the crowds outside – 450 young people were once turned away from the queue, mostly for making too much noise. Since Sunday was such a difficult night to control audiences, in the middle of September the Gaiety replaced *Rock Around the Clock* with a light musical called *Rainbow 'Round My Shoulder*. The audience might have been lower in numbers but at least the show was trouble-free. Indeed, the Rank Organisation decided to suspend the notorious film at all its venues on Sundays. It seems that on Saturdays teenagers also had football matches to help burn off their energy but on quiet Sundays the film was providing bored youths with a unique opportunity to let off steam.

The Capitol Cinema, in Edge Hill, Liverpool, decided to display notices banning lads in Edwardian dress. In some London cinemas groups of teenagers were simply barred, whatever they were wearing. Sometimes lads were allowed in only if they were in pairs or accompanied by a girl. If a gang of youths was refused admittance they would threaten to go to another cinema down the road; managers responded by phoning neighbouring picture houses to warn them and the lads would again find themselves refused entry. Some managers separated the boys from the girls by sending the girls upstairs to the circle where the seats were more expensive. In Finchley, North London, local youths were barred by the manager from seeing any films that attracted large audiences but were allowed in to see what most people did not want to see. In Lancashire, at the Savoy, Cleveleys, two Alsatian dogs were led down the aisles as a warning to would-be jivers. Some London cinemas hired professional wrestlers to keep the peace, such as burly Len Britton, who worked as part of the anti-Teddy Boy squad at a London cinema in the sport's off-season.

By 1959 cinemas, particularly those in the Manchester area, were trying more novel approaches to quell potential trouble. The manager of the Empire Theatre in Middleton invited his adult patrons, including Teddy Boys, to become manager for the day. He wanted to show the Teds what members of his staff had to put up with. The invitation came after Teds fought and slashed seats, causing £30 worth of damage. It is not recorded how many Teds took up the offer or whether it changed their behaviour. The manager of the Capitol Cinema in Bolton banned Teddy Boys for three months to stop further damage to the furniture and fittings. After a truce the Teds were re-admitted, only for the manager to find that another fifteen seats had been slashed. Perhaps the most sensible solution to the problem came from a Ted who said, 'I wish they would show the film in a dance hall, without seats, then we could really enjoy it.'

Cinema managers were forced to act since there were financial penalties for allowing bad behaviour to take place on their premises. Also in Greater Manchester, at Rochdale, the manager of the Victory Cinema was summoned to court on a variety of charges, including failing to maintain order at the venue, not keeping the gangways free and using seats not secured to the ground. Giving evidence, a cinema attendant claimed that when he had ejected Teds for misbehaviour the manager let them back in again. The attendant also said that he was not allowed to phone the police and therefore had to contact them in secret. He had even been assaulted as he tried to stop a lad dancing on the stage. Police confirmed that they had been called many times and found gangs standing and chatting in the aisles and girls screaming. They made so much noise that it was difficult to hear the film. The manager also admitted that he had been assaulted while trying to keep order. He reported that 180 seats had so far been damaged and there were fifty people on the banned list. The manager was fined £45 and the company £90 for the offences.

The ultimate sanction was to completely ban a film. Local Councils or cinema chains would sometimes refuse to show a controversial film. *The Wild One* (1953), an account of America's lawless motorcycle gangs starring Marlon Brando, was banned nationwide by the British Board of Film Censors due to its potentially corrupting influence. It was not shown in the United Kingdom until 1967. During the middle of August 1956, *Rock Around the Clock* was also prohibited in many places, including Belfast, Birmingham, Blackburn, Bolton, Bradford, Brighton, Bristol, Carlisle, Gateshead, all of Gloucestershire, Ipswich, Preston, Reading, Smethwick, South Shields and West Bromwich. The Blackpool Tower Company postponed screenings indefinitely after unfavourable reports from around the country. The management called for a special 'audience reaction' report. Some people certainly supported the ban. Two teenagers from Surrey wrote to the *News Chronicle* to register their disgust at repeated reports of riots following the showing of the film. They asked whether the film selectors needed even further proof that it should be banned.

When Taunton banned *Rock Around the Clock*, after reports of trouble in other districts, youths painted 'We Want Rock and Roll' in foot-high green letters on the Shire Hall and on several local business premises. It wasn't only the young who objected. The secretary of Taunton YMCA dismissed the complaints and claimed that nobody objected when thousands of people thumped and stamped at the Last Night of the Proms concerts. The chairman of Taunton Liberal Association also objected to the ban and felt that if the music was to be outlawed from the cinema it might also be banished from the radio and dance halls. He felt that such a move would be the beginning of an Orwellian slippery slope to controlling what people enjoyed. The ban was reversed in January 1957 and the film shown at the local Gaumont. The only condition was that the movie was not allowed to be the last feature on the programme. This was to give the young audience the opportunity to cool down before they hit the streets to go home.

Banning the film didn't always have the desired effect. When Lancashire towns Wigan and Leigh refused to show

Rock Around the Clock, Teds simply jumped on buses and trains to catch the film in Manchester.

* * *

In spite of the bad publicity surrounding *Rock Around the Clock*, the film industry was keen to capitalise on its success. A sequel, *Don't Knock the Rock* (1956), was shown on local screens at the same time. Such was the speed of manipulation of the teenage market. *The Girl Can't Help It* (1956) and *Rock, Rock, Rock!* (1956) continued the trend. The films were mostly thinly plotted excuses to showcase the talents of such rockers as Little Richard, Eddie Cochran and Gene Vincent. It was the music that sold the movies. By 1957 over twenty-five major films with a rock 'n' roll theme were being shown in cinemas. *Jailhouse Rock* and *King Creole*, featuring Elvis Presley, followed in 1958.

Unfortunately, the tendency towards violence also continued, including several incidents throughout London. In 1957 two policemen were injured after a fight with Teds at a cinema in Sydenham. After a showing of *Jailhouse Rock* at the Hornsey cinema, rival gangs of Teds threw bottles at each other. There was also a disturbance at the Palais Cinema, Kensal Green, during a showing of *Disc Jockey Jamboree*. Youths ripped out seats and threw them at the screen. Fireworks were also thrown at the audience. A year later a seventeen-year-old Ted attacked a man who told him to be quiet in the cinema. The Lambeth magistrate told the lad that he must be dealt with severely. Borstal would not do. Detention centre would not do. He jailed him for six months.

Despite the widespread trouble, the whole affair must be put into perspective. In spite of the subsequent uproar, *Rock Around the Clock* was originally screened in 300 cinemas the length and breadth of the country, including tough venues at Sheffield and Glasgow, without any trouble. It was only after disorder in South London that trouble spread. Indeed, there were complaints about misbehaviour at only 25 of the

400 cinemas that continued to show the film. A Newcastle journalist was sent on a mission to report on the London disturbances. After watching the film in Bethnal Green he witnessed nothing more than the occasional 'Yippie' and a few delighted squeals. He concluded that the whole affair smelt strongly of a publicity stunt.

Future Beatle John Lennon was disappointed to find that nobody at the Liverpool cinema where he saw the film was singing or dancing. He was all set to tear up the seats but nobody joined in. His experience echoes that of a London lad who claimed to have seen the film at the Elephant & Castle and found that everyone was as quiet as a mouse. Andrew Loog Oldham, who later became manager of the Rolling Stones, watched the film in the Haverstock Hill Odeon. Sitting among twenty uptight viewers who tut-tutted and shifted uncomfortably in their seats, the middle-class Oldham quietly slashed his own chair.

Nevertheless, after witnessing disturbing scenes both during and after a screening, the Bishop of Woolwich was another of those calling for the film to be banned. He felt it a tragedy that the cinema riots had started just when Teddy Boy activity had begun to die down. Looking optimistic about the future, he boasted of having confirmed some former gang leaders in the previous few years.

The Teddy Boys were far from finished but it was not outrageous cinema riots that would keep them in the public eye. Two years after *Rock Around the Clock* whipped teenagers into a rock 'n' roll rage, a more disturbing series of riots would propel the Teds back onto the front pages. Bored with slashing cinema seats, some Teds were turning their pent-up aggression on black immigrants.

15

RACE WARS 1: NOTTINGHAM

'The man who can win the allegiance of the Teddy Boys can rule this country.'

(Andrew Fountaine, National Front member)

In September 1956 a West German youth magazine called *Bravo* heralded the arrival of *Rock Around the Clock* but pointed out that English youths had wrecked cinemas showing the film. The magazine explained that the 'wild rhythm' of Haley's music originated in the traditional ritual music of black Africans. Furthermore, since rioting was judged to be the typical behaviour of black people, it seems that Englishmen had turned into 'white negroes'. German audiences were warned not to follow suit.

While British Teddy Boys enthusiastically adopted elements of black zoot suit fashion and revered the sound of Afro-Americans such as Little Richard and Chuck Berry, some Teds held racially prejudiced views about the black immigrants living in their own communities. Although most of the time their aggression was focused on rival gangs, they also directed their violence towards 'foreigners'. There is some irony in this, although the Teds were probably uninterested in the black origins of their music. They inherited the shape of the drape jacket directly from the English spivs and Edwardians rather than the black American Zooties and heard a great deal of their rock 'n' roll performed by white singers. While rock 'n' roll music was a marriage between black R&B and white country music, young British listeners would have been exposed mainly to the white exponents of the genre such as Haley, Buddy Holly, Eddie Cochran, Gene Vincent and

Elvis Presley. Besides, an appreciation of the black roots of rock 'n' roll was unlikely to influence more pressing social concerns, namely the threat that the immigrants posed to the Teds' territorial pride and sense of status.

What is ironic is that the early Teddy Boys themselves were sometimes described in racial terms. In 1955 the *Manchester Guardian* felt that the Teds faced more discrimination than any race group in the country. Journalist Hilde Marchant suggested that the Teds were only the latest in a long line of scapegoats, including Jews, American soldiers, spivs, cosh boys, negroes and communists. In 1957 the explorer and anthropologist Tom Harrison returned from the far-away island of Borneo only to find that Britain was seemingly swarming with its own primitive savages. Explaining what impressed him most on his return, and with tongue firmly in cheek, he claimed that it was the new terror that stalked the land, namely the Teddy Boy. He joked that the first time he went to Hampstead, North London, he was so terrified that he nearly fled back to Borneo and the relative security of tribal head-hunters.

Aware of the risk of sounding far-fetched, T.R. Fyvel explained that following the Irish and the Indians (although at the same time as the Africans), London Teds were engaged in their own small-scale, anti-colonial rebellion against inferior social status. It was this anxiety about 'status' that was behind some of the Teddy Boy violence towards other races. Teds viewed the influx of immigrants as a threat to their already decaying working-class communities. Although they all lived in the same run-down, inner-city areas, Teds were irritated when some of the newly arrived West Indian and Cypriot immigrants were thought to be earning more than them; this despite the fact that many young people were paid relatively well, especially compared to their parents' generation.

* * *

In 1954, white attackers threw a petrol bomb into a house occupied by a West Indian family in Camden Town, North

London. The following year, two Teds attacked a black man in Shepherd's Bush market, West London, beating him about the head with a stool. Girls also accompanied Teds in an attack on an Indian shopkeeper in Bermondsey, South London. Some attacks were inspired by fascist propaganda urging that blacks be driven out of Britain. For many West Indians living in London the threat of violence became a fact of life. Yet it must also be pointed out that some Teds actively sought out West Indian music and style. Ray Gosling notes that Teds would visit basement clubs and unlicensed drinking establishments, known as shebeens, in Brixton, Soho and Notting Hill.

Things weren't so amicable elsewhere. A Wolverhampton dance hall displayed the sign 'No coloured people or Teddy Boys'; the manager explained that the groups did not mix. Nearby in Smethwick, nine Teds assaulted and robbed an Indian. After receiving a rabbit punch the victim was left semi-conscious and bleeding in the gutter. Forty miles away, a fifty-year-old Indian called Labh Singh was also left with deep scars to his face after being beaten with the leg of a bar stool by a gang of Teds in Leamington; he woke up in hospital remembering nothing. In Brighton, Cypriots and Malayans taking part in a march organised by the Movement for Colonial Freedom were jostled and harassed by Teds. And at a Sheffield fairground, three chain-swinging Teds attacked every black man in sight. Four victims were dragged off the dodgems and others attacked behind the caravans.

It might be that the prejudice directed against other nationalities was closely bound up with the bleak social conditions and desperate sense of exclusion experienced by a demoralised section of the white working class. It wasn't simply about skin colour. In North London when a night-watchman was beaten up by three Teds in the Caledonian Road, Islington, an eyewitness reported: 'I think they mistook him for a foreigner.' Indeed, any 'foreigner' was game for a beating. T.R. Fyvel identified a lack of self-confidence when Teddy Boys met foreigners in the streets. Americans, Poles, Cypriots and West Indians were all seen as alien invaders on their manor.

On the dockside streets of Wapping, East London, in 1957 local Teds beat up Hungarian refugees outside their hostel. Jealousy over local girls was the cause. During the same year, Littleborough, Lancashire, endured a Sunday-night battle between Teddy Boys and Hungarians. Knives, bottles and coshes were used. Since music and entertainment licences were banned on Sundays in neighbouring Rochdale and Milnrow, youths began to travel to Littleborough looking for excitement and trouble. One young bystander had his skull fractured. A year later, at Rochdale, tensions were still running high between Teds and Hungarians. To prevent trouble, the owner of one cafe once had to eject about fifty English youths and keep back twenty Hungarians. Nevertheless, a girl brought the Hungarians a message: 'You are expected out in five minutes.' The two sides then set to battle using bottles, bricks and rubber hoses. Again bystanders were injured. One man was stabbed and another suffered a fractured skull after being hit with a bottle.

In Berkshire, Teds fought a street battle with a bunch of Irish lads outside Reading's Majestic Ballroom in 1958. The following year there was a clash between Teds and Arabs in the Eccles area of Salford. A witness saw Teds running from a dance hall where they met a group of Arabs and started fighting. After a ten-minute brawl, one Ted was stabbed and an Arab left with scalp injuries.

* * *

Coffee bars and cafes deemed to be run by 'foreigners' were particularly vulnerable, which is ironic since they provided a valuable service to bored young people. When Italian Pietro Pineschi took over a coffee bar in Hampstead, North London, Teds began to invade the place to slash seats and threaten Pineschi. Over time, though, the ex-lightweight boxer eventually tamed them and gained their respect. Elsewhere, an Italian waitress spoke of her fear of the Teds after a nineteen-year-old was shot while sitting in her Holborn cafe. She related how they would sit there, twenty to forty of them, over a 7d cup of coffee, annoying customers and threatening to smash up the place. The police would remove them only for them to return.

The London Teds spent much of their time in cafes run by Greek Cypriots, part of a wave of post-war immigration of Greek and Turkish Cypriots. In 1956 500 Cypriots arrived in England to join the 30,000 who had already settled. All British subjects, about 7,000 were of Turkish extraction while the rest were Greek-speaking. By opening up cafes and coffee bars the Cypriots provided the Teds with venues to dance and socialise but some Teds hated the fact that the cafe owners were thriving on the money they spent in their premises.

The idea that cafe owners were exploiting young people is conveyed in a description in the novel *Cosh Boy*: 'Being Saturday night, the place was crammed with teenagers, mostly earning money out of all proportion to the work they did and only too eager to part with it to the Italians and Greeks and other admirers of the British way of life, astute enough to transfer it to their own pockets.' In the novel the Cypriot proprietor's 'single-minded ambition was to extract as much money as possible from the gullible English with the minimum of trouble and eventually to return to his native land with a large bank balance and a solid hatred for the country where he had acquired it'.

The Cypriots had to be able to handle trouble. One cafe was run by two broad-shouldered brothers who looked like they could fight. According to T.R. Fyvel, anybody making trouble would soon be carved up with a knife. From 1954, the death of many servicemen during hostilities between British armed forces and members of the Greek Cypriot nationalist guerrilla organisation EOKA didn't help race relations. One Greek Cypriot restaurateur claimed that Teddy Boys would sometimes open his door and accuse him of murdering British 'Tommies'. In 1957, a gang of up to ten Teds had a tense stand-off with Greek Cypriots in Kilburn High Road, North West London, after the Cypriots allegedly sneered at the Teds. The groups then waded into each other. At least one Ted used a metal studded belt as a weapon. London gangs would also make special forays to Commercial Road in the East End to attack Cypriots.

Teddy Boys found a new form of entertainment in smashing up cafes owned by the 'Cyps', as they were called. In April 1960 up to ten Teds walked into the Espresso Bongo coffee bar near Victoria Station in Manchester. Terrified women fled screaming as the youths wrecked the place. A lamp thrown across the room hit Greek waiter Costas Sophocleous on the head, sending him crashing against the counter. Tables and crockery were smashed and a large plate glass window shattered. Another South London Ted boasted that he was once in a Greek cafe on the Walworth Road when the owner assaulted a boy because he was sitting on the corner of the table. The Ted warned the man that if he did that again he would get the boys to smash up the place. He claimed that he didn't have anything against foreigners but he didn't like to see them hit a white man, particularly one sharing his own nationality.

* * *

In addition to smashing up Greek and Cypriot cafes, Teds directed their hostility towards West Indians. One Ted recalls the time a six-strong gang went after a black man. The Ted couldn't recall what he'd done to annoy them; his colour was enough motivation. If a gang of Teds came across black people in the street they would try to provoke them by calling them 'black bastards'. In Brixton, South London, gangs would try to stop black people getting off the buses, to frighten them. 'We'd often go for the Blacks. We don't like them round here, we hate them,' was the stark verdict of one young gang member. Teds would also cruise in cars looking for lone victims.

Under the British Nationality Act of 1948, UK citizenship had been granted to all members of the Commonwealth meaning they now had a right to enter and settle in Britain. Since the post-war British economy needed additional sources of labour, rising numbers began to exercise that right. In 1951 the total black population of Commonwealth origin settled in Britain totalled 74,500; by 1961 it had risen to 336,600.

Britain, however, was not the Promised Land that the immigrants were expecting. Many had to accept low-status, ill-paid employment and were forced to live in overcrowded, insanitary conditions. The 1957 Rent Act left them open to exploitation and squalor. Black people also faced hostility and prejudice. By the late 1950s, abusing and attacking black people became something of a sport for some youths. Rudy Braithwaite, originally from Barbados, was reading a book on the London Underground one evening when a gang of Teddy Boys marched down the carriage. Two of them sat next to him, one on either side, and began taunting him. Braithwaite ignored them but some elderly white passengers, fearing trouble, hurriedly left their seats.

In two districts in particular, Nottingham and West London's Notting Dale, simmering tensions between blacks and whites eventually erupted into violent unrest. Teddy Boys were in the thick of the fighting during both disturbances. Nottingham was once famous for its lace-making but also boasted other, light-engineering industries such as the manufacture of shoes, drugs, textiles, and also coal mining. Workers from India and Pakistan had been settled in Nottingham for several years. The first black people to arrive in considerable numbers were the West Indians and West Africans during the war, most recruited to the Royal Air Force with some also employed at the Ministry of Defence Ordnance Depot. On demobbing, some servicemen married local girls and settled in the area. By 1958 over 3,000 immigrants (2,500 West Indians and 600 Asians) had settled in Nottingham, about one per cent of the total population of 313,000, making it one of the largest West Indian communities outside London. By 1958, however, the economic boom that had attracted post-war Caribbean migrants to the UK was over. Nottingham began suffering a local recession; factories went out of business and redundancies increased. This did not bode well for the local immigrant population, particularly when local industries refused to take on black workers.

As well as employment difficulties, there was a problem with housing. For generations the centre of the city had traditionally housed local workers, but as they began to move to better homes in the suburbs most of the area degenerated into a vast slum, with cheap rents in decaying properties attracting immigrants. Since they preferred to live near each other, the West Indians began settling in two particular run-down districts. One of these was St Ann's where two-storey tenements, built in the nineteenth-century, rose steeply on either side of a valley intersected by the main thoroughfare and shopping centre called St Ann's Well Road. Apart from a tree-lined promenade called Robin Hood Chase (known as The Chase), St Ann's was a tightly packed heap of soft-brick houses which, by the 1950s, were beginning to crumble.

There were also cultural problems. The local white population accused the West Indians of being lazy and slow to learn new skills. Black people were also rebuked for their habit of spitting. Particularly disliked was a small minority with bright, gaudy clothes and off-hand manners. Known as 'wide boys', they had a habit of pushing in on the queues of white people at the Employment Exchange. Unhappy about the type of jobs being offered to them, some also became abusive to the staff. A particularly serious incident happened in April 1957, when some 'flashy' black men tried to push into the queue at the Exchange. A heavily built white worker took one by the shoulder and turned him away, ordering him to get in line. The West Indians produced knives, shouted abuse and hurled fire buckets. After a tense stand-off, the group departed.

There was also 'bad blood' between blacks and Teddy Boys. In addition to pressure over jobs, Teds were envious that some black men appeared to be doing quite well living off the earnings of white prostitutes, some of them brought in from Manchester and Birmingham. They also objected to seeing local white women visiting public houses popular with the black community. While the women welcomed the attention, the Teds felt aggrieved and used this atmosphere of hostility, resentment and sexual jealousy as an excuse to intimidate, assault and rob blacks whenever the opportunity arose.

Immigrant Edward Scobie recalls the tension in Nottingham created by lawless Teds from the St Ann's Well Road area. Wielding knives, they barked 'fascist' orders to black people not to travel in groups or they would be attacked. One demeaning ploy was for a group to stop a black man and ask for cigarettes. If he handed them over he was humiliated; and if he didn't he would likely be beaten up.

During the few weeks before the final flare-up, at least a dozen black men were attacked and robbed. A black miner leaving the cinema with his wife was mobbed by whites shouting, 'Go back to your own country.' During an argument in a pub a West Indian assaulted his white woman friend. This led to a scuffle and resulted in white men thumping the few blacks present in the pub. The police were accused of showing little interest or concern in these assaults. In the summer of 1958 a West Indian complained that he had been beaten up and his best sixteen-guinea suit ripped to bits. The police inspector investigating is alleged to have told him to go home and put on another suit. News of such incidents spread and heightened the sense of frustration and helplessness felt by the black community.

Violence against blacks was reported periodically during 1957 and 1958. The number of assaults, however, was relatively small, and since white people were also often attacked by Teddy Boys there wasn't always direct indication of a racist motive. Up to the time of the major outbreak of disorder in Nottingham, there was no local political activity against blacks from right-wing groups. By the summer of 1958, however, there was a self-imposed curfew for black people in the St Ann's district. Black men walking after dark felt vulnerable to attacks. Although the assailants were vaguely labelled 'Teddy Boys', some of the culprits were men aged up to thirty years old. Four out of five attacks on blacks were made by adults for racist rather than hooligan motives. It has been estimated that there were about twelve such adult attacks before the main trouble broke out.

During the July and August, tension mounted in The Chase. The incident locally credited with kick-starting the chain of events happened when a black man made a visit to a late-night chemist to get a prescription for his wife. On his way home he was assaulted by a group of Teds. As usual the police were unable to find the culprits. Black people were incensed. Eric Irons was a West Indian who worked for the local Ordnance Depot and was later to become Britain's first black magistrate. He recalls that vengeful blacks set out the following week looking for Teddy Boys, although nothing happened.

On Saturday 23 August the simmering disquiet finally came to a head. Accounts differ as to the exact events, but all place a black male and a white female at the centre of the evening's troubles. One version has it that a young West Indian man was assaulted because he had the audacity to be seen enjoying a drink with a local blonde woman. Another version is that outside a public house in the St Ann's Well Road area, just after closing time, a black man bumped into a white woman, whether on purpose or by accident is not clear. The woman took it as an assault and a brawl developed among the crowd leaving the pub.

Whatever happened, within a few minutes West Indians had produced knives and stabbed six or seven white men before disappearing up an alley. One man was stabbed five times and another needed thirty-seven stitches to a throat wound. News of the fight spread throughout the neighbourhood and by 11 p.m. a crowd of about 1,000 white men had gathered in the area between Peas Hill and The Chase. Some, armed with razors, knives and bottles, were intent on attacking the West Indians and soon there was a pitched battle between blacks and whites. By 11.36 p.m. the police had the area under control, although an officer was injured after being run down by a car. As a safety precaution police used vans to escort blacks to their homes. By midnight the crowds had dispersed. At this point there was no evidence of Teddy Boy involvement, nor were any spotted in the milling crowds. However, the initial hostility towards black men regarding their alleged exploitation of white prostitutes now turned to anger over their ready use of knives. In all eight people, black and white, ended up in hospital.

The following weekend, on Saturday 30 August, a crowd of 3,000 to 4,000 white people gathered at the junction of St Ann's Well Road, Peas Hill Road and Pym Street. Some were reporters and sightseers, ferried in by cars from outlying districts, and one enterprising bus company in Leicester displayed chalked notices advertising tours to see 'the terror spots of Nottingham'. Hoping to provoke another disturbance, sections of the crowd shouted, 'Let's get the blacks.' Since most West Indians had wisely followed police advice and stayed indoors, sections of the crowd turned on each other instead.

Some made up for the lack of visible targets by launching missile attacks on the homes of black people and residents responded by hurling milk bottles from the upper floors at the crowds below. Around this time some Teds attacked five black men in a dark side-street off St Ann's Well Road. Twenty Teds also threw milk bottles at two black men before chasing them. One escaped but Alphonso Walton was caught and given a kicking. In another incident a crowd, including many Teds, surrounded a car containing three black people, shouting, 'Let's lynch them.' Attempts were made to overturn the car but police intervened and told the driver to 'go like hell'. The vehicle managed to speed away. The police also became targets for attack. Individual constables were assaulted for protecting the blacks the previous Saturday.

The following week was quiet but on the evening of Saturday 6 September a crowd of up to 200 white people gathered at the bottom of The Chase. All was quiet until five West Indians, who had been drinking at a wedding, walked past and shouted remarks at the crowd. Police had to escort them from the area. The crowd followed but then turned off towards the homes of blacks. Again the tenants from the upper floors threw milk bottles at them. The crowd responded by dismantling a wall to use the bricks as ammunition to hurl back at the windows.

At a press conference, Nottingham's Chief Constable, Captain Popkess, dismissed claims that the disturbances were caused by prejudice and denied that they were racial riots. He blamed the trouble on 'irresponsible Teddy Boys' and drunks and said that the black population in general had behaved well. Although the riots stopped in Nottingham, the initial disturbance on 23 August inspired three nights of copycat disorder in London. Known as the Notting Hill race riots (even though they took place over a wider area and were more a series of racist attacks by sections of the white community), the disturbances once again put the spotlight on the Teddy Boys.

16

RACE WARS 2: NOTTING HILL

'Keep Britain White'

(Slogan used by right-wing group, the League of Empire Loyalists)

On Friday 29 August 1958, almost a week after the first Nottingham disturbance, the *Kensington News and West London Times* was keen to alert its readers:

> Nottingham must be a warning to North Kensington, to Paddington, to Brixton, wherever coloured people in large numbers are living and working side by side with long-established Londoners.

The caution was already a little late. After a week of press reports about the troubles in Nottingham all the elements were firmly in place for a fresh wave of disturbances in North Kensington, where the social problems were much worse than those in the Midlands. The disturbances, when they erupted, were also more serious than those in Nottingham, being spread over a wider area and covering several days. In fact the riots commonly attributed to Notting Hill spread to Shepherd's Bush and nearby Notting Dale, to parts of Kensal New Town, Paddington and Maida Vale.

At that time Notting Hill was a neglected district in the inner belt of London, between the business centre and the suburbs. A short distance away was Notting Dale. To the west was the White City area of Shepherd's Bush. To the east of Notting Hill was Paddington, housing a sizeable black population, most of its residents having settled before the peak influx of 1955–56. With few available properties remaining in Paddington, Notting Hill became an overspill area for West Indians, the total black population being about 7,000. While the Nottingham riots broke out in a district densely settled with black people, the London disturbances erupted beyond the reaches of the more concentrated black settlements. There were 2,000 to 3,000 fewer blacks in Notting Hill than in Brixton.

The area between Notting Hill and Hammersmith was already a magnet for gangs of Teds from Fulham, Battersea and Elephant & Castle who would invade the area looking for a fight. Notting Dale and nearby White City also housed many young Teds. As one contemporary writer put it, 'their creed – if it can be called a creed – [was] one of self-assertion and a resentment of all discipline, restraint or organization'. Crime and fighting were part of the culture of such areas. In the two years before the troubles broke out, while the black community was still growing in Notting Dale, Teddy Boys were responsible for several assaults, although black people were not the only target. The usual pattern of such attacks was for Teds to take offence at the behaviour of passing strangers who looked easy prey. The violence was indiscriminate and needed only the suspicion of an insult for its justification. A fortnight before the disturbances rival gangs fought a pitched battle in Cambridge Gardens, off Ladbroke Grove. The local population had had enough. Angry residents from several streets united to present a petition to the London County Council, pleading for something to be done about the violence, the rowdy parties and the unlicensed bars known as 'mushroom clubs'.

Along with its illegal drinking dens, rough public houses, gangs and prostitution, the area also had multi-occupied houses with families of different races on each floor. It was an ideal location for those wishing to exploit those newly arrived in the country. Blacks, gypsies and Irish were crammed together in squalid properties run by racketeering landlords who bullied and intimidated tenants. The infamous Peter Rachman was one of the few who would let properties to black tenants. Local white families, who had endured the war years but missed out on the exodus to the suburbs, were left to stagnate in squalid properties and poorly paid jobs. Some of these people had their reasons for objecting to immigration. There were issues surrounding unemployment, particularly competition between blacks and whites for unskilled jobs. One young boy put it crudely, stating that it was all 'the Queen's fault' for visiting black countries where they did their war dances for her. They then thought that they could come over here 'and take our jobs'. Others objected to the generous benefits system that enabled supposedly idle immigrants to collect money from the Assistance Board. Tales circulated of blacks coming off the boats and claiming £5 for the week.

A shortage of housing after the war led to competition for accommodation and resentment when immigrants managed to find properties over white prospective tenants. Overcrowding was also an issue, particularly the practice of immigrants banding together to share a single property. This enabled them to afford to pay a higher rent than a single white person. A young ex-Ted explained that he didn't agree with injuring people but that the 'Spades' had brought it upon themselves. He blamed the immigrants for having no consideration for others. They moved into areas and bought up properties before evicting families. He also argued that it was impossible to reason with black people.

As in Nottingham, the perceived sex lives of black men were another cause of concern. There were allegations of sexual misconduct, including accusations of rape and of white men's wives being accosted. The growth of brothels and the running of prostitutes also caused tension. In the two years before the troubles, twenty-two black men from the area were convicted of living off immoral earnings.

Black sexuality and its effect on white men were familiar themes. The film *The Wind of Change* (1961) deals with racism among Teddy Boys, although by the time it was released there were few Teds left. Named after Prime Minister Harold Macmillan's Cape Town speech in 1960, the film explores the problem of race within the context of Teddy Boy violence. Set around Notting Hill, main character Frank is a disgruntled and racially prejudiced Ted whose hatred of blacks is driven by sexual jealousy. The earlier film *Sapphire* (1959) also depicts Teds as racist thugs.

* * *

Political tensions also played their part. Various right-wing organisations such as the Union for British Freedom, the White Defence League and the League of Empire Loyalists were active in the area, inciting white residents to 'Act Now to Keep Britain White'. In what was fertile ground for racist propaganda, meetings were held, leaflets distributed and ominous slogans such as 'Down with niggers' and 'We'll kill the blacks' scrawled on walls. The right-wing groups, however, did not create the racism. They merely exploited and encouraged views that were already held by an agitated section of the community. Adult men in pubs, for example, had traditionally sung 'Old Man River' and 'Bye Bye Blackbird', improvising the lyrics with racist slogans.

This sort of racism filtered down to the young. In the week before the disorder a drunken fifteen-year-old approached a black man in a railway carriage at Liverpool Street station and was reported as shouting, 'Here's one of them – you black knave. We have complained to our government about you people. You come here, you take our women and do all sorts of things free of charge. They won't hang you so we will have to do it.'

The abusive language might not have been reported accurately, having been filtered down through various official channels, but it was the type of message spouted by right-wing orators such as Oswald Mosley, the founder of the pre-war British Union of Fascists. Mosley, now heading the Union Movement, helped articulate and exploit the resentments of discontented white people living cheek by jowl with the black population in the most deprived areas.

Some disenfranchised Teds were certainly susceptible to racist propaganda. Perhaps because they saw no reason to conform to a society they felt did not value them, they turned instead to peer leaders who incited them to vent their feelings of alienation through anti-social means, particularly violence, racism and anti-semitism. Ex-Ted Eddie Adams explained that although some Teds did support Mosley, there were many that didn't and many of his supporters were the old pre-war Fascist members of his organisation. These were the ones organising events.

Nevertheless, there was certainly right-wing support for the Teds. Jeffrey Hamm, the secretary of the Union Movement, refused to condemn the Notting Hill Teds, who, he argued, 'were the target of those who had grown old too early and have forgotten or prefer to forget the wild indiscretions of their own youth'. Oswald Mosley also sprang to their defence, calling them 'fine types'. The Teddy Boy movement, he said, 'is vital and, in comparison with many of its critics, also virile, which is what youth should be'. He also praised the 'high intelligence' of Teddy leaders. He stated that their reactions 'are mostly the normal, healthy reactions of vigorous young men [to the] corrupt and finally destructive values of a rotten society'.

* * *

Hostility increased during the summer of 1958 as Teds from White City began to target black people. The first incident was not in Notting Dale but in Shepherd's Bush. On 14 July a gang of white lads from the White City estate wrecked a West Indian-owned cafe in Askew Road. They escaped before police arrived. A fortnight later up to thirty returned and used sticks to break furniture and crockery. Six youths were later conditionally discharged and ordered to pay £40 compensation.

In Notting Hill the Teddy Boys were said to have chased black people for sport, like fox hunting. Tryphena Anderson, who arrived in Britain from Jamaica in 1952 to train as a nurse, remembers people coming up to her and saying that the Teddy

Boys were out last night and were going 'black burying'. She misunderstood and thought that they were going blackberry picking. Yet Teds were not the only ones responsible for such attacks. For weekend entertainment some older, respectably dressed white men in cars would try to run over black people at night. Nevertheless, sixty per cent of those arrested for the London disturbances were aged under twenty; only fifteen per cent were over thirty.

On 17 August a white crowd smashed the windows of two houses occupied by blacks in Stowe Road, Shepherd's Bush. In retaliation seven residents came out and stabbed a man. Also in August, four youths entered a black-owned cafe in Shepherd's Bush and began throwing chairs around. This was merely a prelude to a more serious attack three hours later when about twenty Teds entered the place and spent five minutes trashing the place. Five young men, all from respectable families and in full employment, were later found guilty. Hammersmith was another area ripe for racial unrest. In the week before the main disturbances in Notting Hill several policemen were injured when they went to investigate a group of youths who were causing a nuisance in Fulham Palace Road. Teds also spent their weekends scouring the area looking for black faces.

Dozens of racist incidents were perpetrated in the last week of August, any one of which could have kick-started the chain of events that led to the main disturbance. Three incidents in particular stand out. On Saturday 23 August, as the group of black men in Nottingham were stabbing whites outside a public house, there was parallel trouble in Notting Hill. A West Indian was attacked in a North Kensington pub by white men who battered him with dustbin lids and jabbed him with broken milk bottles. At 1 p.m. bottles were thrown at two houses occupied by blacks in Bramley Road, Notting Hill. Perhaps the London Teds were embarrassed at being upstaged by their provincial colleagues in a distant Midlands town.

The third incident was the most serious. Within hours of the Nottingham news filtering through to the rest of the country, early on Sunday morning, groups of Teds in Hammersmith began to cruise the streets searching for Africans and West Indians. One nine-strong group, armed with iron pipes, table legs, starting handles, knives and an air pistol, packed themselves into a car and went on a 'nigger hunting' expedition. Blacks walking alone or in twos were targeted and attacked. The first victim was chased down a street and cracked over the head with an iron bar before his attackers calmly returned to the car and continued their entertainment. Some intended targets managed to escape but at least five men were seriously injured and some left sprawling unconscious on the pavements in Ladbroke Grove and Shepherd's Bush.

Of the nine lads, eight hailed from the White City estate. They were aged between sixteen and twenty-one. Although largely inspired by the Nottingham riots, one claimed that he was seeking revenge for his friend who had been recently been knifed by a black man. Two had only met by chance on the evening concerned and agreed at the last moment to come along. The leader of a youth club, to which several of the group belonged, explained the attacks by stating that the club was not open that night – so the lads did not know what to do with themselves. Normally, to break the boredom, they would battle with neighbouring gangs but in their absence they turned upon black people.

The culprits, not all of them Teddy Boys, were each sentenced to four years' imprisonment, a punishment that was meant to act as a strong deterrent and maintain Britain's reputation in the Commonwealth. Commenting on the case former Lord Justice of Appeal, Lord Denning, remarked, 'Occasionally there should be severity – one might say extreme severity – for the good of all.' One young observer at the time, however, commented that the sentences were excessive and would cause more trouble.

Even with this latest spate of specific attacks it was still not obvious that they were leading up to a major event: they were just the latest in a long line of racist incidents all over London. Six days passed without incident, although tensions grew as rumours of forthcoming action spread throughout the area. On

Friday 29 August a gang of white lads attacked a white Swedish woman called Majbritt Morrison who had been seen arguing the previous night with her Jamaican husband, Raymond, at Latimer Road underground station. The boys, feeling it their duty to protect her, had shouted racial abuse at Raymond and were angry when Majbritt turned on them. The boys no doubt felt that she was a traitor to her race. When they saw her the next night they pelted her with bottles and stones and struck her in the back with an iron bar. The police rescued her and she was escorted home, although she refused to go inside and ended up being arrested. The incident inflamed white feeling and later that night a mob of 300 to 400 white people, many of them Teddy Boys, were seen on Bramley Road attacking the houses of West Indian residents.

By Saturday 30 August the Teds in West London suspected that something was about to break in Notting Dale and began to converge on the district. Youths pursued black men and broke the windows of houses where West Indians were known to run businesses or where white women lived with black men. Shortly before midnight a crowd of 200 attacked the homes of West Indians near Bramley Road. One house was set alight and two more were pelted with bricks and milk bottles. Another house had a bicycle thrown through the window. In the ensuing clashes, iron railings, bicycle chains and choppers were used as weapons. Barbadian Rudy Braithwaite had a friend whose teeth were knocked out by a group of Teddy Boys. He also remembers Teds taking their chains and twirling them in the air before smacking them on the ground. White reinforcements arrived from other parts of London and if they couldn't get at the blacks, who were being protected by police, they turned their violence on the officers.

One Notting Hill Ted told a reporter from the *West London Observer*, 'We've come to join in the fun ... We'll come to get the blacks all right ... Believe me, mister, we are going to drive the blacks out of this area ... First we are going to get them out of North Kensington, then Ladbroke Grove, then "The Town" and finally Westbourne Grove, where it all started.' The next night a mob, 500 to 700 strong, converged on Bramley Road chanting, 'We'll get the blacks', 'Lynch the blacks'. They used knives, bottles, crowbars and dustbins to attack houses. Another armed mob of 100 youths gathered under the arches of Latimer Road station. There were also clashes on the Harrow Road and in Kensal Rise. Hundreds of youths, many dressed as Teds, roamed streets in the Lancaster Road district, jeering whenever they saw black people. Normally regarded with horror by the local white adult population, during the disturbances many Teddy Boys came to be regarded as heroes. Some black people certainly felt that violent and racist Teds had the support and sanction of many adults.

Other groups, some fifty-strong, waited outside the houses of black people. A 'mushroom party' in Blechynden Street attracted a large crowd who flung bricks at the building. The police asked the partygoers to stop playing the music and move elsewhere. Later on, petrol bombs were thrown at other houses where there were clubs or parties taking place. A group of blacks was attacked and a woman stabbed in the shoulder. Elsewhere, a ten-year-old boy, caught up in the trouble, was hit in the mouth with a broken bottle. A police car with a prisoner inside became the target of bottle-throwing youths. One man was pinned against a wall by police only for the crowd to throw bottles at them, chanting 'Down with the dirty nigger'. Empty bottles from a passing milk float became missiles. In one incident a white man called Bert Harper was slashed across the neck, receiving a five-inch cut. At midnight a Jamaican was attacked in the Harrow Road area.

On the afternoon of Monday 1 September the Teds returned and the crowds began to gather. Until now the disturbances had been confined to the Notting Hill area, the participants being mainly young, working-class men from the immediate community. On the Monday the trouble took a new twist as media reporting and word of mouth helped attract outsiders to the area. Traditional rivalries between areas such as Shepherd's Bush, Paddington and Hammersmith were put aside as whites united against a common enemy.

By the time darkness had fallen, the hordes in Notting Hill had reached worrying proportions as some residents also took to the streets to prowl for suitable victims or simply watch events unfold. A howling mob of 300 Teds who had attended Notting Hill's first fascist meeting left energised and stirred up for further trouble. 'Let's get the blacks,' they shouted as they began attacking properties housing immigrants – only to be met by showers of milk bottles thrown from the upper storeys. At one house a brave Jamaican woman, armed with an axe, stood guard at the door. 'We are a decent family here,' she declared. Barbadian Ivan Weekes recalls watching a raging battle in Powis Terrace involving black men, policemen, Teds and white hooligans. Blood was everywhere and the street was ablaze with Molotov cocktails.

The fighting also began to spread to other districts. A house was torched in Paddington and a West Indian cafe in the Harrow Road was besieged by 800 bottle-throwing men and women. Terrified blacks cowered inside as the premises were pelted with over 300 milk bottles. In another incident a young man slashed a West Indian across the face. When he was arrested he coolly told the officer: 'So a darkie gets chivved [knifed]. Why all the fuss?'

Most black people avoided leaving their homes, particularly after dark. Black London Transport employees who had to work late shifts were given escorts. Notting Dale nevertheless housed a high proportion of daring and reckless young black men who were not afraid of trouble. Some formed vigilante groups to patrol the area in cars. Black reinforcements also arrived from surrounding areas, including Brixton, Shepherd's Bush and Paddington. A group of West Indian militants organised themselves and made pre-emptive attacks on a local fascist headquarters.

On Tuesday night trouble kicked off in Kensal Town and North Paddington with skirmishes between whites and blacks using milk bottles. Around the same time, mobs up to 700-strong inflicted damage in Notting Hill. Five white men drove through the streets shouting, 'Stir them up' and 'Get stuck into them'. On Wednesday a welcome rain shower dampened people's spirits. The crowds thinned and the violence temporarily subsided. However, as the sun shone again the next day, familiar bouts of racist abuse and bottle-throwing continued, along with petrol-bomb attacks on the homes of West Indians in Notting Hill and Paddington.

A few days after the worst disturbances a young lad, who had earlier been part of a gang attack on a West African student, revealed that he had heard that some Teds from the Elephant & Castle were coming over to help them finish off the job – though he felt that the Notting Hill lads could handle their own problems. Although trouble in Notting Hill began to decline, over the next fortnight further assaults on black people were reported in various areas, including Harrow Road, Southall, Stepney, Harlesden, Hackney and Islington. Tensions in Brixton remained high for days. A rumour circulated around a Shepherd's Bush dance hall that a black cafe owner was refusing to serve whites. Twenty-five Teds, armed with sticks, paid him a visit to trash the place.

Despite the siege-like atmosphere, the violence had petered out by 5 September. At the end of these twin outbreaks of racial violence the number of arrests was as follows: 177 in London and 25 in Nottingham, a ratio of 149 whites to 53 blacks. Various factors helped bring an end to the troubles: extra police officers assigned to the areas, the increasing number of arrests and the heavy sentences imposed upon some of the rioters. By the end of September both Nottingham and London had almost returned to normal, although race relations in Britain were to be changed forever.

One consequence of the disturbances was that the various black immigrant groups, Trinidadians, Jamaicans, Africans and Guyanese, became a more united community, bound together by a common defensiveness and with a much stronger black political identity. If the Notting Hill and Nottingham clashes marked a new beginning for Britain's black population, they also signalled the beginning of the end of the Teddy Boy movement in its original form.

There were, however, a couple of isolated incidents where Teds appeared to be making a last stand. Nine months after the clashes, in late spring 1959, a young Antiguan carpenter called Kelso Cochrane was stabbed to death by youths in North Kensington. A black resident of the area revealed that after midnight she had heard banging on the fence outside her house. She claimed that Teds often did this to attract attention before starting a fight. Although Teds were implicated in Cochrane's murder, nobody was brought to justice.

In April 1959 a Pakistani-owned cafe in Walsall Street was invaded by twenty Teds after the owner displayed a chalked notice: 'Teddy Boys not allowed in here'. The sign, which was put up after previous bouts of disorder by Teds, was ripped up and tables and chairs placed upside down. Around the same time, two black men entered café in Gloucester that was full of Teddy Boys. Gilbert May hadn't even sat down when a Ted hit him over the head with a sauce bottle; his wound required eleven stitches. A week later, at Blackheath, Birmingham, thirteen Teds returning to the Pavilion Dance Hall after having a last drink, attacked seven black men parked in a large car outside the venue. The disturbance began as a fight between the Teds but ended with a chair being thrown through the car window.

* * *

As residents of Nottingham and North Kensington cleaned up their mess and made efforts to restore racial harmony, there were various attempts to look for causes and explanations. A group of young men were interviewed by Barry Carmen of the BBC for the radio programme *Black and White*; they were billed as 'Teddy Boys at Shepherd's Bush' though they denied being Teds. Nevertheless, the transcript of the programme lists various justifications no doubt shared by many Teddy Boys and indeed other white working-class people at the time. Unfortunately the transcript does not identify the individual voices and the reader is unaware of who is speaking at any one time.

The young men being interviewed feel that black people should be kept out of Britain. They do not like them going with white girls. One blames the London disturbances on blacks beating up his friend – he claims that on the night of the disturbances fifteen blacks jumped his mate, slashed his back open and broke his arm. The whites, in retaliation, torched one of the culprits' homes. One lad particularly dislikes the idea of mixed-race children. The outrageous view that black people should be shot is voiced. It was believed that blacks gained jobs because they worked for lower wages. An example is cited of one factory that refused to hire white men because blacks were cheaper to employ. In contradiction, blacks were thought to be lazy and content to let white men do the work. At the labour exchange, blacks were said to draw more benefit money than whites. Blacks were said to attract white women because they were more virile and were able to spend more money on them. It is also claimed that blacks grew prosperous off the backs of prostitutes, both black and white. One lad estimates that ninety-five per cent of Britain's black population are ponces or run brothels. While black ponces are detested, white ponces are deemed acceptable.

Others also suggested reasons for the disorder. A *Sunday Times* reader claimed that unlimited immigration was a threat to the standard of life of the British working classes and that rioting Teds were meeting the challenge in the only way they were able. Labour MP Charles Pannell stressed that the disturbances were race riots. He explained that when a gang set out with the idea that the only criterion whether they bash in a man's face or not was that his skin was not white, that was a race riot. Senior police officers, however, assured the Home Secretary, Rab Butler, that there was little or no racial motivation behind the disturbances. *The Times* felt that the local black population had become a 'novelty' target for gangs out to cause trouble. A London policeman explained that black people were merely the latest victims of the sort of violence which the Teds had traditionally meted out to cafe owners and rival gangs.

Black people did not escape blame. Labour MP George Rogers felt that the riots were not the work of Teds, as was commonly believed, but the legitimate response of the local community to undesirable elements within the black community. Speaking of the disturbances in Notting Hill, Conservative MP Nigel Fisher declared that society must recognise that there were bound to be faults on both sides in these matters. There were bad immigrants just as there were vicious Teddy boys and violent youth gangs. The troublemakers of both races ought to be ruthlessly dealt with and severely punished. He felt that there was probably a perfectly good case to be made out for deporting convicted criminals and, by agreement with colonial Governments, even restricting immigration to Britain of people with a known criminal record in their country of origin. Unease at the disturbances enabled those who favoured stricter immigration controls to gain the political advantage. Legislation duly followed. The Commonwealth Immigrants Act, introduced by the Conservative Government in 1962, tightened the regulations, permitting only those with government-issued employment vouchers. This effectively limited the number of immigrants allowed to settle.

On 3 September the *Daily Mail* published a cartoon showing Teds soiling the British flag with blood. Although the disturbances were often portrayed simply as the work of racist Teddy Boys and hooligans, such a view ignores the role of right-wing fascist groups who helped orchestrate events. There were also various social and political factors lurking in the background. These seemingly spontaneous explosions of white anger were rooted in urgent post-war social problems, including issues of housing, employment and cultural ignorance – along with insensitivity on both sides.

A *Manchester Guardian* reader was concerned that the racial disturbances were being laid mainly at the door of the Teds. He pointed out the role of economic insecurity in aggravating racial prejudice and gave figures to show that in the London area unemployment among men under eighteen years of age had more than doubled between July and August

1958 (a rise from 399 to 910). In Nottingham unemployment had increased over six times (from 49 to 314). These were not seasonal fluctuations but a product of recession.

Another reader wrote to *The Times* pinpointing almost the opposite reason for the riots, blaming the high-wage-earning economy for the lack of social responsibility among youths. When young people realised that their big money could not buy the social status they craved, they instead gained prestige and self-importance among their mates through acts of violence and bravado. The writer particularly felt that social and economic improvements had destroyed the traditional basis for self-respect by giving young people too much independence before they were ready for it.

As author Edward Pilkington observes, the focus on the Teds helped to diminish the wider significance of the riots by deflecting attention away from the authorities, who had allowed racial resentment and violence to escalate. A young white rioter further explained that it was adults who started the disorder: the Teds merely jumped on the bandwagon. Those who viewed the Nottingham and London troubles as Teddy Boy-driven hooliganism turned the Teds into scapegoats, while helping to divert attention away from British society's own prejudices and failures in managing its immigrant population. For this, the media must share some of the blame for it had long singled out the Teds as a major social problem.

17

TEDS AND THE MEDIA

'A great deal of the stimulation of the teddy boy cult had been due to the press.'

(Ronald Goldman, lecturer, 1960)

In the 1950s popular media expanded rapidly. For many households the wireless was the focal point for home entertainment. Families would gather silently around the radio to listen to *The Goon Show*, *Hancock's Half Hour* and *Housewives' Choice. Dick Barton, Special Agent*, was a particular favourite of young boys. In the early 1950s about 350,000 households also had access to television. The population's burning desire to watch Queen Elizabeth's coronation in 1953 boosted the popularity of TV in Britain. From 1955 commercial TV franchises offered an alternative to the BBC. By the end of the decade ten million homes were glued to such programmes as *Dixon of Dock Green*, *Double Your Money* and early 'soap opera' *The Grove Family*. As well as offering light entertainment and factual documentaries, television producers also turned their attention to the flourishing teenage culture, offering 'pop' programmes such as *Oh Boy* and *Six-Five Special*, which featured performances by stars such as Cliff Richard and Marty Wilde. Television dramas also focused on the activities of teenage gangs. *Teddy Gang* (ITV, 1956), *Tearaways* (BBC, 1956) *The Wharf Road Mob* (ITV, 1957) and *Strictly for the Sparrows* (ITV, 1958) portrayed the brutal social realities of life as a Ted.

Popular newspapers such as the *Daily Mirror* and *Daily Express* boasted daily circulation figures of over four million copies. Sunday papers such as *The News of the World* and *The People* spread sexual scandal and salacious gossip to sensation-hungry readers. From the beginning both local and national dailies took great interest in the shocking behaviour of the Teddy Boys, highlighting in particular episodes of extreme violence. This was the very first youth movement to come under the intense spotlight of the mass media and the saga was as much played out on the pages of the newspapers as it was on the streets and in the cinemas of the tough inner cities. Indeed, it has been argued that press coverage of the Teds merely encouraged their anti-social behaviour.

In its investigation into the racial disturbances in West London's Notting Hill, *The Times* acknowledged that a range of factors were involved but still felt the need to highlight the role of the Teddy Boys. The point was hammered home by further descriptions of youths in Edwardian dress gathered outside the Magistrates Court during the subsequent trial of those involved. It was noted that those arrested had surrendered an arsenal of flick-knives, stilettos, razors, bicycle chains, choppers, a club and a carving knife – weapons that were already associated with daily Teddy Boy violence.

While the working-class Teds were easily singled out for censure, the authorities wriggled free of any suggestion that they had failed to help accommodate and integrate the immigrant population over the previous ten years. Few commentators blamed the disturbances on the wider social problems affecting white working-class culture, or the effects of concentrated immigration on already deprived neighbourhoods. The recent troubles were presented merely as the latest manifestation of the sort of teenage hooliganism more usually displayed in inter-gang warfare and the smashing up of cinemas and cafes. By highlighting the common themes that had already made the Teds notorious in the minds of the public, the media managed to avoid examining the deeply rooted institutional racism and prejudice of the rest of British society.

While the media blamed the Teddy Boys for the riots, others were turning the tables and blaming the media for helping to inspire the disturbances. In a letter to *The Times*, both the press and the entertainment industry came under fire from a reader for their glorification of violence, which, it was said, was having a damaging effect on 'socially illiterate' youngsters with too much money and not enough responsibility.

Others blamed the mass media for inspiring all Teddy Boy criminality. Politicians, in particular, blamed cinema and the new medium of television for helping to create a generation of young ruffians such as the Teds. Labour MP Maurice Edelman claimed that the media romanticised criminals. He asked: 'What is the use of police patrols in Richmond, hauling in gangs of Teddy boys, when night after night the whole of television constantly exalts violence in one form or another?' The fact remains, however, that the aggressive Teddy Boys originated before the supposedly violent influence of American rock 'n' roll and before the advent of widespread TV in working-class homes.

The adverse influence of the cinema was a different matter, having been seen as a contributory factor in the rise of juvenile crime since the First World War. Before the rise of the Teds, the Ealing film *The Blue Lamp* (1949), together with *Cosh Boy* (1952), introduced the theme of post-war adolescent violence. It was felt that addiction to such films made impressionable youths think that crime and violence were natural. Journalist Cyril Dunn certainly felt that the Teds were deliberately aping screen villains. Watching some Teddy Boys talking to each other, he noted how they never stopped 'acting'. Refusing to smile, and with their face muscles held rigid, they projected a mood of controlled and intense hostility.

Such influences aside, press reporting of the disturbances arguably helped inflame tensions in the riot-torn areas. After the disorder in Nottingham on 23 August, thirty-five newspapermen arrived in the city to report on events and interview local people. Their often sensational second- and third-hand accounts of the fighting made the area a magnet for budding anti-black rioters the following weekend. Banner headlines in the *Nottingham Evening News* spoke of gangs of

Teds scouring the St Ann's Well district armed with knives, and warned blacks that they must not travel in groups. The newspaper used the expression, 'Teddy-boys, self-appointed guardians of the peace' and reports like this might have helped excite and motivate youths from neighbouring districts to invade the area. One London teenager, for example, was arrested at Nottingham Midland Station early in September, carrying a suitcase containing a lead-filled rubber cosh and a bicycle chain. Sensational reporting also attracted inquisitive sightseers, whose presence only hampered police efforts to restore order.

Television footage also helped publicise Nottingham's racial clashes – with one episode proving to be particularly damaging. According to Nottingham's Chief Constable, in the absence of any actual fighting a TV cameraman lit a bright magnesium flare to film a mock scuffle between a small group of youths. The excited crowds, which had already begun to disperse, rushed back believing that there was a fire. In the ensuing pandemonium a very real white versus white clash developed and in the fierce fighting that followed police reinforcements were attacked as they approached from the side alleys. Twenty-four people ended up being arrested due to what began as a manufactured 'race riot'. Five were jailed for three months. The cameraman later denied orchestrating the incident and claimed that he lit the flare only after the disturbance had started.

One difference between the rise of the Teds and previous gang-related crime was that the 1950s were an age of mass publicity. It has been suggested that the public did not react to the Teddy Boy, 'they reacted to their conception of him'. This 'conception' was largely founded on what they had been told in the newspapers and other media. To illustrate the point, in 1958 a member of the public was nervously trudging through the foggy and deserted streets of London's St Pancras at 1 a.m. expecting to be beaten and robbed. His fears were about to be realised when two Teds stopped him, only to politely ask him directions. The moral of the story was that it 'shows how unjust one can be after a diet of crime columns in the papers'.

Dennis Vosper, Parliamentary Secretary to the Ministry of Education, pointed out that it was easy to exaggerate the importance of 'jungle' schools and Teddy Boys, since most young people were well behaved. He felt that the problem was that Teds attracted the glare of publicity, and that damaged the reputation of all young people. Liverpool MP Bessie Bradock also lamented that Teds received so much bad publicity, saying she was sorry that the newspapers couldn't spare a headline for the Teds who organised their own Sunday football teams.

The Teds were not only making the news, they were acutely aware that they *were* news. In a sense, the media helped create the very phenomenon on which they were reporting. Chris Steele-Perkins, the author of a book on the Teds, puts it neatly: Teds 'had created outrage: outrage had created Teds'. It was newspaper publicity that initially helped spread the Edwardian style to the rest of the country. It was press publicity that also contributed to the wave of rock 'n' roll riots in the nation's cinemas after 1955. In 1956, after a showing of *Rock Around the Clock* in Manchester, about 100 teenagers gathered in the street – but in the national newspapers there were a reported 1,000 rioters. Owing to such exaggerated reporting, teenagers around the country were inspired to stage their own full-blown riots. In Birmingham, before the film was banned, one Ted was boasting, 'We will show Manchester what Birmingham can do when the film comes here.' He never got the chance.

The publicity given to the rioters was a source of pride rather than shame. Opposite a Manchester cinema was a newspaper placard describing the previous night's disturbance. Passing Teddy Boys scrutinised the poster, trying to identify themselves in the photographs. 'That's us brother. That's us!' they shouted in delight. Excited by the publicity, the gangs felt that such behaviour was expected of them.

* * *

As always, the press plays an important role in creating a sense of moral outrage. The manner in which certain 'facts' are reported can help generate public anxiety, indignation and alarm. There were certainly instances of press hype. Management at the Gaumont in Shepherd's Bush, West London, were forced to deny reports of near riots and a police presence to prevent Teddy Boys dancing during a screening of *Rock Around the Clock*. It was admitted that some lads did jump on stage to jive but returned to their seats when reprimanded. In an incident already referred to, the assistant manager confessed that although a group of lads did lift him onto their shoulders to carry him through the cinema, their behaviour was considered good-natured fun – but the newspapers made it seem more serious.

Home Office files reveal that one newspaper's claim that the interior of a cinema had been trashed was a gross exaggeration; the 'trashing' amounted to little more than damage to three light fittings. It also turned out that in another incident a press photographer had encouraged a group of young people to dance in the street to gain photographic proof of rock 'n' roll hysteria. When the *Daily Express* reported that the audience at the Avon Theatre in Glasgow had smashed glass display panels in the foyer, to loot photo stills of the Haley film, it failed to mention the manager's report that only one panel had actually been smashed and that hooligans had been smashing the same panel every week, regardless of the film being shown. The *Yorkshire Post* reported that a fight between a large group of Teds had broken out behind the Gaumont in Saltaire and that a 'vanload of police' had swung into action to break up the brawl. The cinema manager, however, reported that no fight had ever taken place and the 'vanload of police' was merely three constables standing by the side of a small commercial van just in case they were needed.

At a meeting of the northern branch of the Cinema Exhibitors' Association, delegates blamed the press for the cinema riots. One claimed that there had been no trouble when *Rock Around the Clock* had been shown at Newcastle, Darlington and other North-East venues. It was also revealed that the trouble at London's Elephant & Castle had nothing to do with the cinema and started only after the venue was closed.

Mr Rockett, the branch secretary of the Association, decided to send a letter to the authorities pointing out that there hadn't been as much trouble as the press was suggesting. He claimed that the newspapers had offered a challenge to the Teddy Boys by the publicity they were giving them. Other cinema managers blamed the spread of the riots on exaggerated reports of isolated incidents.

Young people were also quick to blast media reporting of the cinema disturbances. In a letter to Newcastle's *Evening Chronicle*, 'Three Disc Spinners' blamed the press for publicising hooliganism and insisted that those who liked to rock 'n' roll should not be classed as rowdy, irresponsible and stupid. In court, one Manchester lad admitted there was clapping and foot stomping at the Gaiety performance but no 'larking about'. He felt that some newspapers had blown the incident out of proportion by plastering their pages with accounts of hosepipes being used. He declared that no one in their right senses would behave like that – though, of course, he might simply have been playing down the incident in his own defence.

In London in 1956, the Palace Theatre, East Ham, staged a play called *Teddy Boy* starring Malcolm Knight. In the same year, Knight also starred as 'Nick' in the ITV Playhouse drama, *Teddy Gang*. While walking along the street one day the actor was punched and kicked in the stomach by two Teds who were unimpressed by his portrayal: 'You cannot take the "mickey" out of us and get away with it,' said one of the attackers. The play's manager reported that as the play toured the country they had received several anonymous threatening telephone calls. Ironically, in the play Malcolm's character is beaten up and slashed.

Around eight miles away, in the same year, a Walthamstow journalist locking up his premises was threatened by three Teds weeks after he had published an article headed, 'Are they potential traders in vice and violence?' In this case the answer was probably 'yes'. The newspaper reported that all over the country newsmen were being threatened by Teds. One well-known Fleet Street journalist was even slashed with a razor.

* * *

Colourful reports on the Teds were well-established newspaper fodder by May 1954, but from then on the press intensified their focus, introducing them to the wider public and setting a journalistic pattern which was followed throughout the decade. By April 1955, the *Widnes Weekly News* was warning that there was too much Teddy Boy publicity. Of all the newspapers, the *Daily Mirror* least saw the Teds as a threat, being generally sympathetic and indulgent towards the craze. The same cannot be said for many other newspapers, whose daily headlines offered fearful accounts of the terror posed by juvenile gangs and the robust measures required to tackle to them. In May 1954, for example, the *Daily Herald* reported that in Reading, Berkshire, 'war' had been declared on Edwardian hooligans. In November of the same year the *Sunday Chronicle* spoke of 'Terrorism by "Edwardian" thugs'. The terms 'war' and 'terrorism' were popular among headline writers reporting on Teddy Boy activity.

A conference organised by Bromley Council of Youth in 1955 discussed whether the Teddy Boy problem in the district had been exaggerated by some newspapers. Speakers seemed to think so. Various youth club leaders condemned coverage of Teddy Boys and girl gangs in both the national and some local papers, with the exception of the *Kentish Times* which had been 'most fair on the subject'. They maintained that sensationalist articles only encouraged the hooligan element to seek the limelight and also made it appear that every youth dressed in Edwardian clothes was automatically up to no good.

Various techniques were used to intensify the Teddy Boy menace. By lumping together separate crimes the press increased the perceived seriousness of the threat. On 1 May 1954 *Reynolds News* linked three unrelated incidents: the St Mary Cray gang battle, a threatened gang attack on staff at a Wandsworth cinema and the violent robbery of a shop assistant by two thugs. 'Spotlight on a Grave Social Evil In Our

Midst', ran the headline, even though only one story, the St Mary Cray fight, actually involved Teddy Boys.

It is significant that a few days after the St Mary Cray incident, the first cinemas and dance halls started to ban Edwardian clothing. Similarly, after three men were slashed at the Regent Dance Hall in Brighton later the same year, the manager responded by banning all dancers from wearing Teddy Boy clothes. It was as if they were panicked into doing so. On 6 May, Home Secretary David Maxwell Fyfe informed the House of Commons that the police were ready to suppress any signs of hooliganism by 'Teddy boy Edwardian gangs'. He also admitted, however, that only twenty-four young people, acting in groups of three or four, had been arrested for violence in London in the six months before the end of March. This was hardly the 'crime wave among the young' that readers of the popular press had been led to expect. And as George Melly points out, the Teds were only a small minority, a fact difficult to appreciate when looking through the newspapers of the period, which tended to suggest that Teds were lurking menacingly on every street corner. To put this into context, it is worth remembering that the biggest youth movement in Britain after the war was not the Teddy Boys but the Young Conservatives.

Nevertheless, the public's anxiety about rising juvenile crime in the 1950s found in the Teddy Boy an easily recognisable 'folk devil' that could take collective blame for a whole range of crime and anti-social behaviour problems. At the very beginning of the Teddy Boy phenomenon, *Tailor and Cutter* magazine, in satirical mood, protested about the intense publicity that was being given to the relatively few violent assaults committed by youths dressed as Edwardians. What the magazine objected to was the continued media association of that particular clothing with criminality. The point was made that there would be a similar uproar if the fashion preferences of murderers and other criminals were given equal publicity.

After the phrase 'Teddy Boy' was first used in print in September 1953 the number of references to them increased rapidly. Between January 1954 and December 1959 Teds were mentioned 400 times in the *Daily Mail* alone, with most articles carrying negative connotations. After 1954 young criminals were no longer described as 'spivs' or 'cosh boys' – it was as if a fresh shorthand label had to be invented to portray what was considered to be a new type of violent and delinquent behaviour.

Once the menacing figure of the Teddy Boy had been established in the media the violent behaviour of a few virtually transformed all adolescents into delinquents, or at least potential delinquents. There came a point when the labels 'Teddy Boys' and 'hooligans' became synonymous, so that the misdemeanours of either group were lazily merged. The phrase 'Teddy Boy' became a general term of abuse. 'Angry' playwright John Osborne was labelled 'the original Teddy Boy'. Irate yachtsmen branded the owners of high-powered motor boats 'marine Teddy Boys'. One town councillor described disorderly National Servicemen as 'Teddy Boys in Army uniform'. After an ill-tempered football match in 1958 the Burnley FC chairman claimed that Manchester United 'played like Teddy Boys'.

The *Daily Sketch* even argued against those who believed that the term 'Edwardian' was not a synonym for 'thug'. 'Not yet, perhaps', the paper explained, before warning that it could become so, if the Teddy Boy movement was allowed to spread unchecked.

* * *

The reported activities of the Teds were increasingly lumped together with everyday delinquency problems, as the press began reclassifying random episodes of hooliganism, brutality and rowdyism as Teddy Boy behaviour. Soon they were being blamed for rapes, burglaries and any assaults committed by young people, particular if the perpetrator could be identified by some conspicuous item of Teddy clothing. It was not necessary to wear the entire Edwardian bespoke suit to be identified as a Ted. In 1956, for example, when a South American was mugged and stabbed outside a Liverpool pub at closing time, the fact that one of his attackers was wearing narrow trousers, a Slim-Jim tie and a leather jacket was enough for them to be labelled 'Teddy Boys' in the local press. So appalled were they by the crime that dozens of genuine Teddy Boys came forward voluntarily to help the police with their inquiries. The public were equally to blame for loosely identifying Teds. The following year, a boy who had been assaulted and thrown into the Thames claimed his assailants were Teds because they wore 'black Edwardian trousers and open-necked white shirts'.

Whether they favoured Edwardian fashions or not, young hooligans were classed as Teddy Boys. After four youths threw a safe into the Thames in 1955 a witness described the culprits as Teddy Boys simply because they had crew-cuts. A year later a thirteen-year-old had a firework thrown in his face and the two offenders were described as Teddy Boys in the press although the only description given was that they were wearing duffle coats.

Isolated incidents were tenuously blamed on Teddy Boys even where the identity of the offender was doubtful. In May 1955 a 60-year-old Cypriot man called Christos Tsapparelli was killed in Camden Town, North London. The victim was walking home with his wife when he saw a girl being harassed by four youths. The wife shouted at one boy to leave the girl alone but he then swore at her. Her husband then told him off for swearing and went to help the girl. The same boy then punched and kicked him while he was down on the pavement. Although there was nothing to link the killing to Teddy Boys, a witness initially referred to the culprits as Teds. Press headlines such as 'Teddy Murder Hunt' followed. Scotland Yard ordered officers to get an alibi from every Teddy Boy in the district. Despite the police and media focus on the Teds, a Detective Superintendent later admitted in court that the culprit had no association with Teddy Boys. David Carew was found guilty of manslaughter and sentenced to three years' imprisonment.

Even when the facts were accurately reported they could be selectively sensationalised. A Yorkshire youth club leader claimed that after a disturbance on his premises he was pestered by reporters into admitting that the damage had been caused by youths with tight trousers and elaborate hairstyles even though this was not the case. The report appeared regardless.

In 1958, at a time when incidents involving Teds were major news stories, any gang fights, however loosely linked, were destined to make the headlines. In a case already mentioned, Ronald Marwood, an ex-grammar-school boy said to have 'old Teddy Boy connections' was hanged for the murder of a policeman. The connection was somewhat slight. The *Daily Mirror* reported that Marwood's headmaster had said that the boy had worn Teddy Boy clothing to school, but it later transpired that the headmaster had made no such statement. Nevertheless, Marwood was held up as evidence that the Teddy Boy gangs were not yet dead. In fact, he had no real association with either of the gangs involved in the brawl that led to the stabbing of the policeman. Right to the end the newspapers were still looking for a Teddy Boy angle to the story: as Marwood was about to be hanged press photographers outside the prison were keen to capture Teddy Boy-types taking part in disturbances.

Even at the beginning of the 1960s, when the original Teds had largely faded from public view, the idea that they were all hooligans remained, even if they now wore a different uniform. A visitor to Burnham-on-Sea, Somerset, in 1960 wrote a letter of complaint to the Urban Council after witnessing motorcyclists speeding along the Esplanade. They were referred to as 'Teddy boy louts', although they were probably so-called 'Ton Up Boys'. In the same county, the same year, a seventeen-year-old, found guilty of causing trouble at the Taunton Vale Hunt barbecue, was described in the press as wearing 'traditional Teddy-boy uniform' of black leather jacket with white piping, drainpipe trousers and white paint on the toes of his shoes. All this was a far cry from Edwardian finery.

It has been claimed that throughout the 1950s the official response to the Teddy Boys was consistently ill-timed. Sometimes the reaction was too slow; sometimes the response was premature. The authorities would anticipate non-existent dangers, resulting in the press creating unnecessary public alarm. The very efforts by police, politicians and the press to demonstrate that something was being done to curb the Teddy Boys actually gave them a sense of structure and significance that many of them probably never had.

As their reign drew to a close, Ronald Goldman, a lecturer in educational psychology, began to reflect on the media demonisation of the Teds. At a United Nations Congress on crime prevention in 1960, Goldman claimed that the British press, on the whole, took a very unsympathetic view of the adolescent. He felt that a large majority of Teddy Boys merely adopted the dress and that the term 'delinquent Teddy Boy' was unjust and inaccurate in most cases.

Others also sought to redress the balance. Dr Josephine Macalister Brew, an experienced youth worker, defended young people, who had never before endured so much abuse for their manners, their fashions and their love of music and dancing. She felt that although the post-war rise in delinquency had halted, cases of violent gang behaviour were still being blown up out of all proportion. Although Brew was wrong about the halting crime statistics, she was perhaps right about incidents of gang-related violence (most of it attributed to the Teds) being exaggerated.

Newspaper readers were made to feel that Teddy Boy gangs were on the rampage. Indeed, the number of reports highlighting the Teddy Boy menace far outweighed those attempting to promote positive images of the group. Other forms of media were guilty of the same prejudices. When Free Cinema film-maker Lorenza Mazzetti proposed making a film about Teddy Boys, the British Board of Film Censors told him that the work would only receive a certificate if it clearly condemned its subject. Since Mazzetti refused to comply, the film was never made.

While the Teds were continually demonised by sections of the media, there were others who were keen to join Goldman and Macalister Brew in defending their reputation.

18

DEFENDING THE TEDS

'Only social workers, tailors, barbers and intellectuals had a good word for the Teddy Boys.'

(Hugh Latimer, *Observer* journalist, 1955)

Despite all the column inches of negative press, not everybody saw the Teds as a threat. In June 1955 Labour MP George Isaacs opened the Dulwich College Mission's 'Teen Canteen' at the Elephant & Castle – an experimental youth club in a cafe setting. Isaacs admitted that there were some bad Teds but said he also felt that there were some fine lads among them who were also members of youth organisations such as the Sea Cadets and Boys' Brigade. Isaacs felt that the Teds had suffered a bad press and particularly saw a problem with the term 'Teddy Boy', which he said had begun to 'stink'. It was largely the media that created the stench around the Teddy Boys and so Isaacs tried to redeem their reputation by suggesting a more fragrant label, one associated with nationalistic pride and looking forward to a bright future rather than back to a murky past. He proposed an alternative name: 'the New Elizabethans'.

Not surprisingly this did not catch on but there were others who also saw the label 'Teddy Boy' as a problem. One solicitor felt that it was unfortunate that it was ever devised, arguing that 'without the label the problem might not exist'. The Chief Constable of Liverpool, Sir Charles Martin, sought to clarify the label: 'I dare say that nearly all hooligans are teddy boys, but I think it would be quite false to say that all teddy boys are hooligans.' A Somerset newspaper reader also defended the Teds and felt it a pity that society ever gave them a name. 'There was no need to classify them,' he reasoned. He felt that Teds were not abnormal and if they wanted to look smart then that was their business.

Others also tried to present the Teddy Boys as harmless figures maligned by the press and misunderstood by the public. As early as 1954 journalist Hilde Marchant tried to calm the public's fears. During several visits to the Mecca Dance Hall in Tottenham, North London, she found little to criticise, besides a touch of vanity and a little exhibitionism. She acknowledged that some Teds had 'evil ways' but felt that the vast majority were not violent and merely wore their uniform as a relief from boiler suits and factory overalls. She was supported by the dance hall's manager, who claimed that the boys were no trouble at all. In Hertfordshire a speaker at the St Albans Debating Society listed a catalogue of violence committed by Teds but still managed to conclude that they 'should be more pitied than condemned'.

Some Teds were also keen to inform the newspaper-reading public that they were not what they seemed. One, who was fed up with adult moans that lads spent all their time in cafes or on street corners, wrote to the *Daily Mirror* to outline his busy social diary which included evenings practising his fencing, table tennis at the youth club, drama practice, weekend football and supporting the local netball team. Another young man wrote to the same newspaper to reveal that he washed up three nights a week, did DIY, ran errands and cooked meals. All very praiseworthy, yet he ends his letter by declaring that he is no less than a Teddy Boy! The domesticity of Northern Irish Teds was also confirmed by a schoolteacher who was told by his daughter that she had seen a Teddy Boy in full regalia doing his mother's washing. Before getting carried away, it must also be pointed out that in 1955 a youth from Huyton, near Liverpool, appeared in court dressed in a drape jacket, blue jeans and check shirt. His mother had called the police because she was at the end of her tether and could no longer control him. She had asked him to tidy his room but he replied, 'You're the — housekeeper,' before assaulting her.

In an effort to erase the stigma attached to the Teds, rival gangs joined together to organise a three-day fete in Leamington Spa, Warwickshire, in 1958. It not only attracted 10,000 visitors, but raised £1,000 for the League of Hospital Funds. An organising committee, among them youths with police records, helped manage attractions including fashion displays, five jukeboxes with 1,000 records and competitions for Teddy Boy suits and hairstyles. A Ted spokesman declared, 'We will show that we are not the layabouts which the older generation think we are.' Another added, 'We are sick of being got at because we dress differently. OK, we're Teddy Boys but we can give a hand for a good cause, can't we.'

Teds were nevertheless aware that people were still afraid of them. One complained that when he got on a bus people would edge away from him, fearing that he was carrying a knife. When a London woman boarded a packed underground train, nobody offered her a seat until a Teddy Boy stood up for her. Another member of the public reported that she had seen four lads sitting at a bus stop when three elderly ladies passed carrying bags; the lads got up and let the ladies have their seats, before helping carry their bags to the bus. She took great delight in revealing that they were Teddy Boys. On a crowded Brighton to Victoria train, four businessmen spread themselves out and refused to budge for a *Daily Mail* reader. On the other side of the carriage, four Teds kindly shuffled along to make room for the man to sit down. In Bury, Lancashire, Teds were seen helping a woman with a pram.

There were constant reminders that not all Teddy Boys were thugs. A reader saw two drunks brawling in the street when along came three Teds. Fearing further trouble, the witness was pleasantly surprised to see the lads break up the fight and send the drunks on their way. When she went to donate blood a woman found that most of the donors were Teddy Boys. A lady selling emblems for Princess Elizabeth Day was impressed by the number of Teds who gave money. The annual event helped raised funds for the Children's Society Appeal.

Despite the hype, some children saw the Teds as harmless. A

concerned mother wrote to the *Daily Mirror* to reveal that her ten-year-old son had recently announced that he had formed a secret gang with five others. Searching his pockets she found a sheet of paper headed 'Teddy Boy Gang' listing several gang rules. Her horror soon turned to relief as she discovered that the rules included being kind, helping each other, not telling lies and loving animals. In 1954 a class of eleven-year-old pupils were asked to write a letter to Santa telling him what they wanted for Christmas. Three girls asked for a Teddy Boy.

Figures of authority also came to the aid of the Teds. Scout Commissioner J. Dodds Drummond sympathised with the Teds, reflecting that it was a fearful thing for youngsters to feel that they were merely tiny entities among millions of people. Yet that was the world that adults had created for these children. No wonder some became Teddy Boys. Drummond wished them good luck. A councillor in Lewes, East Sussex, opposed a recommendation to ban Teddy Boys from the Saturday night dances in the Town Hall. He explained, 'There are plenty of respectable men who wear Edwardian costume. If I were to dress up this way and present myself at the Town Hall, I should feel put out if I were not admitted.' Salford Brewster Sessions refused an application for an extension of the music licence of the Devonshire Ballroom in Broughton, after rowdy incidents by youths. The manager denied that the trouble was caused by Teds – he thought that the Teds were as well behaved as any boy you could meet, as well as being well groomed. He also claimed never to have seen one of them fighting. In 1960 Manchester's Chief Constable reported an overall downward trend in crime even though juvenile offending and crimes of violence continued to rise. However, he thought it wrong to blame the increase in crimes of violence on Teddy Boy gangs.

It was noted at a 1955 conference of East Midland probation officers that the term 'Teddy Boy' never cropped up during discussions of juvenile delinquency. A Nottingham officer claimed that this was because they were 'not a serious problem'. He admitted that a lot of them started fights at dances, but then youths always had done: it was simply that they were dressed differently. In the same year, Lancashire Probation Area Committee reported favourably on the Teds. Although some youths under supervision favoured Edwardian dress they were not considered a serious problem. Those that brawled in the streets and outside dance halls had always behaved that way, whether in uniform or not.

Sometimes Teds were actually presented as heroes. In 1955 one took off his jacket and jumped into the Thames at Teddington, South West London, to save an eight-year-old girl who had fallen in. Two Teds also dived into the River Brent in Middlesex in a vain effort to save a young girl. Somerset's Chief Constable pointed out that at Weston-super-Mare in 1957, Teds were the first to assist during an accident. In South East London, after the 1957 Lewisham railway disaster, in which ninety people were killed, twenty-five Teddy Boys were among the first to take off their coats and help. In Devon, when severe flooding damaged parts of Exeter in 1960 many young people, including Teds, showed extreme gallantry in coming to the aid of those in trouble. When a fire broke out on a Cheshire farm at Wheelock, Sandbach, the farmer's wife reported that it was teenagers, including Teddy Boys, who helped drag twenty tons of smouldering hay from the barn. Taking the theme of Teds as heroes one step further, one *Daily Mirror* reader likened them to Francis Drake and Walter Raleigh, for daring to be different.

The press did occasionally report heart-warming stories of Teddy Boys turning their lives around. One called Harry had become disillusioned and, after starting and finishing various jobs, was successfully interviewed for a YMCA scheme called British Boys for British Farms. Harry liked the tough agricultural life so much that he gave up his former life and became a hard worker. One reader was worried sick when her son started spending all his money on Teddy Boy clothes and staying out late. However, the boy's concern over his parents' health led him to throw away his Teddy suit and replace it with sensible clothes. Declaring that he needed some discipline in his life he then joined the Army.

Some commentators viewed the Teds optimistically, as a sign of something positive and creative. Rev. Leslie Davison, President of the Methodist Conference, argued that instead of criticising them and mocking teenage fashions people should realise that young people were at the budding point of a new age. Teds were also defended at a London conference organised by Christian Action. Leslie Paul, Vice President, failed to see why sartorial originality was thought wicked. He viewed the movement as something hopeful, a move towards independence and a signal that the new generation had rejected being spoon-fed, to make its own future.

Speaking at a conference of the Somerset Federation of Townswomen's Guilds, Rev. W.T. Cowlan spoke highly of the Teddy Boys: 'I think some of them are delightful people. They are very refreshing and unconventional, and they are prepared to do and say the things some of us would like to but daren't.' Mrs F.W. Penny, speaking about the work of the Taunton Welfare Society, asked: 'We grumble about teddy boys and delinquents but who can blame them?' Lady Brabourne, a cousin of the Queen, told the NSPCC that Teds were often maligned. Although some behaved atrociously, others were decent and upright. To see one in the street did not mean that you were going to get knocked on the head.

The broadcaster Nemone Lethbridge was another who praised the Teds, claiming that with few exceptions they did not want to fight each other. Their ambition was merely to play a musical instrument, if only in a skiffle band. In fact, hardcore Teds hated skiffle, which quickly became, in the words of writer Dick Bradley, 'the acceptable, even slightly "cissy", face of youth, patronized by vicars, teachers and youth club leaders'. Bradley had a point. After playing at a community dance hall in Smethwick, Staffordshire, the seven-strong West Side Skifflers from the Methodist Church were ambushed by twenty Teds. 'We want rock 'n' roll not skiffle,' they shouted as they beat the group with their own instruments.

Liverpool promoter Sam Leach recalls the night The Blue Diamonds skiffle group played at a first-floor ballroom. The gig was invaded by a gang of Teds, including, rather dramatically, one on a motorbike. During the ensuing battle a female follower of the band suffered a broken ankle after she was knocked through a plate-glass window. Fortunately for her, but unfortunately for him, she landed on a policeman stationed outside. On another occasion the band was attacked by more than sixty Teds at Carr Mill, near St Helens. The group had to be rescued by their female followers who waded into the fray wielding spiky-heeled stiletto shoes.

In response to Lethbridge, a teacher with a more negative experience of Teddy Boys wrote to *The Times* to point out a problem with the lads. Teds were said to attack any privilege, real or imagined, in any other social group. Their reactions usually took the form of intolerance, hooliganism and violence. A Liverpool newspaper put it more starkly: 'Those idealists who view the Teddy Boys as misplaced angels or "victims of an indifferent society" ought to realise that the next victim of the "boot in" brigade could be someone dear to them.'

Across the Irish Sea, opinions on the Teds were similarly divided. When J.D. Hornsby, the National Secretary of the Belfast YMCA, spotted some of the city's first Teds he viewed them not as delinquents but as boys needing guidance and understanding. Yet even in Northern Ireland attempts to defend the Teddy Boys were met with resistance. Mrs Haughton, the chair of the Child Welfare Council, became upset after listening to a BBC radio programme devoted to a discussion of the Teds. She felt that the programme not only portrayed them as non-delinquent but actually promoted the membership of such gangs: 'It was really made out that if one joined the Teddy Boy gangs, it would be alright.' She felt compelled to complain to the BBC.

If the Teds could not always be defended, attempts could at least be made to explain their behaviour. In the words of child expert Donald Ford, 'We must attempt to give the Teddy boy the tolerance of our understanding.'

19

UNDERSTANDING THE TEDS

> *'What Makes A Teddy-Boy? ... homes where the parents are themselves often criminals ... the lack of a strong relationship based upon affection and discipline between the parent and the child.'*
>
> (Richard Whittington-Egan, writer, 1956)

In 1957 a newspaper claimed that there were plenty of experts in almost every subject, but on the Teddy Boy problem they were strangely silent. This was not strictly true.[1] Throughout the 1950s many attempts were made to understand and explain the phenomenon, and the Teds were subject to a torrent of sociological, psychological and cultural analysis. Their behaviour was blamed on everything from boredom to the Welfare State, from poor parenting to the threat of atomic warfare. Speaking at a literary lunch at the Dorchester Hotel in 1962, romantic novelist Barbara Cartland offered her own theory. She believed in pre-natal influences of hooliganism – the behaviour of the Teds was, she said, the result of their pregnant mothers reading 'sensational filth'.

The press led the way in the analysis. On 5 May 1954, the *News Chronicle* published an article examining the Teds,

1. So claimed the *Somerset and County Herald* on 29 June 1957. Yet while the popular media was obsessed with Teddy Boys there was little academic interest in the phenomenon. It has been noted that from 1953 to 1960 there was only one reference to Teddy Boys in the *British Journal of Delinquency* and that was from a German source. See Springhall, *Coming of Age*, p. 200.

featuring contributions from psychologists and other experts. In the same month, *Picture Post* revealed 'The Truth about the "Teddy Boys" and the Teddy Girls'. The magazine's Hilde Marchant visited the Teds in their natural habitat, a dance hall in Tottenham, while a psychologist provided expert analysis of her findings. In May 1955 Liverpool's *Evening Express* ran a series of articles on the Teddy Boy phenomenon, with mandatory interviews with probation officers, churchmen and social workers, while in October 1955 the BBC broadcast a *Special Enquiry* report into Britain's teenagers; included in the discussion were two Teds, a schoolgirl, an undergraduate and a cosh boy. From 23 January 1956, the *Evening Standard* published its own four-part investigation into the Teds, and from February 1957 *The Sunday Times* began a weekly series of articles written by Donald Ford entitled, 'Who are the Teddy Boys?' (reprinted in his book *The Delinquent Child and the Community*). Over five days in March 1958 *The Manchester Evening Chronicle* jumped on the bandwagon. Twelve months on, and rather late in the day, *John Bull Illustrated* ran a feature on 'The Mysterious Cult of the Teddy Boys and Girls'.

These attempts to explain the Teds were part of a wider post-war project to discover the causes of juvenile delinquency. Indeed the debate still rages among left- and right-wing political commentators. In 1950, before the Teddy Boys had even hit the streets, London magistrate Basil Henriques laid some of the blame for children's moral deterioration on working mothers, the increase in divorce and the corrupting influence of the cinema (and, by implication, imported American culture). In 1952 the Archbishop of York, Dr Cyril Garbett, blamed juvenile delinquency on a variety of causes, among them cinema films, comics, two World Wars, family breakup and a lack of parental discipline.

With the arrival of the Teds a year or two later, experts readily provided medical and psychological explanations for their behaviour. 'A family doctor' examined the 'Edwardian insanity' and judged the Teds to be of 'unsound mind', suffering from forms of psychosis and paranoia, with an inferiority complex to boot. The feeling of inferiority, he said, was compensated for by an attempt at superiority which then led, ultimately, to them becoming criminal psychopaths. The doctor concluded that it was a desire to do evil, rather than a lack of moral understanding, that led Teddy Boys to carry vicious weapons.

Elsewhere, a psychiatrist claimed that Teddy Boys were not essentially delinquent – they were simply seeking security, while freeing themselves from an over-dependent position at home. Continuing a familiar theme, Dr Christopher Lack insisted that the wearing of Edwardian clothes was an attempt to compensate for unrecognised feelings of inferiority. He thought that Teds were socially inadequate, emotionally insecure, of weak character and of subnormal intelligence. Although the leaders might be vicious, their humble followers carried weapons merely to assert their masculinity.

Such fancy explanations cut no ice with the Conservative MP for Bromsgrove, James Dance. Speaking of a need to redress the balance of the criminal justice system, he dismissed the criminal psychologists, claiming that there were far too many people looking into the minds of the Teddy Boys and not into the minds of the old ladies who had been coshed. Lord Goddard, former Lord Chief Justice, agreed that too much attention was being paid to the offender rather than the victim. 'It is no good talking to them about reformation: they live by crime.' The *Daily Mail* also felt that the craze could not be stamped out by training and psychological treatment. What was needed was 'severe punishment'.

* * *

Explaining the actions of the Teddy Boys was to become something of an industry. T.R. Fyvel highlighted various features of the psychopathology of the Teds, including disappointment with the dreariness of street corner life, the brooding threat of violence in defence of a new-found *persona*, a cynical worldview about their own as well as of other classes, together with low employment aspirations. Fyvel identified, in particular, a young sub-group of Teds which he labelled 'drifters'. These boys were cast adrift with no direction in life and no moral standards. Rejecting all authority they lived only for immediate gratification. Seeking security in gangs they were destructive, with an urge to vandalise. All attempts to guide them into worthwhile pursuits were seen as an attack on that security. Fyvel also looked for sociological explanations, believing that the roots of post-war delinquency were to be found in contemporary social ills such as the breakdown of the family and traditional authority patterns, materialism, too much sex and the boredom inherent in affluent society.

Boredom was a familiar theme in any analysis. *The Somerset County Herald* tried to explain the growth of the Teddy Boys by suggesting that society had failed to give young people a sense of purpose. In particular, dull routine jobs gave youths a sense of emptiness. The vacuum was consequently filled with a youthful desire to dress up, parade the streets and cause trouble.

The search for excitement, however, was often fruitless. Others noted how the Teds were infected by a sense of aimlessness and post-war tedium. A *Manchester Guardian* journalist witnessed Teds 'up west' on a Sunday night. They were said to be a sad sight as they stared vacantly at the shop windows. They kept moving, but not as though they were going anywhere. Such boredom was thought to make young people vulnerable to evil influences. In 1954 a report into young people's leisure opportunities feared that the 'drifting youth of the Welfare state' became the 'inevitable prey of the gang-leader'. At best they grew up 'to lead, despite all the material opportunities of our age, inert, stunted and purposeless lives'.

Speaking at a conference in 1956, Ewart Bell, County Youth Officer at Surrey County Council, divided young people into three groups. The 'socially-conscious' made up twenty-three per cent. Thirteen per cent were labelled 'anti-social' – these were selfish, aggressive and loutish youths with a chip on their shoulder and a grudge against society. From this group sprang the gangs of hooligans. The majority of Teddy Boys, however, belonged to a third group, the 'apathetic' which made up the remaining sixty-four per cent. Bell felt that members of this group were neither naturally aggressive nor particularly eager to collaborate with authority. All they wanted was something to relieve their boredom. Left to themselves they would probably burn off their nervous energy in jiving and other noisy youthful pastimes.

* * *

It is too simplistic to say that boredom produced the Teddy Boys. For some, they were the result of a deadly combination of boredom *and* affluence. John Montgomery, writing in the 1960s, felt that 'until children were taught to overcome greed with responsibility there would always be Teddy Boys of some kind, or their descendants, standing around on street corners looking for trouble, whatever people called them.' In particular there was a growing feeling that young people, including the Teds, were earning far too much money, particularly during the later years of affluence between 1957 and 1963 when youths enjoyed greater spending power. In 1961 Labour MP for Northampton, Reginald Paget, claimed that throughout the world the younger generation was behaving badly because it had plenty more money in its pockets. The Conservative Party agreed. A 1963 pamphlet declared that in almost every country (Denmark and Italy were the exceptions), where there had been a rapid improvement in material prosperity, there seemed to have been a significant increase in crime, particularly juvenile crime.

The Teds rose to prominence at a time when the wages of adolescents were, for the first time, rising significantly faster than those of other age groups. Real earnings were more than fifty per cent higher than before the war, a rate of increase half as great again as that achieved by adults. A *Times* reader cited two reasons for the rise of the Teddy Boys. The first was the more indulgent attitude towards children of the past few generations; the second was that higher wages meant that youths were paid more than necessary to meet and maintain their standard of responsibility. The result was that Teds felt that they had the right to adopt any attitude of life and had the economic power to do so.

K.D. Robinson, headmaster of a Birkenhead school, told a conference that high wages without corresponding responsibilities were the main cause of the Teds. He proposed a reduction in wages by taxation and a compulsory savings scheme for those under the age of twenty-one. Complaints by adults that the younger generation was being paid too much were nothing new. What was new was the youthful consumption of goods, such as clothes, magazines and records, that were aimed specifically at the teenage market. What distinguished post-war youths from their parents and grandparents was this increasing consumerism, which some believed was sapping young people's moral fibre.

From the mid-1950s this important new teenage market was mostly aimed at the wage-earning working classes, since most middle-class youths were either still at school or college gaining qualifications or serving low-paid apprenticeships. Almost ninety per cent of all teenage spending was conditioned by working-class taste and values. The Teds, in particular, were open to the novel attractions of the growing teenage culture. In their fashions, language, musical interests and behaviour, youths became so outlandish that they could no longer be understood by their parents and teachers. Increased spending power gave the young an economic independence and resulting assertiveness that unsettled many adults. With economic freedom, teenagers now demanded their own spaces separate from adults. They also sought leadership and guidance from each other rather than their parents, meaning the generations began to grow apart. The traditional wisdom of your elders was no longer relevant. In 1956 the *Daily Mirror* held a Teenagers' Parliament attended by twenty youths, some of them Teds. Many cited a generation gap, with parents resentful of their freedoms, entertainment opportunities and money.

It was a familiar theme. In Stan Barstow's short story 'The Desperadoes' (1961), tough gang leader Vince explains to a girl the reasons for his anger: working to line somebody else's pockets, distrust from the police just because he wears his hair differently, poor relations with his father who calls him 'a layabout an' a ted'. It is as if the war-wounded father is jealous that his son has escaped the horrors of combat and, to rub salt in the wound, even manages to earn more money than him. The generation gap looms large, for, according to Vince, his father's generation has made a mess of the world with their wars and bombs. Vince reacts with a violent rejection of authority, claiming that he cannot rest until he has smashed something, until he has shown them that he doesn't give 'a bugger' for any of them and they realise that they cannot boss him around. As the certainty and stability of the old world order crumbled, the looming figure of the Ted became a bogeyman on which adults could focus their deep-seated fears about the new social order.

* * *

The new Welfare State was coming under increasing scrutiny. Fully implemented after the war, its aim was to care for citizens, in Winston Churchill's famous phrase, 'from the cradle to the grave'. Compulsory National Insurance contributions enabled child allowance and financial protection against the pitfalls of disability, sickness, unemployment and old age. Yet according to one *Times* reader, although welfare provision promised young people full economic security, it produced instead a sense of boredom.

In 1961 the British Medical Association also hinted at the adverse effects of the new welfarism:

> The society in which today's adolescents find themselves is one of bewildering change ... the whole face of society has changed in the last 20 years ... a decrease in moral safeguards, and the advent of the welfare state has provided a national cushion against responsibility and adversity.

It was a point not lost upon those in the criminal justice system. When King of the Dudley Teds, John Avey, appeared before local magistrates the Recorder, upon hearing that the young man had drawn £4 a week from the Labour Exchange for nearly a year, exclaimed, 'This is absolutely appalling ... where are we heading when this sort of thing can happen?' It was also thought that the Welfare State tended to diminish the responsibility of parents, thus reducing their control over their children. Men who no longer cared for family life were considered more likely to leave their wives and children, knowing that they would still be looked after. For mothers who put their own pleasures before those of their children, extra money meant that they were more often away from home enjoying a good time. Such parents no longer seemed to care where their offspring roamed at night. Indeed, children with more money in their own pockets could roam further afield. It was feared that these youngsters would grow up into lawless Teddy Boys. A neat solution was proposed by Mrs M.A. Cumella, a Liverpool barrister, who suggested withholding Family Allowance payments until parents made their children behave.

As standards of living continued to rise, so the spectre of deprivation largely disappeared. Children in the 1950s were healthier, better fed, better housed and better educated than their parents and grandparents. Since poverty had long been cited as an obvious cause of crime, particularly in the mid-nineteenth century and even the hungry 1930s, both the authorities and the public might have expected a decline in crime rates. It is perhaps ironic that crime began to rise significantly after 1955, as increased national prosperity, combined with the safety net of the Welfare State, began to banish grinding poverty into an increasingly remote past.

With the elimination of Victorian-type squalor and deprivation, commentators were forced to look for social and personal, rather than simple economic, reasons for the growth of lawlessness. As London magistrate Basil Henriques explained, 'Children used to steal because they were hungry. Today their pilfering is becoming one of "I see, I want, I take".'

Whether the Teds were created out of poverty or increased prosperity is a good question since their growth certainly coincided with rising crime rates and the expansion of the Welfare State. It was not difficult for some to see the connections.

Other reasons cited for juvenile delinquency included a weakening of religious influences and lower moral standards among adults, together with a general lack of discipline at home, at school and in factories. At Tory Party conferences throughout the second half of the 1950s speakers would don their rose-tinted spectacles to praise the honest workers of the Depression and the camaraderie of the Blitz. All this, of course, was in direct contrast to the appalling behaviour of the spivs and Teds. It was felt that the problem with post-war youths was that they were no longer subject to the strict discipline of the war.

Others, however, felt that Teddy Boy criminality was rooted in the very horrors of the wartime experience and its aftermath. Psychologist Sir Cyril Burt explained that the generation that grew up during the Second World War was restless and unsettled, lacking moral principles and ideals. At a London conference, organised by the charity Christian Action, Canon L.J. Collins claimed that Teddy Boys reflected the failure of the older generation and a post-war society still living on violence and insecurity. One of the Plough Boys, from London's Clapham Common, explained the psychology of the times. Now that the war was over there was a feeling among the young that they had missed out on a major event, even though echoes of the conflict still seemed to pervade the atmosphere. If they had been born ten years earlier the lads would have had the chance to fight abroad, perhaps becoming heroes. In the 1950s, however, their violence and aggression was no longer acceptable or commendable. Young men were left feeling redundant, with no proper channel for their aggression or opportunities to claim military honour and respect.

Labour MP George Rogers pointed out that the Teddy Boys and other young men in his constituency were children when the war was being fought. They also visited cinemas to watch films in which the commandos and bombers were seen as heroes. Young, impressionable minds were being taught that there was some virtue, at least at some time, in killing your enemies. Rogers asked a pertinent question: 'Have we no responsibility now if, in that atmosphere of violence, so many of those boys have grown up believing that violence is not wrong?'

Child expert Donald Ford also felt that the Teds had grown up in the shadow of the war and felt cheated of the heroism achieved by others. Their senseless acts of violence stemmed from a false and embellished picture that they had gained from parents and older brothers of what the war was like. He also claimed that the more vicious type of Teds were socially insecure individuals who lacked purpose in their lives. The war attracted them because it involved one great overriding purpose – victory. Unfortunately, there was no equivalent sense of purpose in the relatively peaceful 1950s. Despite the introduction of National Service in 1948, peacetime left some young people without a legitimate means to test the limits of their courage and masculinity.

The war must have brutalised and damaged the minds of some children, particularly those experiencing the nightly bombings and the loss of family members fighting abroad. Even years later, its effects could still be felt. Elizabeth Stucley, who ran a youth club for London children in the 1950s, asked the boys to paint pictures but was shocked at the subject matter. The images largely depicted violence in various forms: bombs exploding, ships sinking, space battles with hideous monsters. One child had painted a Teddy Boy, accurately capturing the lad's typical scowl of defiant exhibitionism. Violence, both gang-related and military, became fused in the minds of 1950s youth. A teacher at a secondary school asked one of her pupils, a budding Teddy Boy, to draw a tank going into battle. The boy sketched a realistic-looking vehicle manned by two Teds. Labelled 'Teddy Tank' the missiles shooting from its gun barrel were not shells but a broken bottle and an open razor. Such was their obsession with war and weaponry that the Director-General of the Imperial War Museum reported trouble from visiting gangs of Teddy Boys.

The likelihood that a generation of children growing up in wartime had a greater tendency to commit offences was given credibility by research conducted for the Home Office by Leslie Wilkins and published in 1960 as *Delinquent Generations*. After analysing masses of crime statistics Wilkins concluded that children born between 1935 and 1942 were more prone to delinquency than those born in any other seven-year period. He argued that the highest delinquency rates were to be found among those who were between four and five during the war, an age when they were more likely to be disturbed by the horrors of conflict and other forms of social upheaval than children of any other age.

Wilkins's calculations and conclusions were, however, seriously flawed.[1] The difficulty with the 'delinquent generation' argument was that as time passed children who were born after the war became criminals at an even greater rate. By the 1960s the generation of youngsters born in the years following the war had begun to record rates of delinquency even higher than their immediate predecessors. By 1970 the number of recorded crimes per million of the population was more than twice the 1960 figure (38,030 compared to 18,474).

Wilkins acknowledged that wartime conditions alone could not account for subsequent rises in levels of juvenile crime, particularly regarding lads aged seventeen to twenty-one. He felt that there was a particular issue that contributed to rising delinquency among young men in the early 1950s: the adoption of the Edwardian uniform, which for the Teds operated as a means of maintaining and preserving group identity. Because the clothing was such a visible and easily recognisable symbol, the group was at risk of being shunned and isolated by the rest of society. Such harsh treatment was likely either to destroy the group or increase its sense of solidarity. For the Teds it was

1. Not only were Wilkins' statistical inferences unsound but he failed to consider variations of delinquency rate between different types of offence and completely overlooked non-indictable offences. See Osgerby, *Youth in Britain Since 1945*, p. 15, note 10.

the latter. As Wilkins puts it, 'the delinquents become more delinquent'.

* * *

Issues of home life and child rearing were yet more sources of explanation for the growth of the Teddy Boys. At a meeting of the Howard League for Penal Reform, Dr Peter Scott identified three types of father responsible for producing Teddy Boys: those who couldn't identify with their sons; downtrodden, henpecked husbands; and aggressive drinkers. Poor parenting and the inadequate home backgrounds of young people were often cited as factors in turning children into delinquents. It was another familiar theme, pre-dating the Teds. In the early 1950s Rev. Griffiths traced delinquency to family background, and particularly to those who had experienced illegitimacy, family conflicts, step-parents, uninterested or ignorant parents, overcrowding and poverty. Likewise, Basil Henriques claimed never to have met a boy who was intrinsically bad. The vast majority of delinquents were, he thought, 'unwanted and unloved in their own homes'.

When the Teds arrived, commentators continued the common theme. In Bruce Walker's *Cosh Boy*, Mrs Collins, the mother of the young Ted Alfie, knows only two child-rearing techniques: let the children do as they please and then beat them for it, or not be bothered at all. A *Times* reader maintained that Teddy Boys were made in their first five years through lack of loving care and moral guidance. K. Hutton, chief welfare officer for Wolverhampton, blamed working mothers for rearing Teddy Boys and children who ran wild. A senior borstal officer claimed that in his experience of Teddy offenders more than half came from backgrounds which were 'absolute hell'. Mrs Unmack, a Taunton town councillor, spoke of fathers who neglected their parental responsibilities and children who treated their homes like hotels for eating, sleeping and occasionally watching TV. She concluded, 'If young people felt at home in their homes, there would not be so many teddy boys.'

The Tory solution was to improve the family. A One Nation Group Conservative pamphlet admitted that we 'shall not turn all today's Teddy Boys into tomorrow's Boy Scouts'. The report felt, however, that more could be done to help families, so that home life provided young people with a better alternative to 'caff society'. Against such views, however, one of the Plough Boys admitted that although some of the lads came from 'bad homes', the worst ones often came from the best homes, albeit the best working-class homes.

* * *

For others it was not simply domestic life but the wider social environment that was to blame for the rise of the Teds. Sir John Hunt, leader of the 1953 British Mount Everest expedition, blamed society for producing the Teddy Boys. Rising juvenile crime statistics and the 'cult of Teddyism' were said to be a reflection of a sick adult society. While some previous studies of the causes of crime focused exclusively on individual psychology and levels of intelligence, attention increasingly began to turn to the social context of delinquency. Just after the war the Conservative Party report *Youth Astray* blamed children's misbehaviour on social, economic and, to some extent, hereditary factors for which they could not be blamed: 'The blame – for blame there is – rests largely upon society.' In 1956 the Economic Research Council was still saying very much the same thing: 'Society is largely responsible for the environment in which the adolescent grows to maturity. A growing tendency for anti-social behaviour in this period is an indictment of society rather than of youth.'

Yet by 1959, after years of Teddy Boy delinquency, attitudes had dramatically changed. *The Responsible Society*, another Conservative report, raged: 'We reject the notion, propagated by sincere but misguided idealists, that society shares the guilt of its criminals; that most malefactors are the victims of their environment. If this is true it was much more true before the war when unemployment and bad housing offered greater excuses than they do now – and crime was less prevalent and less violent.'

Nevertheless, the idea that poor social environments helped create young criminals held sway. Deprived inner-city communities certainly changed spectacularly in the post-war period. The original Teds hailed from working-class neighbourhoods that had long traditions of community spirit, vital for survival when times were tough. After the war, the redevelopment of areas such as South London, particularly in the form of new housing estates and high-rise developments, contributed to the breakup of formerly tight-knit communities.

Throughout the 1950s sociologists and criminologists argued that criminal behaviour was part of a traditional, generational and cultural response by a section of the working-class community in conflict with wider society. Certain inner-city areas, blighted by slum properties, overcrowding, unemployment and a lack of recreational facilities, were seen as breeding grounds for crime and juvenile delinquency. This sort of research shifted the blame from individual moral shortcomings to wider social inequalities and political failings.

Some also argued that frustrated and disadvantaged working-class youths became delinquent because they were unable to gain recognition and prestige in a society dominated by middle-class ideas of respectability and achievement. Crime and anti-social behaviour became alternative, even if illegitimate, means for such youths to acquire the status denied to them by society.

But what about the *legitimate* means that Teddy Boys had of achieving status and social mobility, for example through education and employment?

20

CLASS WARS: WORK, NATIONAL SERVICE AND EDUCATION

'Most teddy boys are victims of the present-day system which gives better education, but so often offers no prospect of better opportunities.'

(Sir Charles Martin, Liverpool Chief Constable, 1957)

Although some blamed rising crime rates and the growing popularity of the Teddy Boys on the mollycoddling of the Welfare State, it would be wrong to think that the early Teds enjoyed bountiful government handouts. Nor did they benefit from the commodities offered to teenagers by the new consumer society. The original Teds, many from the slum neighbourhoods of squalid working-class districts, were the product of the austere years of the early 1950s rather than the later era of affluence experienced under Prime Minister Harold Macmillan's Conservative government. In 1956 Harry Moore, Superintendent of a London Methodist youth club, explained: 'Wherever there are poorer homes you will find Teddy Boys.'

Many youths of the time were small, skinny and undernourished, having been brought up on rations. They left school early and worked as market porters, van boys and labourers in unskilled or semi-skilled dead-end jobs. Some remained unemployed while awaiting National Service – and some employers would not hire them for that reason. Those who opted to become Teddy Boys were further disadvantaged. William Prendergast, mentioned earlier bemoaning society's discrimination against the Teds, felt that he had no chance of getting a job. Employers, he explained, would sneer at him and refuse to hire him. He was not alone. Eighteen-year-old Bill Foster, from Lancashire, had the best qualifications for a job in a laboratory but was nevertheless turned down. His rejection letter pointed out that his winkle-picker shoes and narrow trousers turned off the interviewers. Foster, who had science A-levels, denied being a Ted.

In 1956 A. H. Downward, youth employment officer for Bootle, warned school-leavers that there were 'no openings for boys who arrive for an interview wearing draped suits, narrow trousers and shoe-string ties'. This was reinforced by a 1958 report on the shortage of jobs for school-leavers, which suggested that the situation was made worse by employers being choosy, particularly in regard to candidates turning up for interview in Edwardian clothes. In the same year, youth employment officers in several Midlands towns reported that many employers were turning down youths who turned up for interview in Teddy Boy dress.

The Stock Exchange had banned Teds from working there in 1954. Members were warned not to employ them as runners or office boys after six months of noisy behaviour and fights came to a head when fireworks were let off outside the Exchange. Since menial employment was in abundance, many youths failed to value their jobs and consequently drifted in and out of work. One Ted from Tipton, Staffordshire, left eighteen jobs in two years. It was also claimed that boys did not take their jobs seriously when they could claim 26 shillings a week from National Assistance.

Labour MP James Idwal Jones felt that nothing was more likely to produce Teddy Boys than allowing youngsters to leave school without finding them interesting and suitable work. Perhaps with these sentiments in mind, a scheme to rehabilitate the young long-term unemployed was carried out in Liverpool in 1959. Twice a year the Liverpool Boys' Association camp at Heswall, Cheshire, invited up to fifty lads who had been unemployed for five months or more for a three-week residential stay. Many were Teds with convictions for theft and drunkenness. Using sport, classroom work and handicrafts, together with the strict discipline of early wake-ups, the course was designed to restore the boys' sense of purpose. The success rate is not recorded.

For those in work, however, the financial rewards were relatively good. Despite being unskilled or semi-skilled, many young workers could earn more than their more ambitious peers who sought apprenticeships or white-collar jobs, or those who stayed on at school hoping to go to university. They certainly had more money to spend on clothes, with many Teds putting money down for a suit with their first wages. They also had enough money in their pockets to buy records and visit cafes and dances.

One career option was the Merchant Navy, though this path became blocked for some. In 1956 the General Secretary of the National Union of Seamen explained that since employment on the ships meant exemption from National Service, they had attracted their share of young men who were anxious to avoid being called up. This included some seagoing Teddy Boys who had brought only dishonour and bad publicity. In the same year, the Cunard and Canadian Pacific shipping lines both announced that youths wearing Edwardian clothing would no longer be employed on their ships. Youth employment officers advised drape-suited applicants, 'nothing doing until you go home and change'.

After all, if Teds could cause trouble in dance halls and cafes they were just as capable of wreaking havoc in the middle of the ocean. When a brawl broke out among the crew of the British liner *Georgic* in 1955, Liverpool Teddy Boys were blamed. They were said to be fighting over girls smuggled aboard. The previous week, when the ship was docked on the other side of the world in Melbourne, thirty-one seamen were arrested for being drunk and disorderly. A ship's officer explained that Teddy Boys had been allowed to sign on in Liverpool after it had proved impossible to muster an experienced crew in time. Former liner steward Robin King confirmed the recruiting crisis in his account of life on merchant ships in the 1950s. He confirms that due to a shortage of skilled men ships sometimes had to employ 'undesirables'. He reveals that on his first voyage he had to work alongside two convicted burglars, ten perverts, two petty thieves (still active), two ex-borstal inmates and three Teddy Boys (dance hall types).

Two years after the *Georgic* incident a quarter of the 600-strong crew of another British liner, the *New Australia*, walked off the ship as she was about to set sail from Sydney. The men claimed to have been terrorised by thugs. Ever since the ship set sail from London there had been feuds between Teddy Boys, Irishmen and Scotsmen. In one incident more than a dozen men were battered with fire-hose nozzles as they lay in bed. A sixteen-year-old on his first voyage was also beaten up. While the ship was berthed in Malaya armed police and two armoured cars were needed to control some of the crew. One seaman who walked off claimed to have heard men screaming at night. The protesters only returned to their ship when four young men were paid off and put on another vessel.

Teddy Boys continued to be a problem on ships into the next decade. In 1962, the Merchant and Airline Officers' Association reported that discipline was so bad on British merchant vessels that they were considering permanently banning troublemakers from seafaring employment. The blame was placed on a minority of Teddy Boys who were behind 'all too frequent reports of assaults, fighting, knifing and insubordination'.

* * *

It sometimes seemed as if the Teddy Boys not only lacked career aspirations but also resented others getting on. In 1959, a quiet eighteen-year-old called Peter Butler died after a fight at a Portsmouth dockyard. On leaving the yard the student engineering apprentice was caught up in a brawl between rival groups, about five on one side and twenty on the other. His father claimed that Teds working on the docks disliked the student apprentices who were studying for managerial positions. The Teds, who outnumbered them, would attack the students.

Motivated by the same envy of those who were getting on in life, some Teds also saw an easy target in university students. There have always been town versus gown conflicts in Cambridge, but in 1958 the trouble took a new twist when violence flared between local Teddy Boys and undergraduates. It was believed that up to sixty Teds were involved, most drawn to the city from surrounding villages and attracted by the entertainment on offer. When the cinemas shut, they were left hanging about the streets and there were reports of attacks on students, some being chased late at night by gangs. One undergraduate was stopped and threatened with a razor if he didn't hand over some money. The university's undergraduate newspaper, *Varsity*, admitted that the attitudes of the students probably aggravated the local Teds as much as the Teds' behaviour annoyed them. It was pointed out that, after all, the eccentricities of the Teds' Edwardian style of dress were matched by the students wearing their gowns. Labour MP Reginald Paget suggested that undergraduates of the past probably behaved like far bigger hooligans than the Teddy Boys of the present.

It wasn't just university students who were held in contempt by Teds. Younger schoolboys, particularly those from 'posh' schools, were also the victims of attacks. In 1959 a gang of Teds jeered and shouted at 400 schoolboys as they marched back to Fortescue House School after a church parade at Strawberry Hill in Twickenham, Middlesex. 'Chicken!' they shouted. 'They won't fight.' One Ted, aged about fourteen, darted over and punched one of the pupils on the nose, leading a sixteen-year-old rugby-playing prefect to break ranks and batter three Teds before rejoining the march.

In 1957, after a catalogue of incidents, police were called to protect rowers from Eton as they sculled the Thames between Windsor and Bray. Not only had the boys been ambushed and fired at with rifles but local Teds were even diving under the boats to overturn them. The Eton College cricket pavilion was also wrecked by a gang of Teds.

In 1961 a fourteen-year-old Somerset boy was fined after pushing a cigarette into the face of a public schoolboy returning to class from church. The attacker claimed that his victim had called him a 'thieving Teddy boy'. In the same county two years later the Headmaster of King's College in Taunton spoke out after an unprovoked attack by Teddy Boys on some of his pupils. He was probably referring to an incident where fifteen pupils fought a half-hour running battle with youths wearing winkle-pickers, drainpipes, leather jackets and Slim-Jim ties. Also in 1963, at The King's School, Canterbury, boys in traditional straw boaters fought with local Teds after two pupils were nudged off the pavement. There were soon thirty pairs of fists flying. A passing doctor intervened, shouting, 'We don't want this sort of class warfare in Canterbury.' He was promptly punched.

Although some grammar school boys such as Ray Gosling adopted the clothing and embraced rock 'n' roll music, they never faced the same bleak futures as working-class Teddy Boys from the tough secondary moderns. Teds were seen as the social leftovers, excluded from the upward mobility of post-war affluence after their brighter peers had been filtered into skilled apprenticeships or channelled into the grammar schools. A *Daily Mail* reader blamed the hot-house education system for failing less able pupils and turning them into Teds. Feeling rejected, some created their own world with its distinctive clothes, hairstyles and weapons. The reader urged a return to an education system that fitted all children for whatever station in life they were best suited.

The intention of the 1944 Education Act had actually been that every child should be given an education suited to his or her age, aptitude and ability. For some, however, the hidden purpose of the selection, streaming and examining process was that a chosen minority of pupils should do well while the majority failed. What critics of the 11-plus exam system believed it actually did was to cream off roughly twenty per cent of eleven-year-olds for the grammar schools and an almost-certain path into higher education and high-status occupations. The rest were consigned to the secondary-modern 'scrap heap'. In a sermon to parishioners in Warwickshire, Rev. James Begg of Leamington Baptist Church defended the Teds.

He felt that from the day these lads started school they were overshadowed by the 11-plus exam system. He felt that they were rebelling against a system that classified them as failures.

The 1950s education system was certainly not a hit with everyone. After Bank Holiday clashes between Teds at Weston-super-Mare, Somerset, in 1958, Bristol's Lord Mayor flung out a challenge to the Education Committee: 'Examine your own education system to see whether the roots of the Teddy Boy menace may not lie there.' A grammar school master also spoke out in favour of comprehensive schools, attended by all children regardless of ability. He felt that the selection system contributed to the large number of Teddy Boys and cited in support the view of a psychologist who suggested that their aggressiveness was due to a sense of inferiority, partly caused by their failure to pass the 11-plus.

Speaking at a Summer School on delinquency, Liverpool sociologist John B. Mays claimed that given a different social, educational and home background, the Teddy Boy would probably be the type to be captain of the fifth form at Greyfriars, Frank Richards' fictional English public school, home to Billy Bunter. In 1959 the President of the NUT, Miss A.F. Cooke, also spoke of the benefits of a good all-round education. She told the Union's annual conference that many of today's Teddy Boys and Girls could have been turned into useful citizens had their energies been directed into the right channels by the provision of county colleges planned to provide for their social, as well as educational, needs.

* * *

If the education system was seen to be inadequate in inspiring young working-class lads, there was at least another compulsory system, National Service, which promised to turn them into upright, decent citizens. Yet what was seen by some as a certain cure for Teddy Boy hooliganism was, ironically, also cited by others as one of its major causes. To teach the Teds a lesson, one newspaper reader suggested that they be put in the

Army and packed off to Cyprus and other international danger zones. As a panellist on the BBC radio show *Any Questions?*, Lord Boothby, speaking at the time of the Suez crisis, quipped, 'Send them off to Cairo and let them Teddy Boy there.'

Forcing young thugs to do military service has always been a popular antidote to hooliganism. After seeing a picture of a Ted in the *Daily Mirror* in 1953, one reader claimed that a sergeant-major would do him a lot of good in a few hours; another reader felt that it would at least ensure that the lads would get their hair cut. Yet most young men over the age of eighteen in the 1950s were already forced to undertake up to two years' National Service. Between 1948 and 1960 compulsory military service disrupted the lives of over two million young men. This spell in the Forces was meant to teach lads the benefits of self-reliance, comradeship, the capacity to work in groups and the acceptance of discipline. Admiral Sir Mark Pizey, Vice-President of the Somerset National Association of Boys' Clubs, spoke of the benefits of National Service. Looking back at his own military career he remembered how boys would arrive with no discipline and wearing drainpipe trousers; before long they were 'licked into shape' to become worthy members of the community.

On the downside, National Service wrenched lads from their ties to home, work and neighbourhood. In some cases it led to excessive drinking and sexual promiscuity. Horror stories abounded of soul-destroying duties such as whitewashing coal. Defaulters would end up on 'jankers', punishment which might involve being confined to barracks or camp or some other restriction of privileges. More serious misdemeanours might result in a spell in the 'glass house' (prison). In 1954 Private Anderton was forced to polish the guard room floor on his hands and knees. He was further punished when his sergeant tried to push his face into the tin of polish. In this case it was the sergeant who ended up in detention for fifty-six days, despite claiming that he had tripped and fallen on the unfortunate soldier. For those who later cited the absence of Army discipline as a factor leading to rising crime, it is perhaps telling that British crime figures began to rise significantly only after 1955, at which time the nation's healthy young men were still undergoing National Service.

Just as there are today, in the 1960s there were frequent calls for its return to deal with delinquency. In a debate in the House of Lords on rising crime, Lord Auckland said that whatever other defects National Service might have, he was sure it had saved many a Teddy Boy from prison or worse. It is more likely, however, that delinquent youths, when conscripted, simply became problems for the Armed Forces instead. The worst of them ended up court-martialled, held in military prisons and discharged in disgrace.

Still, military life certainly did appeal to some. The fighting qualities of the Teds were noted by the Rev. J.H.A. Charles: 'In the event of another war, teddy boys might earn a larger number of decorations than calm law-abiding citizens.' In 1954, at the annual meeting of the a body called the North of Scotland Centralised District of the British Order of the Ancient Free Gardeners Friendly Society, Harry Armstrong gave a rousing defence of young people, particularly the Teds: 'Change the drape suit for the battle dress ... the crepe shoes for Army boots, the dance halls for the battlefield of Korea, Malaya and Kenya, and what do we find ... youth in all its glory, all its confidence, still prepared to accept all the responsibilities of life, and even prepared to die for the free expression of their beliefs.'

Major C. Relf, a Commanding Officer in the Territorial Army, felt that a spell as a volunteer would turn violent Teds into men and satisfy their longing for a uniform, comradeship and discipline. Despite this, Teds were not always welcomed into the Forces. Princess Louise's Kensington Regiment advertised for Territorial Army volunteers in 1956 but made it clear that Teddy Boys need not apply. It was explained that this did not simply mean young men in Edwardian dress but those with a Teddy Boy attitude; these were said to be cowards who only operated in gangs and lacked the courage to stand alone. Times certainly changed for by 1965 Julian Snow, MP was claiming that Mods and Rockers weren't bad people and that some

Territorial Army units could be composed of them. It was felt that their aggressive attitude and mechanical skills could be put to good use.

Military life and the Teddy Boy lifestyle were not, however, mutually exclusive and some managed to remain Teds while serving in the Forces. In 1955 a Birmingham airman was slashed across the face by a Teddy Boy soldier. Around the same time, two soldiers in military custody tied up their guard at Peninsula Barracks in Warrington, Lancashire, then locked him in a cell before escaping in their Teddy Boy suits. A year later in Shropshire, a Shrewsbury man was attacked by six Teddy Boy soldiers from the nearby Nesscliffe Army Camp. When a seventeen-year-old Ted from Yeovil, Somerset, was charged with insulting behaviour, the father complained that his son had never been so much trouble until he came out of the Navy. He felt that his deterioration was the result of the company he had kept while at sea, for his son had previously written home to state that every other boy in the billet was a Teddy Boy.

Paul Adlington, a nineteen-year-old National Serviceman wearing Edwardian uniform, was arrested and searched at a dance in Grantham, Lincolnshire. He was found to be carrying an open safety razor-blade in his pocket. The lad denied brandishing it to threaten a member of the Royal Air Force the previous week. It seems that the RAF man had called the Ted and his mate 'tough guys'. At King's Lynn, Norfolk, there was trouble when airmen from the nearby RAF base at Marham went on their weekly night out. Some of the men at the base were in a Teddy Boy gang that was involved in a feud with local Teds. The leaders of the rival groups had a fight while their gangs formed a circle. In the resulting scrap an airman was knocked unconscious and a farm worker had part of his ear bitten off.

Despite their fearsome reputation for violence, Teddy Boys did bring something positive to the Armed Forces. A Lieutenant-Colonel of No. 7 Training Regiment of the Royal Signals found that while the average national serviceman came into the Army naturally untidy, the Teddy Boys took great pride in their uniform.

Some maintained that conscription into the Forces was actually part of the Teddy Boy problem. A *Manchester Guardian* reader believed that adolescent boys naturally modelled themselves on men a little older – but these potential role models were being shipped off to Germany or Cyprus. When they returned, the age gap was too great for them to be of any influence. It was suspected that the reason there was so little Teddy-Boyishness in rural England was that young men in these areas were exempt from National Service and instead engaged in agriculture. They therefore proved better role models for local young people.

For some Teds the prospect of conscription was a threat to their individuality and a potential cause of their disaffection and anti-social behaviour. Child expert Donald Ford believed that the young were trapped in the gap between leaving school at fifteen and beginning National Service at eighteen: while they were relieved at escaping classroom authority, they dreaded the military authority that awaited them. These three wasted years, or 1,000 nights, have been called 'The Battle of the Gap'. It was during this time that some youngsters, left in limbo and with no sense of direction, became Teddy Boys. There was little incentive to find a permanent job. Many employers will have seen little point in training lads, or even employing them at all, in skilled work while they were waiting to be called up. The *Star* newspaper, however, rejected the claim that Teds couldn't find work by pointing out that tens of thousands of decent London lads managed to hold down jobs until they reached eighteen.

King George's Jubilee Trust, initiated in 1935 by the Prince of Wales on behalf of the country's youth, also felt that National Service interrupted the transition from school to work and prevented lads from planning and working for the future. This artificial interlude helped create a period of 'irresponsibility' and even 'deterioration' in young people. At a loose end, some youths used their remaining years of freedom to cause mayhem. Birkenhead headmaster K.D. Robinson also believed that Teds were having a last fling before National

Service cut their earnings and freedom. A youth club leader in Finchley, North London, further maintained that Edwardian gang warfare was caused by young people's insecurity, created by the prospect of conscription. An interesting point was made by Mrs M.A. Cumella, a Liverpool barrister, who revealed that some boys were committing offences in the hope of being sent to borstal in order to avoid their National Service.

Whether National Service was the cause of, or the solution to, the Teddy Boy problem remains a matter of opinion. For some, military discipline and skills proved useful in later life; for others, conscription was an oppressive system to be rebelled against.

Cyril Dunn of *The Observer* suggested that a spell in the Armed Forces might actually aggravate the problem of disaffected young people. He felt that the aimless, unintelligent youth with no civilian training was likely to be given the most boring jobs and left feeling even more useless. It was these directionless, poorly educated, working-class young lads who had already either rejected, or been failed by, the education system.

Described by one historian of the period as semi-literate 'intellectual and spiritual morons', many Teds admittedly lacked educational qualifications. Having left school at fifteen, they later found themselves trapped at the bottom of the heap, unable to rise further up the career ladder and enjoy better incomes. The warden of the Senior Detention Centre at Blantyre House, Kent, said of the Teds: 'One very noticeable factor has been, the more exaggerated the dress, the greater the degree of illiteracy; rarely do we see an intelligent "Teddy".' Lord Moynihan felt that Teds normally showed little intelligence and even less desire to improve themselves in any way. According to one Liverpool headmaster, 'the would-be Teddy Boys that spring up here and there in my senior classes are a menace. They are usually the work-shy boys, I notice.' Psychiatrist Dr Peter Scott concluded that Teds were bad workers and made appalling apprentices.

It is possible that many working-class children found the education system meaningless because it was based on middle-class values and aspirations that clashed with their own working-class outlook and culture. Finding no prospects through education or work, leisure became important, particularly for the Teds. It was through leisure that they gained the excitement and self-respect which they failed to find through satisfying work.

For some commentators the violence of the working-class Teds was a strong reaction to middle-class values. In his book *The Young Pretenders* (1965), John B. Mays offers a 'rough and ready' classification of adolescents. Group 1 consists of the Teddy Boys and others who react aggressively against the limitations of their environment. They lack support and affection at home and are the products of an inadequate education system which fails to allow them access to worthwhile, highly ,paid employment. In a society which greatly stresses the importance of success, as measured by making money, these lads are the ones who tend to be written off as failures and misfits.

For Mays, Teddy Boy delinquency was a form of protest against being the also-rans. The anti-social behaviour usually took the form of hostility towards 'respectable' society and its institutions. At the same time, this behaviour offered lads some kind of compensatory fantasy existence in which violence, nonconformity and general obstinacy enabled them to prove themselves and achieve their own, somewhat warped, kind of social status.

* * *

In one sense, the Teds acquired this sense of status not through education or skilled employment but through the purchase and adaptation of upper-class Savile Row suits and style. Donald Ford believed that the 'vicious Teddy-boy' compensated for his disadvantaged life by achieving self-esteem through his clothes and his association with others who dressed the same.

For Rev. Walter Lazenby, however, their uniform was much more than this: it was a gesture of defiance. Likewise, for social historian Harry Hopkins their clothing was a half-conscious, class-based reaction designed to prove that the lower classes could be just as arrogant and high and mighty as the snobs on the other side of the Thames. It was meant to be provocative, worn as a badge of insubordination. The Teds' sense of aloofness was linked to the insolence of social aspirations – for no matter how hard they worked, the council estate youths who parodied the look of Edwardian dandies could never hope to attain the lifestyle of the upper classes. Instead, they attempted to buy status by hijacking the sartorial style of their social superiors.

Their clothes were a highly visible sign that the Teds rejected the strict class codes of English society. It must be remembered that in 1951 the Conservative government was re-elected under Winston Churchill, signalling the restoration of a class-based hierarchy and sense of privilege. It was against this background that the Teds rose to prominence. For the press, politicians and many other commentators their lifestyle became a celebration of the yob, of alienated working-class youth hell-bent on wreaking revenge against society.

Still, the Teddy Boys were more than just ordinary working-class ruffians in the tradition of nineteenth-century gangs such as London's Hooligans or Manchester's scuttlers, or even pre-war mobs such as Glasgow's razor gangs. In 1953 the *Daily Mail*, while acknowledging that juvenile delinquency was nothing new, maintained that Teddy Boy criminality was nevertheless a 'new' and worrying social trend. So what exactly was 'new' about it? Teds were unique not least because they were a national rather than merely a local phenomenon. Also, unlike earlier delinquent tribes, they were not directly spawned from mass poverty, slums and unemployment. The later Teds, at least, were the product of a new economic revolution that had put spending money into the pockets of working-class youths. This was an entirely new social phenomenon. It was the threat of this growing army of financially independent youths who had seemingly rejected the values and traditions of adult and middle-class society that so troubled the authorities and led to vigorous campaigns not simply to punish them but, more importantly, 'de-teddify' them.

21

PUNISHMENT

'The opening of a Detention Centre was an unfortunate blow to the undisciplined "Edwardian" but an ideal answer to the Court that had to deal with these irresponsible exhibitionists.'

(Warden at the Senior Detention Centre, Blantyre House, Kent, 1955)

A month after the Notting Hill race riots of August 1958, the 78th annual Conservative Party Conference was held in Blackpool. Crime was on everybody's mind. What follows is a compilation of comments made by various party delegates on the rise in youth crime:

> this sudden increase in crime and brutality which is foreign to our nature and our country ... Over the past 25 years we in this country, through misguided sentiment, have cast aside the word 'discipline', and now we are suffering for it ... smooth, smug and sloppy sentimentalists who contribute very largely to the wave of crime ... [young people] no longer frightened of the police, they sneer at them ... lack of parental control, interest and support ... the leniency shown in the past by the courts of this country.

The familiar themes are all there: crime was getting worse; moral values were deteriorating; the criminal justice system had gone soft. Thirty motions on crime and punishment were submitted. In London, at a Conservative meeting in Chelsea,

Home Secretary Rab Butler was asked what the government was going to do about Teddy Boy crime and whether it should be tackled with corporal punishment. While admitting that there had been an increase in Teddy Boy disorder, he did not accept that the problem of juvenile delinquency could be solved by flogging offenders. Butler instead aimed to de-teddify the Teddy boys with the short, sharp shock of severe discipline in detention centres.

Butler's White Paper, *Penal Practice in a Changing Society* (1959), introduced a programme of prison-building for young offenders, together with plans for the introduction of new detention centres and borstals where youths would endure 'a maximum of hard work and a minimum of amusement'. Detention centres administered a short, sharp spell of three months' custody to offenders aged between fourteen and twenty-one. Borstal training was given to lads aged between seventeen and twenty-one. Sentences ranged from one to three years, although inmates could be released on licence after six months.

This was a time when the prisons were already bearing the brunt of the Teddy Boy crime wave. A Prison Officers' Association conference in 1959 heard of increased violence and chaotic scenes in the nation's jails. The violence was put down to the fact that more than a fifth of the prison population was at the Teddy Boy stage.

Between 1956 and 1960 the borstal population increased from 2,800 to over 5,000 inmates. Not everybody welcomed plans to open more establishments – particularly those living near proposed sites. Local farmers in West Hatch, Somerset, opposed a scheme to build a new approved school because, understandably, it was feared that the institution would attract 'the Teddy boy type'. One farmer explained, 'We don't want them teddy-boying with our local girls.'

In 1959 it was claimed that it cost £581 a year to tame wayward Teds. This was the cost of holding each youth at the four new detention centres and was more than the fees at a public school. Whether the institutions did any good is the subject of debate. It has been argued that pre-war delinquents, whose criminality was perhaps rooted in poverty and who were therefore eager to find employment, responded well to the vocational and educational programmes offered by borstals. The Teddy Boys and their successors, however, regarded these programmes as rather obvious efforts to initiate them into the dull grind of working-class adulthood. The post-war decline in the effectiveness of the borstals might therefore reflect some shift in ideology among the youths they served. Boys who were steeped in an adolescent culture that saw no value in the middle-class idea of a career were unlikely to embrace remedial educational and vocational programmes.

Some also doubted the usefulness of prisons. In a 1965 radio programme one lad claimed that the only ex-Teds he knew who had not gone on to live good lives were those who had been to prison. It was as if their experience of jail had further corrupted them. For one listener the programme certainly brought into the question the reformative value of imprisonment but it could be that these Teddy offenders were determined to follow a criminal path, regardless of the consequences.

Prisons, borstals and approved schools were not the only institutions that took Teddy Boys off the streets. Detention centres and remand homes also offered short spells of punitive detention. Efforts to de-teddify youths were similar across all institutions. In detention centres, which held young prisoners for up to twenty days, the staff gave boys severe haircuts and made sure boots replaced their fancy footwear, a look ironically adopted by the Skinheads a decade later.

With their strict discipline, such institutions were certainly feared. After being told by a magistrate that he was being sent to an approved school, a fifteen-year-old Ted broke free of his escort and shouted, ‘They’ll not hold me,’ before diving headfirst through a window, falling twelve feet onto the pavement and knocking himself unconscious. The boy, from Radcliffe, near Bury, had been sentenced for stealing and selling his mother’s gramophone records.

In 1959, at Carlton Approved School, near Bedford, about eighty boys, armed with knives and chisels, smashed up the place before going on the run. The day after the mutiny a journalist inspected the damage. A member of staff confided, 'You mustn't forget that each one of these lads is a true Teddy Boy. What happened last night? They reverted to type.' At a Home Office inquiry into the disturbances one optimistic ex-Ted suggested various improvements for the school: more television sets, better clothes, extra cigarettes and money from home to be sent without restriction.

Perhaps a more liberal regime would have been the solution to the Teddy Boy problem. Approved-school headmaster C.A. Joyce had some advice on how to break Teddy Boys. He found that wayward lads given a tough regime in solitary confinement came out heroes. To prevent this he decided to pamper them in specially furnished cells with carpets and easy chairs – so the inmate could no longer come out boasting to the other boys, 'They can't break me. I can take it.'

Another type of institution was the attendance centre, usually catering for younger boys. Manchester's attendance centre formed an annexe to the police station on Plymouth Grove. Part of the same experiment to de-teddify the teds, it was the only establishment in the country to take older youths between the ages of seventeen and twenty-one. The centre dealt with forty-seven youths who had been sentenced to two hours each Saturday afternoon for six weeks. The first hour consisted of physical exercise followed by an hour's cleaning and scrubbing. Out of thirty-two youths who had completed the course, only two had appeared back in court. The principal officer in charge bluntly explained the centre's aims: to give young offenders a good, sharp kick up the backside.

* * *

Penal institutions were well aware that one solution was to strip away the very thing that defined the Teds – their clothing – as a means of re-modelling them into better citizens. The

Captain of the Heswall Nautical Training School, in Cheshire, explained that Teddy Boys sent to his institution were shorn of their Edwardian finery and kitted out with a naval uniform: 'The only thing that can elevate him above his fellows now is his own personality.'

C.A. Joyce used to allow boys to wear their own ties. With the advent of Edwardianism and Slim-Jim neckwear, he put a stop to this. Joyce was also unhappy to see boys returning to school from home leave wearing Edwardian suits paid for by their parents. These were also banned. His objection was not so much to the clothing itself but what it so often stood for. And what it stood for was trouble. Elsewhere, when a team of footballers from Twickenham, Middlesex, went to play a borstal team they were told not to wear their Edwardian suits. It would be a 'bad influence' said a league official.

An inspector at a juvenile attendance centre in Salford explained that the boys, some of them admirers of Edwardian fashions, were put into shorts, vest and gym shoes. In this way they were reduced to little boys. After breaking them down the aim was to build them up again in a better image. At Stamford House Remand Home for boys in London there was a room housing all the outfits, including Edwardian suits, confiscated from the boys when they first arrived. On admittance the boys were put into an institutional uniform. 'No bloody shorts' was the horrified cry of some of the lads. More than one reader wrote to the *Daily Mail* declaring that keeping youths in short trousers until they were sixteen prevented them from becoming Teddy Boys. Another reader, however, suggested that making older boys wear shorts made them rebellious and helped turn them into Teds.

The de-teddifying process did claim some success. In August 1953, as the cosh boys were mutating into Teds, a Detention Centre for young offenders at Kidlington, near Oxford, promised tough discipline for youths under the age of twenty-one. One cosh boy, clad in padded shoulders, painted tie and drainpipe trousers, arrived at the centre thinking that he was going to run the place. He was in for a shock. The discipline included 6.15 a.m. wake-up calls followed by a 'liver shake-up' in the playground. Nevertheless, the night before his release the lad confessed to the warden that he was glad of the experience. As he was about to leave the next morning he was asked how he was feeling. Looking down in disgust at his gangster uniform he replied, 'Damned spivvy, sir.' At a Prison Officers' Association Conference in Dover, Kent, in 1959 one delegate claimed that seventy-five per cent of lads at Goudhurst Detention Centre wrote to their mothers asking for a decent suit for their release because they had been made conscious of what 'twerps' they had looked when they first came in.

* * *

Infantilising youths was one novel method of transforming the Teddy Boys into more socially acceptable human beings. Elsewhere, especially in schools, every effort was made to ban their distinct look. In 1954 the headmaster of Canvey Island Boys Secondary School, Essex, asked parents to ensure that boys sporting Teddy Boy hairstyles arrived in school with their hair cut in a 'more English manner'. In 1956 A.E. Nichols, Secretary of the Incorporated Association of Headmasters, felt that without some sort of uniform policy children might arrive in school in bushmen's jackets, dazzling shirts and Teddy Boys suits.

He had a point. A year later, twelve-year-old Stuart Beetson was sent home from school in Sheffield for wearing a purple shirt, tight black jeans and luminous green socks. His fashionable look was topped off with a black jacket carrying the slogan 'Rock 'n' Roll' and a bright blue tie inscribed with the words 'Hep Cat'. Barred from classes, he ended up missing sixty days of schooling and his parents were eventually taken to court. Even after being fined, his father was unrepentant and vowed to fight the ruling even if it meant selling his car. In 1959 the Headmaster of St Mary's Roman Catholic Secondary Modern in Blackburn, Lancashire, announced that boys turning up for lessons in Teddy Boy clothes would be sent home. A year later seven boys were barred from Skelmanthorpe Secondary School, near Huddersfield, for wearing denim jeans. The headmaster claimed that wearing jeans gave children big ideas and turned them into Teddy Boys.

Dance hall owners were equally wary of the uniform. In 1954 a Derby ballroom announced that it would turn away dancers in Edwardian dress. Three months later in East Sussex, after a triple slashing incident at the Regent Ballroom, Brighton, a sign went up: 'No Edwardian Dress'. The manager revealed that he didn't have to bar everybody who looked like a Ted, but he would sort them out and reject those wearing big rings on their fingers. At Liverpool's Grafton, patrons would be refused entry if their trousers were less than sixteen inches wide or their jackets too long. Door staff would use a ruler to measure the distance between the jacket and the floor. At the Palais de Danse, New Cross, in South East London, the manager, flanked by his commissionaires, told a group of Teddy Boys: 'You cannot come in. You're not properly dressed – and you know it. You will not be allowed in if you wear velvet lapels, drainpipe trousers, Slim-Jim ties or other Teddy Boy outfits.'

It was cinemas that were most sensitive about the Edwardian uniform, particularly after the riots following screenings of *Rock Around the Clock*. Teds were often banned from cinemas for wearing even single items since what constituted Ted uniform was a matter of opinion. One Blackpool cinema manager declared: 'I'm the one who decides whether a youth is wearing Edwardian dress or not. My decision is final.' The view was that the lads behaved better when they weren't wearing it. The manager of a Liverpool cinema found that Teddy Boys were ruining trade and driving others away. They were told: 'You get into more civilised dress and you can see the film with pleasure.' The manager discovered that once out of uniform, the lads 'were quite human'. He explained: 'These clothes seem to have a psychological effect on these fellows. Old troublemakers now put on a decent suit before they come in here and are well behaved.'

The Armed Forces were also anti Edwardian dress. In 1955 Lieutenant-General Sir Lashmer Whistler, chief of Western Command, ordered the withdrawal of walking-out passes for servicemen wearing such clothing. The style was not specified but was thought to include long, drape-fronted jackets with velvet collars and narrow trousers shortened to show white socks at the ankles. The order applied to 60,000 troops. Subsequently, at the Royal Engineers Camp at Malvern, Worcestershire, the commanding officer ordered men of all ranks below sergeant, with the exception of National Servicemen, to parade in their 'civvies' for inspection. One young man was advised that his tapered trousers were too Edwardian. Another youth, wearing a drape jacket nine inches above the knee, was told to ditch the offending item. At Bicester, Oxfordshire, National Servicemen from the 16th Battalion, Royal Army Ordnance Corps were ordered to dress suitably when off duty. The move came after complaints from bus passengers about rowdiness from youths dressed as Teddy Boys.

Upholders of the justice system were also critical when defendants turned up in Edwardian clothing. 'Stop the suit and you would stop a lot of trouble,' was one maxim uttered at the time. In West London the Chairman of Acton Magistrates' Court urged an offender to 'get rid of that suit and try to become a decent member of society'. The lad's father explained that his son had never been in trouble before he bought the suit. Binding over five Liverpool Teds for assaulting two boys, Mr Justice Sellars made it a condition of their probation that they must not wear 'fantastic dress' or belong to any organised gang. In 1954, a Marlborough Street magistrate, sentencing three London Teddy Boys for assault, noticed that the two younger boys were wearing drainpipe trousers. 'That makes it difficult to get them down and give them a hiding,' he replied. Ordering probation for a seventeen-year-old in Edwardian dress, the chairman of the court in Barnet, North London, advised him to burn his suit and get a decent haircut.

Over in West London, when a father from Brentford heard his son described in court as a 'Big Chief' of the Teddy Boys he ripped up the lad's suit. A Bristol parent also hacked his son's suit to bits, telling a reporter: 'Since my son bought this thing a year ago his personality has changed.' One seventeen-year-old Ted even promised to destroy his own jacket. After being remanded for three weeks in a Lincolnshire prison, Michael Higgins promised a Nottingham magistrate that he would burn his long, black coat if only he could be given his freedom. Similarly, John Brankin, of Bradford, assured a magistrate that he would destroy his Edwardian uniform and never again associate with Teds if only the court did not send him to borstal. The plea worked. He was fined and put on probation. Norman Speed, also in Bradford, promised the magistrate that he would destroy his purple drape jacket and never again associate with Teds – but he was nevertheless sent to borstal.

* * *

Magistrates had the difficult task of trying to curb the Teddy Boy problem. They did not shirk their duty. After gang fights in Newcastle upon Tyne, the chairman of the magistrates court promised: 'We are going to stamp this out in Northumberland. You are going to get as much punishment as we can give you.' After a spate of gang violence, a Wolverhampton stipendiary magistrate declared, 'This has got to be stopped, and I'm going to stop it.' Another chairman of magistrates warned a member of a Bristol Teddy Boy gang, accused of wilful damage, that his fellow magistrates would all be very glad to see the breakup of such gangs. The Chairman of Devon Quarter Sessions, worried about the growth of gangs, warned 'smart Alecs, spivs and Teddy Boys' that first offenders would not, in future, necessarily receive lenient treatment from the courts. The Chairman of Dartford Juvenile Court told a group of young offenders that they had turned themselves into a bunch of undesirables known as Edwardians. He called the Edwardian cult rubbish and warned the lads that it would lead to prison or worse. The Chairman of Hendon Magistrates told an eighteen-year-old that the public was getting worked up about the Teddy Boys, and didn't feel that they were being dealt with severely enough by the courts.

Some people certainly felt that the magistrates were ineffective in dealing with the problem. At the 1961 Conservative Party Conference, during a debate on the reintroduction of corporal punishment, a councillor representing Whitehaven, Cumbria, spoke of the many Teds who came to court knowing that magistrates were 'hamstrung', as in many cases all that they could do was bind them over. It was felt that the courts were being ridiculed – and the sentence of probation, in particular, was seen by some as a soft touch. Some probation officers themselves privately felt that the sentence was being used as a cheaper alternative to sending boys to approved schools.

Faced with the rapid spread of Teddy Boy violence around 1957, a probation officer from a Midland town revealed how his department had demanded tougher action. They had to show the Teds that crime was not an automatic passport to probation and therefore recommended that certain characters were packed straight off to borstal, even if they had no previous convictions. This gave them a sharp shock and stunned other gang members. The media publicity surrounding such cases would also have given potential Teddy offenders something to think about.

Some politicians also thought that Teds were getting away lightly. In 1957 Conservative MP Geoffrey Stevens proposed a Bill aimed at curbing the activities of the Teddy Boys and other violent hooligans. The Metropolitan Police Act (Amendment Bill) aimed to increase the penalty for threatening and insulting behaviour which, under the previous Act, was fixed at £2. Stevens tried to clarify what exactly was meant by such behaviour and revealed that when the short title of the Bill was first announced some referred to it as an anti-Teddy Boy Bill. He admitted that while he had Teddy Boys in mind, the Bill was not exclusive to them.

His Labour colleague T.C. Pannell pointed out a potential problem with the interpretation of the Bill, claiming that people appeared to differentiate between the unruly behaviour of Teds and students. At the New Year's Eve celebrations at Trafalgar Square, for example, the police were tougher on Teds than on undergraduates – who appeared to be allowed greater licence to misbehave. Members of the public, however, maintained that it was the Teds who were getting off lightly. A man complained that he had been issued with a £3 fine for a parking offence but on the way home from court read that a Ted had been fined a mere £2 for an assault. Similar inconsistencies in sentences were often pointed out. One Liverpudlian complained that his cyclist son had been given a £2 fine or a month's imprisonment for having a faulty brake light while five Teds with previous convictions were fined a mere 25s each for beating up a cafe owner.

In a debate on Geoffrey Stevens' Bill, James Dance, Conservative MP for Bromsgrove, Worcestershire, pointed out another problem with imposing fines on young people. While hoping that the Bill would curb marauding Teddy Boy gangs, he also wondered how the courts could be certain that convicted youths actually paid the fines themselves. In many cases it was their parents who coughed up the money. Dance believed that the perpetrators should be made to pay and to suffer the punishment, perhaps by having money stopped from their pay packets. He also suggested impounding the Teddy Boys' 'revolting' suits and cutting off their curls until they paid their fines. He claimed that punishments were often far too lenient and suggested to magistrates that if there was a little less binding over and a little more bending over, there might be an improvement in the behaviour of these 'young, stupid men'.

* * *

Flogging offenders was an old favourite with right-wing criminal justice campaigners, disappointed that it had been abolished by the 1948 Criminal Justice Act. As well as banning corporal punishment, except for breaches of prison discipline, the Act laid the emphasis on corrective training and treatment rather than punishment. By the mid-1950s some felt that society was reaping the whirlwind and that the rise of the Teds was the direct result of such misguided leniency.

In 1955 a policeman, believed to be a high-ranking officer, anonymously criticised current attempts at tackling crime and proclaimed that violent behaviour was worse than at any time in living memory. In particular, he blamed the 1948 Act for making life easier for criminals and more difficult for law-abiding citizens. The officer objected to the view from 'intellectual critics' that Teddy Boys were misunderstood and discriminated against by society. He accused those who held such notions of studying the brutes from the safety of an office or the back of a law court, and proposed that they meet the drunken and rampaging hooligans, as policemen did, at close quarters at closing time on a Saturday night.

Other police officers were similarly pro-flogging and anti do-gooder. Tom Fallon, former Chief Superintendent of the Metropolitan Police, said of the Teddy Boy: 'Stripped of his bogus glamour he is merely an apprentice gangster, a spineless young hoodlum who hunts with a pack – a warped ninny with an exhibitionist twist.' Fallon added: 'Sooner or later the public will become surfeited with the aery-faery meanderings of misguided social reformers, psychologists and cranks. Kindliness and good intentions are commendable qualities but they are incapable of changing the heart of a character with the instincts of a killer. These warped sub-humans have no understanding of soft-glove methods. To them such processes are weak and effete. There is one direct mode of access to the heart of a brute – through his hide.'

The truth is that the 1948 Act abolishing flogging was followed by a decline in robbery-with-violence offences, the very crimes for which birching was administered. It was not until the mid-1950s that the decline was reversed. By then some felt that the restoration of corporal punishment was the answer to Teddy Boy violence. In 1958 Conservative Major W. Hicks-Beach believed that flogging would help prevent a great deal of Teddy Boy-type hooliganism. Lord Howe asked how many more women had to be attacked and how many more Teddy

Boy outrages had to occur before corporal punishment was restored. Another Conservative MP, John Arbuthnot, could not help feeling that if many of today's Teddy Boys had been beaten at school, society would not be having trouble with them today.

Even if magistrates could not order a flogging they could advise parents on the best course of action to take. In 1955, at Liverpool City Quarter Sessions, two seventeen-year-olds Teds from Walton were found guilty of assaulting an off-duty policeman. The Assistant Recorder advised their fathers to give them the biggest thrashing of their lives if they continued to hang around with the gang. Labour MP Marcus Lipton also believed that the Teds 'ought to have been smacked on the behind by their parents'. The reliance on parental discipline, however, sometimes proved to be inadequate. Sir Gerald Dodson, Recorder of London, felt that since judges could not order a flogging it was left to the father, who in turn left it to the mother, to punish their son: 'She does nothing, and that is how a Teddy Boy is born.'

Pro-flogging supporters came from all walks of life. Rev. A.W. Butterworth of Hereford felt that, 'The best way to redeem Teddy Boys who attack and rob elderly women is to let them feel punishment on their own skin where it hurts most.' Father Henry Waterhouse, a Jesuit, Rector of St Francis Xavier's in Liverpool, also advocated the birch: 'I certainly believe in corporal punishment for boys, especially Teddy Boys.' The problem, he felt, was that between the two extremes of a long spell in an approved school and probation there was 'no provision for a short sharp lesson to bring the bad Teddy Boy to his senses'. 'It is about time drastic action was taken to put a stop to these scenes of violence caused by irresponsible youths called "Edwardians",' wrote Robert Haddon to his local newspaper. 'The only remedy now is imprisonment and the birch. Fines are useless.' At Rochdale Juvenile Court, the father of two lads, aged thirteen and sixteen, on being told that they had avoided custodial sentences for their parts in robberies, told the magistrate that they should bring back the cat-o'-nine-tails and there would be no need for remand homes or approved schools. The older boy, who had been found guilty of stealing a car, had recently exchanged his £15 suit for Edwardian clothes.

Even ex-prisoners were in favour of corporal punishment. Anthony Heckstall-Smith was sentenced to eighteen months' imprisonment around the time of the Clapham Common murder. He was in favour of flogging for child rapists and cosh boys, believing that it was the only worthwhile deterrent. For as well as being a coward and a bully the cosh boy was 'inordinately vain – a strutting, puffed up little creature, as pleased with himself as a cock-sparrow on a dung-heap'. He felt that Craig (of Bentley and Craig) was one such fellow. Ronald Coleman, the leader of the Clapham Edwardians, was another.

Heckstall-Smith described Coleman as 'the young spiv with his curled quiff, stovepipe trousers and flashy tie'. He was considered too tough, even at sixteen, to be sent to borstal and was jailed instead. Although some thought that Coleman had still got off lightly, Heckstall-Smith didn't think so for the longer such boys were held in prison, the less chance they had of leading useful lives when released. Heckstall-Smith also believed that there was no psychological cure for the cosh boy. 'I do not believe that youths like Coleman and Craig will react to any treatment the psychiatrists can give them.' Just flog them, he believed.

Banning Edwardian clothing, flogging, fines and tougher sentences were just some of the solutions that occupied the minds of politicians, newspaper editors and the general public. There were, however, other means of stopping the Teddy Boys. Before the Teds could be dealt with by the courts they were faced with bobbies on the beat who were increasingly ready to meet the threat.

22

POLICING

'It is to be deplored, but it does not justify national alarm. We should remember that before we get hysterical about Teddy Boys, the police know how to handle these gangs.'

(Superintendent Fabian of Scotland Yard, 1954)

The police were, from the outset, the first line of defence against the Teds. When a Tory MP asked the Home Secretary in May 1954 what action would be taken to stop the hooliganism, Sir David Maxwell Fyfe replied that the Commissioner of the Metropolitan Police had assured him that his officers were on the alert to suppress any trouble. Indeed, the police had already begun a drive to tackle the Teddy Boys. After the murder of John Beckley, Scotland Yard had asked London County Council to clean up Clapham Common, which the Edwardian gangs were apparently using as their private playground. The police also urged the council to end open-air dancing on the Common or at least to maintain stricter supervision.

Fast-forward two years and more than 5,000 Chingford residents had signed a petition calling on the Home Secretary to deal with the Teddy Boys – they were, they said, concerned for the safety of their children after dark. The public needed reassuring and reports of robust police actions and initiatives were constantly used by the authorities as proof that something was being done. In 1955 a number of police forces had already declared war on the Teds. In the military town of Colchester, police liaised with the Armed Forces to rid the town of them.

Action was prompted by a spate of late-night gang warfare. Newcastle police said 'that they would smash the city's Teddy gangs' while the Sheriff of Alloa in Scotland declared that 'no Teddy thugs would be tolerated here'.

As ever the press kept the public informed. In 1955 the *Sunday Dispatch* gave several examples of how the authorities were waging war on the Teds, on the streets, in the dance halls and in the cinemas. The headline boasted that the Teddy Boy 'menace' was at last being cleared up – when it had in fact barely begun. Around the same time, Liverpool's *Evening Express* carried the headline, 'It's Friday night and the Teddy Boys are on the prowl.' The article focused on the need for extra policemen in the West Derby area of the city, which housed the Locarno and Grafton dance halls. The old beat system of policing was felt to be inadequate in dealing with the ferocity and size of the gangs since individual constables stood no chance. Trouble was also flaring up over such an increasingly wide area that police back-up was often too slow to respond. The authorities therefore introduced Land Rover patrols throughout the city to target trouble spots such as the dance halls. The aim was to disperse the gangs before they caused any mischief. The problem was that the lads simply caused trouble elsewhere. It was felt that the squeeze being put on the Teds was driving them to fresh pastures, such as New Brighton on the Wirral. The downside of such tactics had been noted the previous year. London police similarly believed that the clothing ban in certain establishments was driving Teds further afield; barred from their usual haunts, youths were forming train parties to invade areas where they were not known.

Not all policemen were considered to be up to the task of controlling the gangs. The Blackpool Watch Committee decided to forcibly retire special constables over the age of sixty-five. It was felt that the men were liable to be injured dealing with boisterous Teds. It was as if the Teddy Boy threat demanded a new form of policing, or at least greater use of the old techniques. Former Detective Superintendent Hodge revealed his gang-busting solution. 'The drag' was the term used by corner boys for police swoops to pick up suspected persons loitering in the street. Hodge urged more use of 'the drag' to tackle the Teds.

Police dogs came in particularly useful. In 1954, in Kingston, Surrey, the police initiated 'Operation Teddy Boy'. Special patrols, accompanied by a dog team, conducted a 'big drive on hooliganism'. A year later, a group of twenty-five rowdy Kingston youths were forcing people off the footpath. Police spoke to them but eleven refused to move – until a police dog was called in to help shepherd the lads to the nearby police station where they were charged. The following year two police Alsatians were used to break up a jiving mob outside the Gaumont cinema in Lewisham, South East London. In 1956 Liverpool's Chief Constable introduced his own solution, as thirty-two police dogs became full members of the city's Flying Squads, travelling with officers in fast cars and Land Rovers. In 1958, the Chief Constable of East Sussex felt that the psychiatrist's couch was not the place to curb the Teds. He explained, 'In my county I have great faith in the Alsatian dog. They soon disperse when they see a constable with a dog.' In the same year it was announced that Blackpool police would also start using four-legged officers to suppress the violence. Speaking of the usefulness of canine assistance, Captain Popkess of Nottingham police warned that nothing quelled a drunken brawl or stopped a Ted in his tracks quicker than a police dog. Velvet collars and dog collars obviously did not mix very well.

* * *

The London police were extending their robust measures to rid the capital of Teds. In 1957, a Scotland Yard conference involving high-ranking officers met to discuss the problem, and this resulting message went out to the capital's 16,500 constables: get tough with the Teds. Instead of charging youths under the Metropolitan Police Act of 1839, they were advised to use the more robust Public Order Act of 1936 which gave greater powers of punishment in fines and imprisonment. The tough measures came following alarm at the increase in street fighting. If youths were causing a really serious disturbance that threatened to escalate into a street brawl, the police were again urged to use different tactics: they were to seek custodial remands of those arrested at their first court appearance, so that the Yard's legal experts could decide whether to bring more serious charges against them.

Two years later Sir Joseph Simpson of Scotland Yard was again calling for an all-out drive to stop the gang warfare among Teds in London. Measures were to include regular swoops by uniformed officers on troublesome dance halls, along with random checks by CID officers on dance hall entrances to search likely suspects for weapons. Officers were told to stand no nonsense and go for the toughest boys when making arrests. More use was to be made of police informants to find out when gang fights were due to take place. Plain-clothes officers were to be placed in cafes, listening for plans of forthcoming battles. They were also to seek out Teds' haunts, particularly street corners and pubs at closing time. Officers could then watch and listen in so they could swoop on them later when they ganged together at dance halls. Each police station opened a special dossier on Teddy Boy activity in its area.

In 1958, after disturbances led by armed rival gangs from neighbouring districts, police in the Black Country town of Oldbury also declared war on the Teddy Boys. Superintendent Bache announced, 'We cannot tolerate this any longer, we are meeting force with force.' In the same year Manchester's new Chief Constable revealed his own measures for tackling Teddy Boy disorder. As well as using police dogs he was in favour of a large uniformed presence in trouble spots. As a last resort there was a reserve squad (he hesitated to call it a 'riot squad') on standby if needed. In 1959 dedicated police patrols were still operating at weekends in Richmond and Kingston, Surrey, as well as Wandsworth in London. The Richmond 'anti-Teddy Boy squad' included an inspector, a sergeant, ten constables and two police dogs. In four months they arrested 250 Teds.

The clampdown inevitably meant that some young people

felt unjustly targeted and subject to repressive police practices. A group of girls leaving a London coffee bar and simply laughing and joking were told by a policeman to walk in twos or else and such oppressive actions were certainly unwelcomed. In Hampshire in 1958, on a Saturday afternoon in Commercial Road, Portsmouth, a group of about 100 youths 'of the Teddy Boy type' marched through the shopping centre shouting and handing out flyers bearing slogans such as 'Brighton CID cleared up. Now for Portsmouth.' Traffic was held up for an hour. The protest came after a youth called Slack was allegedly beaten up by the police. Protestors also bill-posted the town with posters reading 'Local CID turned thugs'.

There were other reports of heavy-handed action. In 1959, after police raided a Bermondsey coffee bar and made arrests, up to eighty youths marched to the police station to protest. A Birmingham Ted complained, 'They get you while you're alone, or in pairs ... I was walking home from the boozer last month with one mate when a police car draws up. Out jumps these coppers and clobbers us against the wall. Just for singing in the street. It makes them feel big I suppose. Now last week there was a fight. The gang comes out of a boozer with broken bottles in their hands. The police didn't do nothing then.'

In Swindon, Wiltshire, a policeman was acquitted of twice punching a sixteen-year-old in the face, breaking his jaw. The officer was off duty when he noticed an unlit motorcycle under a street lamp. He told one of the youths standing nearby to turn on the lights but he refused. The policeman allegedly tried to punch the lad's mate but missed before attacking the victim. In court the injured youth, who had his jaw wired up, was asked if he was wearing Teddy Boy clothes, as if that would establish what sort of person he was. He replied that he was wearing a leather jacket and cowboy boots since he was on his bike. The court accepted that the policeman acted in self-defence. There was a different outcome, however, for a sergeant from Sheffield who was taunted and abused for weeks by a Teddy Boy. The officer finally snapped and boxed his ears and was cautioned by the Chief Constable.

In 1961, during one of Bristol's worst outbreaks of Teddy disorder, lads from different areas battled with the police in the central part of the city. Trouble began at 9 p.m. after youths started congregating during a pub crawl. One Ted explained, 'We were just drinking peacefully but the cops kept on following us around and moving us on.' Another lad alleged, 'They just rammed into us with truncheons and torches.' No doubt the police had a different story to tell.

* * *

If the police could be rough on the Teds, so could the general public. When he saw two Teds try to snatch an old woman's pension in Islington, a 76-year-old ex-boxer swung into action. With a left hook he floored one of the lads before they fled. A 78-year-old man broke his umbrella on Teds who refused to get off the children's swings at Watchet, Somerset, while another six Teds blocked the path of old Etonian Angus Montague in Park Lane, London. The former Royal Marines Commando put them on their backs.

Public-spirited citizens sometimes came to the aid of the police. When eight Teds damaged a bridge over the River Bollin in Cheshire, next to Wilmslow Rugby Union Football Club, several rugby players got hold of the vandals and handed them to the police. Rugby-playing medical students also helped police outnumbered by Teds in a dance hall in Maidenhead, Berkshire. In Watford's High Street three housewives saw Teds fighting with broken bottles. When a policeman cried for help they waded in with their handbags.

Despite this being a period when police officers regularly patrolled areas on foot, they could not be everywhere at once. In the absence of a 'bobby', members of the public were determined to take the law into their own hands. There were many examples of people taking their own action against the Teds. Vigilantes patrolled the streets of Gillingham, Kent, while in Heywood, Lancashire, a meeting of 100 clergy, parents and youth workers discussed ways of tackling Teddy Boys. A former schoolmaster urged volunteers to become vigilantes, parading pleasure spots and other places where Teds gathered. He got the thumbs-down and was told that his idea resembled a Police State.

In 1955, in the south of Liverpool, a group of fathers threatened to form vigilante groups to keep Teddy Boys from the children's playground. A year later, the local newspaper was bombarded with letters and comments from angry Liverpudlians. There were renewed calls for vigilante action against the Teds and one reader called for fifty volunteers to be drawn from university students, teachers, solicitors and off-duty policemen. Aided by five cars, three gallons of tar, a bale of feathers and some hairdressing shears, the vigilantes were to seek out the Teddy Boys and publicly humiliate them.

* * *

Public shaming rituals have a long history in criminal justice. Some thought that such practices should be revived. In 1956 a group of psychologists and experts met to discuss the Teddy Boys. One speaker, a solicitor called J.A. Reston, thought that the solution was ridicule, particularly for children to laugh at the Teds. This might have been the aim of one magistrate who told a Ted, wearing a long crimson coat, that he looked like 'a cross between a Spanish toreador and a candidate for a gala performance'. A speaker at the 1958 Conservative Party conference thought that the stocks 'have much to commend them'. Five years later Lord Goddard, former Lord Chief Justice, thought it a pity that the stocks could not be used for Teddy Boys, 'who nothing cures as quickly as ridicule'. Since the stocks had not been used for over 100 years, more suitable means of humiliating the Teds were suggested. An alternative shaming cure was that Teds, before being released from custody, should have their beloved locks shaved to the skull with just a tuft of hair left in front.

Other long-discontinued means of dealing with criminals were revived, at least in the fevered minds of the Teds' opponents. In an echo of transportation, an MP proposed deporting the thugs to a deserted Commonwealth island and letting them fend for themselves. Even before the rise of the Teds, a member of the public had suggested sending the cosh boys to the deserted archipelago of St Kilda, 100 miles to the west of Scotland. Allowing them some agricultural tools, along with sheep and cattle, they would be left to fend for themselves. It was felt that a spell without public houses or female companionship would teach them a lesson.

The idea of ridding the country of Teds was not simply wishful thinking, at least over the Irish Sea. The Irish Republic's District Courts introduced a measure to deal with their own Teddy Boy problem: unemployed youths found guilty were given a conditional discharge on the condition that they migrate to England to seek work.

* * *

While some looked to ancient methods of punishment, others sought more futuristic means of controlling the Teds, particularly those who were viewed as having psychological problems. A 'family doctor' offered his own cure for Teddy Boy hooliganism: besides flogging or hanging, depending on the gravity of their crimes, what the Teds needed was rehabilitation in a psychiatric institution. In Colin MacInnes's novel *Absolute Beginners* (1959), set in London in 1958, Teds are seen as 'psychopathic cases' needing medical attention rather than punishment, a theme with sinister echoes in Anthony Burgess's novel *A Clockwork Orange* (1962) where the 'Droog' gang member Alex is experimented on by doctors to rid him of his violent tendencies. Indeed, two American doctors claimed that a heavy tranquilliser and anti-psychotic drug called chlorpromazine, used to treat schizophrenics, could help 'cure' juvenile crime. It was felt that the drug would soothe Teddy Boys and make them manageable for treatment.

Needless to say, all these efforts from politicians, the police, the press and the public, failed to completely eliminate the menace. Fortunately there were other efforts to turn the Teds into socially responsible citizens. By guiding them, offering them moral example and giving them something useful to do, it was hoped that young people would renounce their delinquent tendencies.

23

YOUTH WORK

'So scared are we that boys and girls will become "teddified", promiscuous or Communist, that we try, often unconsciously, to impose upon them our own sets of values, so that they may "fit into" our society and thus not wish to change it.'

(Youth worker, 1957)

Alternative disciplinary methods were mooted in 1956, after Teddy Boys at Heywood, Greater Manchester frequently caused trouble at church social events. At one dance the Master of Ceremonies was hospitalised after being attacked by a Ted. The local vicar, who commanded the local unit of the Air Training Corps, called a public meeting to discuss ways of tackling the problem. He believed that it would be beneficial for Teds to join youth organisations – unlike the cinemas and dance halls, where they more or less behaved as they liked, these were places where adults could help mould young people into better citizens.

Politicians of all persuasions were in agreement. Labour MP John Diamond felt sure that there would be fewer incidents if Teddy Boys had the opportunity to attend youth clubs to be trained in citizenship and responsibility. Conservative MP Edwin Leather pointed out that society spent immense energy and millions of pounds on children up to the age of fifteen before ignoring three-quarters of them by not spending a penny or putting any care and attention their way. He felt that local authorities placed youth services low down on the list of priorities. It was therefore pointless for people to write letters to the newspapers demanding corporal punishment for Teddy Boys, since prevention was the responsibility of society. Colonel R.P. Menday, warden of the Wallingford Training Centre, Oxfordshire, was another advocate of youth facilities. He believed that gangs should be allowed to exist but directed along adventurous and acceptable paths. Believing that boredom was the problem, he claimed that street gangs in 1800 were probably far worse than the Teddy Boys.

If the gang problem had a long history, so did the idea of preventing juvenile delinquency through the provision of youth facilities. The question was whether traditional youth clubs were the answer to the post-war youth problem, particularly the Teddy Boy problem. In 1956, in a House of Lords debate on recreation facilities, the Duke of Sutherland expressed a very Victorian sentiment when he claimed that the provision of playing fields 'would reduce industrial unrest and discontent by giving the workers something worthwhile to occupy their minds and bodies'. Whether this would banish the Teddy Boys from the streets was something the *Manchester Guardian* was not quite so sure about. Ironically, in 1954, in a crowded London park, two Teddy Boys took part in a razor fight, watched by a crowd of about 100 youths and adults. Nevertheless, the General Secretary of Sussex County Playing Fields Association was another calling for more playing fields, reasoning that they would cut down on the number of Teds and juvenile delinquents.

* * *

Teenagers in the early 1950s certainly needed somewhere exciting to go since venues such as the Locarno and Mecca dance halls were aimed at the over-twenties. T.R. Fyvel once made a depressing tour of the desolate late-night London scene, with its clubs, Greek Cypriot cafes, milk-bars, amusement arcades and cinemas. He felt that the drab and uniform entertainment had little to offer. Even the youth clubs, many of them church-run, were considered uninviting, uninteresting, patronising and a bit naff. Most were poorly furnished, badly lit and urgently needed to be brought up to date, in line with the needs and increased spending power of the younger generation. Typically, Teds dismissed such clubs as 'prayers and table tennis'.

In 1958 it was reported that nearly £3,000,000 a year was being spent by local authorities, voluntary bodies and the Education Ministry on a loosely linked youth service. Few teenagers, and even fewer Teds, were using the facilities. Not long after the Notting Hill disturbances, the Countess of Albemarle was appointed to look into the problem of leisure provision for young people. Two years later, the Ministry of Education published *The Youth Service in England and Wales*, also known as the *Albemarle Report*. This landmark document promoted the expansion and professionalisation of the service, leading to a boost in funding and helping adapt youth work to the new age of youth culture.

New approaches to youth provision were certainly needed. One youth leader in a tough London district noted that twenty-five per cent of his fourteen- to sixteen-year-old members had no real interest in the club's activities. These boys, labelled the 'lower stratum' of Teddy Boy society, merely popped in for a game of darts and a cup of coffee, then drifted out. The leaders tried everything to keep them involved, offering judo, badminton and a snooker tournament, but the lads couldn't stick at anything for more than half an hour. One of them would say, 'Comin' out?' and they would all follow like sheep.

One Ted, speaking to Admiral Faulkner, the president of the West Somerset branch of the NSPCC, complained that 'no organisation wanted boys like him, and that a gang was the only thing they could join'. A more important issue perhaps is whether Teds wanted to join youth clubs. Since clubs had rules and regulations, the more rebellious lads avoided them; the Teddy Boys, in particular, would have rejected the middle-class respectable values and ideals of some such organisations.

In the tougher districts a different approach was needed. Rev. Griffiths ran a Methodist Community Centre in Lambeth,

South London, from 1951, catering for those with police records or considered 'unclubbable'. Griffiths noticed the change in youths as the decade progressed. The first sets of gangs, at the beginning of the decade, were still in cloth caps and carried razors to use against rival gangs. They used bad language, condoms were found in the corridors and discipline was difficult to maintain. It usually took about six weeks for the lads to be persuaded to leave their razors at home. In February 1954 the club was invaded by the first Edwardian gangs. These boys were members of much larger groups and, unlike earlier gangs, they now had a loose organisation.

Griffiths issued a challenge to the South London Edwardian gangs, some of whom had smashed windows in his club: he wanted to meet them without police protection to discuss any grievances they had and persuade them to form a brotherhood of Edwardians, dedicated to non-violence. His aim was to replace the excitement of fighting with other kinds of adventure. After traipsing around London's cafes looking for suitable members, Griffiths met with representatives of sixteen Teddy Boy gangs at a West End dance hall. Here they drew up rules for the new club. Only boys who promised not to use violence were to be given a badge of membership. It was proposed that each committee member donate a pint of blood to the transfusion service. They also agreed to a club tie but couldn't decide on a colour except that it should be thin, like a piece of string. Despite initial co-operation, the day after Griffiths met a dozen Teds from Clapton he received anonymous threats from one South London gang. Interest in the club fizzled out.

Other clubs were forced to change with the times. Around 1957, at St Barnabas Church Hall in Finchley, North London, members of the church youth group were playing table tennis when about thirty Teddy Boys and their girls marched in. They didn't care much for ping-pong and asked whether they could bring a record player. The priest agreed and so began the regular Wednesday night dances. Nationally, the authorities were also forced to introduce new initiatives to attract disaffected youth. 'Club Week', held in 1957, involved a series of festivities run by, and for, boys' clubs throughout the country. The event's unofficial motto was 'We're not all Teddy Boys – come and have a look at us'.

* * *

In 1958 there was an attempt to form a National Association of Teddy Boys (NATB). A meeting was held in the Friends' Institute in Mosley, Birmingham, but had to be delayed by half an hour in the hope that enough Teds would appear to outnumber the attendant reporters and photographers. Eventually twenty-two Teds and three girlfriends appeared. The meeting was organised by a youth club leader called Trevor Williams, along with Tom Gauntlet, the Teddy leader mentioned in chapter 9. The chairman, a 76-year-old Quaker called Henry Whittaker, asked that police show more discretion and helpfulness towards the Teds and appealed to youth club leaders not to be frightened of the lads. A charter was drawn up by Gauntlet urging people to differentiate between Teds and hooligans.

It was proposed that if an NATB was to be formed it would establish nationwide centres for Teds run by Teds with recreational and sports facilities. Additional inducements were holiday camps and free legal advice. The newly formed association management committee agreed that the organisation should be open to all Teddy Boys, regardless of race, creed or political beliefs, other than Communism. Before long, however, a faction split away, calling the chief committee officers 'just a bunch of squares'.

Although the NATB was not a widespread success, a more radical type of organisation, created with the Teddy Boys in mind, was quite popular in the two years that it lasted. In 1960 the young Ray Gosling, later to find fame as a broadcaster, left university after one year and founded a revolutionary youth club known as the 'Leicester Experiment'. The club was formed as a response to the Government's *Albemarle Report*, which had criticised the lameness of existing youth services. In 1961

Gosling went on to write a Fabian Society pamphlet called *Lady Albemarle's Boys*, a riposte to the official report.

With 200 members, aged sixteen to twenty-five, paying 6d a week, the Leicester club housed a coffee bar, jukebox, fruit-machine, rock band, quiet rooms, an office with TV, billiards and magazines, together with information and advice facilities. Labelled Britain's 'toughest youth club', its members were largely Teddy Boys. Gosling admitted that there were frequent attempts to wreck the place, with rooms being used as brothels, card schools and places to hide stolen goods. Gosling revealed that there had been committee meetings at which members were frightened to speak up for fear of reprisals. Money once had to be doled out to prevent the office from being trashed and Gosling cut up with a knife.

Gosling warned that improved youth services would not stop all teenage trouble, particularly the street fights. He reasoned: 'Freshers will always be freshers; undergrads will always be undergrads; teds will always be teds.' Yet the club had its successes. An ex-King of the Teds, promoted as a permanent member of staff, revealed that he used to run the town's lads, once leading 250 of them into a mass brawl. He said that people lectured him but he didn't listen. However, he claimed that the club changed him by giving him a sense of responsibility. He now found fun in building something rather than wrecking it.

Young people, wary of traditional youth clubs, were also attracted to the more informal Teen Age Canteens. These were bright and safe meeting places with no membership cards and often no subscription fees. They grew out of the 'In and Out Clubs' developed in London and other large towns during the war and aimed at youngsters who were drifting about in the blackouts and mixing with bad company. Music, dancing and refreshments were provided under the watchful eye of a 'manager'. In 1955 Dulwich College Mission introduced a Teen Canteen in Elephant & Castle, South East London, open six nights a week. It was claimed that before the establishment opened the Teds were bored, wandering the streets and getting into trouble. Now they were redecorating the premises and forming committees. It was also reported that there was no trouble even between different gangs of Teddy Boys, with the lads themselves ejecting any troublemakers.

In 1956 Fellowship Hall Youth Club in Hammersmith Road, London was known as the 'Teddy Boy Club' thanks to the rowdy and unruly behaviour of its members. There were calls to close the place after a spate of anti-social behaviour, including one incident where a passer-by had a bucket of water thrown over him. The leader defended the club and explained to a reporter that the Ted responsible had been expelled. He urged people to volunteer as helpers to stop children turning into Teddy Boys. When the journalist visited the club he was surprised to see the youths helping to decorate the place.

* * *

Ray Gosling was particularly critical of vicar-type youth clubs and welfare workers who sought out Teddy Boys in coffee bars as if they were missionaries venturing into the jungle, although this sort of approach did have its successes. In 1960 the National Association of Youth Clubs set up a pioneer experiment to discover solutions to the problem of 'unattached' youths who didn't belong to anyone or anything. Three young social workers were sent out to different towns to seek out and form relationships with such youths in each area. The project lasted three years but it is unclear whether it was a success.

By 1961 another form of outreach work was being publicised. A Bristol Social Project, consisting of eleven workers, had spent five years exploring the roots of juvenile delinquency. The subsequent report suggested the appointment of missionary 'street workers', who were well-versed in Teddy Boy customs and specially trained to seek out gangs at their meeting places, particularly cinemas, dance halls and fish and chip shops. The workers were even asked to join the gangs to observe them close-up. One worker called Sara joined a youth club and found two groups: the Tip-Tops, who were a bunch of well-behaved youths, and the 'Teds' (so they termed themselves) who, not surprisingly, were a disruptive and destructive group. After some of the Teds had been ejected from the club for their bad behaviour, Sara sought them out on the streets and befriended them. The group had now changed their name to the Calypsos.

Building up a relationship with the youths was difficult. The first meeting that was arranged had to be abandoned when the noisy lads were ejected from the room. The next meeting, at a church hall, was similarly called off when they started smashing windows. Yet the determined Sara did not desert the group. The report on the experiment claimed a measure of success. While Sara was with the group the lads, with one exception, had no court appearances for delinquency – but within eight months of the project ending five lads had appeared in court. The message behind the report was that gangs and juvenile delinquency were symptoms of the stresses and strains of modern living and that a new approach to the problem was needed.

* * *

One big dilemma for youth clubs was whether to accept or reject Teddy Boys. Stan Morris, warden of the Florence Institute boys club in Liverpool, believed that he could tame the Teds even though club dances sometimes had to be cancelled due to their misbehaviour – with one gang leader having the gall to offer him 'protection' against a rival gang. The club was actually losing members to the gangs and Morris admitted, 'They find deeper friendship in the gangs than in the boys' clubs.' He also complained of the poor condition of equipment and lack of money spent on the youth service. It was felt that the clubs had no time for taming the troublesome Teds because they were afraid of losing 'decent' youths. Parents would withdraw their children from camping trips if certain disruptive kids were going.

Stella Baker, a warden at the Liverpool Rodney Youth Centre, welcomed Teds although she once had to disarm a youth of his razor. She nevertheless viewed these lads as 'an opportunity, not a threat to respectability'. Once they had joined, the Teds were placed in pairs in separate classes. That way they were never able to form gangs on the premises.

A National Conference of Youth Councils, held in 1957, attracted 150 delegates, some of whom could almost have been mistaken for Teds. While one young delegate suggested having separate youth clubs for the more anti-social Teds, another claimed that this would only make them stand out, like they did already on street corners. Another young speaker declared that half the members of his club were Teddy Boys, adding that they were not hooligans – although most hooligans were Teddy Boys. In Birmingham, in the same year, four youths met the Lord Mayor to discuss the dilemma of law-abiding Teds being treated with suspicion by the community. They complained that youth clubs would not let them join while in Edwardian dress. Officials from the Birmingham Federation of Youth Clubs agreed to help them form their own club where Teddy Boy uniform was not frowned upon.

In 1959 the warden of the Ancoats division of the Manchester University Settlement spoke of the difficulties in trying to socialise the Teds, who generally disliked being organised, were resentful of authority and uninterested in the activities of traditional youth clubs. University settlements were residential communities of men and women who worked in deprived areas. The warden admitted that such action might be at the expense of the more well-behaved members of the club who would probably leave rather than mix with the rougher element. At Ancoats it had proved difficult to integrate the two groups. The club had up to eighty members, most of them excluded from other establishments. The question was posed whether it was a success to cater for one Teddy Boy at the expense of losing one law-abiding member.

* * *

Despite the good intentions of youth leaders, some lads were never going to embrace the discipline and sense of purpose instilled by boys' club activities. London Teddy Boy Tony Reuter claimed that Teds joined youth clubs only to earn themselves good references in case they were arrested: 'A lot of teddy boys set out to join a Youth club. That means when they get into trouble the club leader will come along to the police and say: "It couldn't be my boys. They wouldn't go in for that sort of thing."'

Many Teds preferred to be members of delinquent gangs rather than youth clubs. Bootle YMCA was forced to cancel its popular dances in 1958 because rival gangs, who were not even members, would regularly clash on the field outside the hall. Genuine members were wrongly getting a bad reputation. Some Teds did not simply ignore the youth clubs, they violently attacked them. In 1954 a youth centre in Camberwell, South London, was wrecked by 'cosh boys' in Edwardian suits armed with razors and knuckle-dusters. Rev. James Butterworth once asked some unruly Teds to leave a dance at Clubland in Walworth Road, London. Their response was to smash crockery, wreck furniture, tear electric fittings and rip a cistern from the wall, flooding the place. Dudley Noble, an ex-member of the Paddington Boys, recalls an incident when a dozen Teds jumped through the open window of a Notting Hill youth club and beat up the table tennis players with bricks and iron bars.

In 1958 members of Teddington's Lockway Youth Club, in South West London, fought a hand-to-hand battle with invading Teds. The club leader explained that previously they had been able to get rid of the Teds by peaceful means. A year later Rev. Gill explained that the Friday youth club night at the Sydenham Community Centre, Somerset, would have to be suspended due to the bad behaviour of Teds, some of whom were travelling from outside the area to cause trouble. In Nottingham, as late as 1961, a group of up to forty Teds, believed to be the Arnold Mob, linked arms across a main road and randomly stopped Rev. Heywood's car before pelting it with mud. Ironically, the boys had earlier visited an abstinence club which aimed at keeping youths off the streets and out of the pubs. The boys simply walked in and threatened to wreck the place before being ejected.

Different arguments have been put forward to explain the Teds' rejection of youth facilities. The chronic shortage of leisure amenities in the 1950s was a great disappointment to young people and resulted in boredom, frustration and possibly contributed to more delinquency. It has also been argued that in some cases the hostility between Teds and the youth club movement was caused by many clubs who were barring lads purely because they dressed in a certain way. By attacking these clubs it was as if the Teds were gaining their revenge. Even when there did happen to be good youth facilities in the area, and the Teds were welcomed, some continued to act anti-socially. Perhaps no amount of clubs and leisure facilities could eliminate the social inequalities evident elsewhere in schools and workplaces.

* * *

Taking up a sport was seen as another potential solution to the Teddy Boy problem. Novelist Nancy Mitford believed these were merely young men who lacked an outlet for their energy. Chris Brasher – who won Olympic gold in the 3000m steeplechase in 1956 – thought that a lack of sports facilities was to blame. Even before the rise of the Teds, one youth worker suggested that a new national sport of gravel pit climbing could be a solution to the cosh boy problem. He felt that organised outdoor pursuits, with an element of danger, could cure delinquency by encouraging lads to work off their aggressive energies.

A psychiatrist took it further, explaining that the likes of table tennis, dancing and conventional sports were failing to divert the aggressive drives of young people. Tough sports such as rugby, together with outdoor educational organisations such as the Outward Bound Trust, stood a better chance of helping to release pent-up aggression. Such a scheme seemed to have worked for lads in the Everton district of Liverpool. Members of the YMCA, half of them Teddy Boys, enjoyed camping, hiking and rock climbing during trips to Windermere in the Lake District. The absence of girls and the need to ditch their flashy uniforms did not seem to deter them from completing the gruelling challenges.

Others argued that boys thrived on danger. Rev. Griffiths complained that modern life was too tame for many children. They turned to crime simply in search of adventure. Record-breaking athlete Roger Bannister, who ran the first-ever sub-four-minute mile in 1954, felt that it would be better for Teds to be channelled into individual sports, even dangerous ones. Indeed, a Sussex doctor claimed that a ban on young people boxing would lead to more Teddy Boys.

Some boys, however, were not interested in the discipline of organised sport. A caretaker from London's St Pancras saw some Teds getting into trouble for playing football in the street. To help them he took out a loan for a kit and formed a football team called Athlone Athletic Club but the boys would not pay their subs and the team was disbanded. The caretaker admitted that they were too tough for him. John Townsend, in his account of life as a teacher in a tough London school in the 1950s, recounts his futile attempts to muster a football team from the lads of Form 4B. He found that games failed to appeal to most of them, particularly the Teddy Boy element who didn't want to ruin their flashy clothes or spoil their shoes.

For some Teds, watching sport merely offered an opportunity for violence and anti-social behaviour. During a 1956 Paisley Pirates ice-hockey match in East Sussex, at Brighton Sports Stadium, scuffles broke out and coins and programmes thrown onto the ice. As the match ended crowds of spectators, led by Teds, attacked the Paisley team. In the same year, second-division side Doncaster played host to Liverpool FC. After the home team scored a dubious goal, Liverpool supporters were incensed that the referee hadn't ruled it offside. Fights broke out and a policeman lost his helmet. A volley of missiles was thrown onto the pitch, hitting two Doncaster players. Table knives, stolen from the train, were later found behind the goal. Liverpool Teddy Boys were blamed. The year also saw a London youth stabbed as fighting broke out among a gang of Teds as they were skating. Two years later rival gangs fought at a skating rink in Forest Gate.

Even the leisurely pursuit of rowing was turned into naval warfare. In 1955 rival Teds fought with oars in the Thames. The skirmish started when one skiff carrying four youths and a girl was rammed by another boat containing three Teds and two girls. The scrap ended with four rowers in the water. Two years later in London's Hyde Park, four Teds took a rowing boat into an area reserved for swimmers in the Serpentine. Swearing and making a nuisance of themselves, they also argued with a lifeguard and struck him with their oars. Incensed bathers swam out to capsize the lads and when the Teds eventually tried to climb out of the water they were repeatedly thrown back in. By the time they reached land one had passed out from the cold and another had a gash on his face.

Sports facilities were also wrecked, such as the cricket pavilion in the Surrey village of Cranleigh, which was set ablaze by Teds who then ran whooping up the street. In Smethwick, four Teds set fire to a golf hut, while in Somerset, Wellington's only swimming pool was forced to close after vandalism by local Teds.

* * *

In 1955 the Duke of Edinburgh's Award scheme appeared to be another answer to the problem. The Duke, as patron of the London Federation of Boys' Clubs, devised the scheme with Teddy Boys in mind. Sir John Hunt, secretary of the scheme, further claimed that the award was ideal for Teddy Boy types who were shunning existing youth movements. Maintaining that they would 'make a very good show under the scheme' he rejected the possibility of setting up a separate format just for Teds. He also claimed that as the scheme succeeded, fewer boys would want to wear Teddy suits.

The Scouting movement also tried to reform the Teds. A speaker told the annual meeting of the Somerset County Boy

Scouts Association that Scouting was not just a 'kid's game' but had an important role in combating the trend towards Teddy-boy-ism. Created by Lord Baden Powell in 1907, one of the movement's original aims was to transform the young hooligans of Edwardian London. In promoting the values of leadership, comradeship and responsibility, the organisation played an important role in forging a sense of self-discipline in generations of young people.

By the 1950s, however, the movement had much the same problem as the youth clubs in dealing with the Teds. Speaking at a conference of Scouts Councils in 1959, the Chief Scout, Lord Rowallan, reported that few men in the movement were capable of redeeming youths such as the Teddy Boys. He admitted that only a small percentage of Teds could be absorbed into the movement without harming the atmosphere on which Scout work depended.

Others saw somewhat dubious affinities between Boy Scouts and the Teds. Teddy Boys were described as 'lost Scouts' by the Commissioner for North West Lancashire. Both groups went about in patrols, wore a distinctive uniform and sought adventure – although one might add that there the resemblance ended. J.W. Ashley Smith, headmaster and Scoutmaster, warned of the danger of destroying the natural virtues of Teddy Boys who became Scouts. He claimed that Teds possessed a strong sense of group loyalty and were willing to help anyone down-and-out, no matter how bad they might be. He did not want to turn such loyal, group-minded Teds into self-seeking individuals.

Concerned that boys were leaving the Scouting movement to join mixed youth clubs when they reached the age of fifteen, the Taunton District Commissioner suggested allowing older Girl Guides to come in occasionally to do some jiving. 'We are not monastic,' he explained. Indeed, girls were also felt to be in need of guidance. In 1959 a Leigh magistrate called on the South Lancashire Girl Guide Association to rescue Teddy Girl types from 'insecure lives influenced by commercialism'.

Although the Chief Executive Commissioner of the Scouts felt that his organisation was for all boys, not just the well-behaved ones, the movement was seen as too middle class and respectable for most Teds. In 1960 the Chief Scout claimed that it was not Scouting's job to collect Teddy Boys and that the work of the movement was about preventing delinquency, not curing it. One leader claimed that one or two nasty-minded thugs could ruin a troop in a short time. Another Scoutmaster had heard colleagues boasting about the boys they had prevented from becoming Teds. He felt this claim to be a slander on the existing members, since how could it be known that such boys would have become Teds? The leader of one particularly tough and rebellious troop summed up Scouting's problem: while the movement was focused on producing 'dear little backwoodsmen', the hooligan element was multiplying in society.

If the Teds didn't appreciate the Scouts they had an equal disdain for another uniformed youth organisation, the Boys' Brigade. In 1954 the Brigade set up their Founders Camp in the grounds of Eton College. Up to 2,000 boys from all over the world pitched their tents but they had to be protected from Teddy Boys from nearby Slough who tried to break into the camp. The Brigade members were told not to enter the town in the evening – and, if they did, they were to travel in groups. It seems that local Teds had been taunting them from the street corners. Four years later, members of the 5th Coatbridge Company of the Boys' Brigade camped up at Monifieth, near Dundee. Police, with batons drawn, had to intervene as twenty-six Teds, armed with bicycle chains and rubber coshes, marched in a long menacing line towards the camp. For their own safety Brigade members were escorted to a nearby YMCA. In 1955 the St John Ambulance cadets' summer camp at Bexhill, East Sussex, also suffered an evening invasion by Teds on bicycles who collapsed their tents and emptied suitcases.

Despite their efforts, if youth workers and Scoutmasters could not solve the problem, there was an army of priests, parsons and pastors driven with a desire to save the Teddy Boys' souls.

24
RELIGION

'Religion must be covered up with "rock 'n' roll".'

(Ray Gosling, broadcaster, 1961)

According to one reader of the *Sunday Times*, society was to blame for the Nottingham and Notting Hill disturbances – but she particularly held the Church liable for not doing enough. Why, she asked, were there no trained youth leaders out on the streets befriending the Teddy Boys? It was felt that the Church should be spending less time organising coffee mornings and more time, money and energy in making friends with 'tomorrow's citizens'. Quite early on, the Teds had the approval of at least one churchman. In 1954 a vicar wrote to the *Evening Express* in Aberdeen praising Teddy Boys for having 'the courage to stand up to the crudities of this modern age'. He felt that the Teds, with their bright waistcoats and velvet collars, were reviving the good manners of the original Edwardian period, particularly courtesy towards other men, chivalry towards women and reverence towards God.

Their growing popularity certainly met with a reaction from the Church, not all of it welcoming. In 1955 a group of girls interviewed by *Picture Post* magazine expressed their resentment at being discriminated against at cinemas and churches. It was claimed that some London clergymen had banned Teddy Boys and girls from their services. It was as if their clothes represented a 'spiritual lack of grace'. A Liverpool parson recalled the time that some Teddy Boys tried to join in a church youth event: 'Fortunately we managed to produce some people who knew how to use their fists.' He admitted that Teds didn't often come their way. The parson would have been proud of a Cornwall vicar called Canon J.H. Parsons. At 69 years of age and six foot two inches, he knocked out a Ted who was insulting girls at his church social club. When the Ted swaggered in shouting and refused to leave, the vicar grabbed hold of his drape collar and the seat of his drainpipes and marched him out of the club, returning with blood on his hands having flattened the lad. The incident came a week after local Teds had broken up a dance.

Other clergymen took a dislike to rock 'n' roll. In 1956 a pastor of a Pentecostal church in Nottingham had a teenage boy and girl give a ten-minute demonstration of jive-dancing to a jazzed-up hymn played by the church band. The purpose was merely to show his congregation that rock 'n' roll music involved devil dancing in the tradition of black magic ritual and was liable to turn its hearers into lawless devil worshippers.

Bath and Wells Diocesan Youth Committee suggested having go-karts and a 'jive service' to attract young people to the Youth Festival to be held at Wells Cathedral at Whitsun in 1963. One vicar promptly resigned from the committee, believing that gimmicks were not needed to attract young people. He particularly objected to 'swinging the gospel' to pack 1,000 Teds and their girlfriends through the door.

He was perhaps being optimistic if he thought that he could attract that many Teddy Boys, particularly as by then they had largely disappeared. Furthermore Teds did not take easily to Christianity. In 1956 the BBC broadcast a programme called *About Religion*, with an Anglican priest from Peckham, South East London, taking on a group of sceptical Teddy Boys and Girls. The result seemed to be a goalless draw with neither side convincing the other. Sadly, some youths treated the Church with contempt. At Mirfield, in the West Riding of Yorkshire, Teds smashed the church window. The Vicar of Chesterfield, in Derbyshire, complained that Teds were stealing the parish magazines from the church and selling them about town. In Manchester some Teds not only held up a church service but, on another occasion, ripped the collection box from a church wall.

* * *

The Church was certainly concerned about the rise in Teddy Boy-related delinquency. 'Let us pray for the Teddy Boys,' urged the vicar of Royston, near Barnsley. In South East London, the vicar of St Paul's, Blackheath, asked from the pulpit, 'Do we condemn the Teddy Boys and think it is better to leave them out on the streets to get into all kinds of mischief and moral danger?' In his parish magazine, a vicar from Bognor Regis, West Sussex, claimed that the Teddy Boy lacked vitamin C – with the C standing for Christianity. Feeling no allegiance to a society that was too complex for him to grasp, the Ted was said to have retreated into a private world. With too much money in his pocket, and taking the Welfare State for granted, his exaggerated dress was subconscious compensation for an aimless personality.

The President of the Methodist Conference clearly had Teds in mind when, in 1956, he criticised a generation that was growing up fearing neither God nor man, and believing neither in itself or in anyone else: 'a generation all dressed up with nowhere to go'. In a letter to *The Times* it was claimed that delinquent youths, including Teddy Boys, were people who for some reason had never been integrated into an effective moral tradition. At an Anglican Young People's Conference, held in 1959, the Rev. E. Ashmore pointed out that most members of the Church Youth Fellowships tended to be grammar-school types. He felt that the Church was failing to touch the Teddy Boys.

For several years there had been various attempts to rectify this by bringing the Teddy Boys into the fold. Teds were certainly encouraged to attend one new Somerset church. At the opening of the building on the Sydenham Estate, Bridgwater, Rev. Gill welcomed Teddy Boys in drainpipe trousers as long as they behaved themselves. The problem was making faith relevant to young people. Some churchmen certainly achieved that. After being invited to the *Daily Mirror* Rock 'n' Roll Party, one vicar announced that he would recommend the music to his congregation in his sermon the following Sunday. In Gillingham, Kent, a vicar welcomed Teds to his dances. There were no reports of trouble.

The Bishop of Tewkesbury, the Right Rev. E.B. Henderson, was known as the 'Bopping Bishop' after he invited a rock 'n' roll singer to his diocese in Gloucestershire to show how to put religious songs and hymns to beat music. In 1954 Pastor Kayes hired a dance hall in Liverpool to run what was described in the press as a 'Sunday School for Cosh Boys'. It seems that some Teddy Boys would go merely to scoff but end up converted to Christianity. Religious songs with a beat were performed by a band led by Billy Bebop, while lads with long criminal records were also invited on stage to talk about their offending. One convert was Andy Barrett, an ex-borstal boy and former cosh-wielding Ted, who had his two nicknames, 'Boogie Amazon' and 'Buddy Jive', tattooed on his hands. After attending one of the meetings, and having a dramatic conversion, he dropped to his knees and prayed.

In 1956 Rev. F. Thewlis of Temple Street Methodist Church in Keighley, organised a series of functions aimed at attracting youths, particularly Teds, 'who don't go anywhere near the Church'. Acts were to include a jazz group made up of students from Leeds University, The Craven Thumpers, who were said to 'sound like a rock 'n' roll outfit', and the Bradford Teddy Boys' Band. The minister even invited the local King of the Teds, hoping that he would bring along his followers – which forced the 'King' to admit that there were only three real Teds in Keighley. It was hoped that once youths started going along to the events they would be inspired to join in the singing of 'The Happy Wanderer' and 'Davy Crockett' before moving on to more solemn classics such as 'Abide with Me'. The minister revealed that the character of each evening would gradually change, culminating in an appeal for new recruits to the Church.

In Oxford, Teds would gather at a cafe housing a jukebox. One night the Rev. Keith de Berry was insulted by a group as he walked past so he decided to strike up a conversation with them. They told him that they had nowhere to go, nothing to do and that the authorities were against them. Although there were youth clubs available, they didn't appeal. The Reverend invited about forty of them to his home at St Aldate's Rectory where they watched films.

Teds and their girlfriends in Southampton challenged a minister called Mr Samuel to preach specially to them. When only two turned up he sent out helpers to round up anyone wearing drainpipe trousers. Soon he had them listening to an hour-long sermon. Afterwards, one Ted admitted that Mr Samuel had guts and was obviously on their side. In 1957 the Rev. Ronald Hicklin, pastor of a church in Middlesbrough, was considering forming a skiffle group to accompany hymns sung by a Teddy Boy choir he had recruited. He explained, 'To attract youngsters you must keep up with the times.' No doubt a Maidstone curate would have agreed. In 1963 he wrote a kitchen-sink-style Nativity play in which a Teddy Boy drew a knife on a man. A 1959 British Pathé newsreel shows a group of Nottinghamshire Teddy Boys helping their local vicar to clean the Parish Church of St Stephen in Sneinton. The vicar, Rev. John Tyson, then rewards the boys by setting up a 'rock 'n' roll club' in the church hall, complete with jive room and coffee bar. Membership is nevertheless dependent upon attendance at Sunday evening mass.

Converting Teds soon became the aim of socially aware churchmen, though the task was not without its dangers. Rev. J. Melville Scutt, Rector of Edgware, Middlesex, formed a Teddy Boy club but was later beaten up in the church hall by some members. In a forgiving mood, the Rector declined to press charges against the boys after they were detained. The vicar of Barlborough, near Chesterfield, Derbyshire, had to arm himself with a walking stick en route to his church, after Teds threatened to punch him in the nose. The vicar was at war with the village Teds after banning rock 'n' roll at the church institute. Club dances had turned into riots with chairs and windows smashed.

When Rev. McCallum Young complained to the local council about the behaviour of Teds outside a dance hall in Greenock, Scotland, he received a threatening letter warning him that 'our chivs [knives] will be working overtime'. The letter was signed 'The Long Jackets'. The minister appealed to the youths for a meeting and received another letter agreeing but on three conditions: he was to come alone, he was not to reveal the venue and no police were to be involved. The outcome of the meeting was not reported.

Gangs of London Teds wrecked Golborne Free Congregational Church in North Kensington twice in two years. They were later won over by the two ministers and helped repair the damage. When Rev. Ernest Marvin took charge of a church in the Lockleaze district of Bristol he revealed how he attracted gangs of knife-wielding Teds. His congregation also included six lads who had been on probation and four ex-borstal boys. By reaching out to youths he ended up with 150 of them attending his evening service, some even putting money in the collection plate. He also managed to get the teenagers to present a controversial Passion Play set to beat music. He asked how the Church could call itself a family of God when part of that family (i.e. the Teds) was left outside.

* * *

Some men of the cloth felt the need to take their message outside of the church. In 1956 Methodist ministers the Rev. Brian Webb and Rev. Cyril Blunt toured mining villages in a caravan, preaching their message through music to young people in pubs and dance halls. At the Forrester's Arms in Doncaster, the pair belted out rock 'n' roll songs to their beer-swilling 'congregation'. Webb reasoned that you had to give people what they wanted, while his colleague maintained that religion and rock 'n' roll fitted well together. One convert was a fourteen-year-old boy who claimed to have given up swearing.

Forty miles away in Bradford there was a spate of gang warfare in 1956 between various groups, including the Abbey Mob, Nick's Lot, the Mau Mau and the Mambo Boys. In one incident, where three girls were stabbed, police made seventeen arrests. Rev. Maurice Barnett, Minister of the Bradford Yorks Methodist Mission, decided to shed his clerical collar and tour the local dance halls looking for gang members. From his pulpit he also appealed to leaders of the gangs to meet him in secret to talk of peace. He even visited lads in their homes. Out of these disarmament talks with seven gang leaders came the formation of a Teddy Boy Club held at Eastbrook Hall in Bradford.

On the first night thirty-three Teds turned up. The sign read, 'Teddy Club second door on the left'. One girl member regularly travelled from Leeds on the back of a motorbike. Rev. Barnett assumed the role of president while nine youths formed a committee. Various rules were drawn up, including no fighting, swearing, drinking or gambling. The club, which boasted a canteen and snooker room, eventually had up to eighty members, with five Teds even turning up for Sunday Mass. Although the club was born out of violence, violence was said to have stopped. One member explained that it was when lads had no money and nowhere to go that they caused trouble.

Also in 1956, churchwardens from Kensington Temple, a Pentecostal church in London's Notting Hill Gate, visited milk-bars to muster Teddy Boys to attend a service by Renee Martz, a visiting sixteen-year-old girl evangelist from Chicago. Converted at the age of four after receiving a vision, Martz had preached in thirty-seven countries. Fifty curious Teds turned up to see if Martz could convert them to Christianity. They were welcomed by 500 regular worshippers – although some weren't happy when a few lads nipped outside for a smoke during the service.

Those who were converted were invited for a chat with Renee after the service. One Ted used the occasion to ask her out on a date but she refused. A photograph of the event later appeared in an exhibition of British Press Pictures of the Year. The print, by Bela Zola of the *Daily Mirror*, was entitled 'Herald Angels' and showed three Teddy Boys clutching hymn books and looking ill-at-ease. One lad looks as if he is singing out of tune while another appears to be having trouble reading the words. Nevertheless, at least one ex-Teddy Boy, Bob Coachman, became an evangelist after listening to Renee Martz.

In Newbury, Berkshire, young Salvation Army members toured the coffee bars on the look-out for teenagers, and offering them a 'youth crush' consisting of a cold soft drink and a helping of the gospel. Major Fred Hopkins of the Wolverhampton Salvationists had a more robust approach:

> We aim to scour the town's coffee houses and dance halls to get the teddies to discard their drainpipes for a blue uniform. Most people think we are a lot of cissies. Our plan is to convince the town's hooligans that we can be as tough as they are. We will invite them to our clubs and give them exhibitions in Indian club swinging. Rough-house types will be more than welcome.

Such novel approaches had their successes. Former Reading Teddy Boy Donald Mundy would appear in full Edwardian uniform at open-air gospel meetings. In 1959 a London church installed a jukebox and offered live rock 'n' roll entertainment as part of its Sunday evening services. The congregation swelled from its usual 12 to about 200, although when the band began to play its first song some regular worshippers walked out in disgust.

* * *

Religion brought unexpected benefits for some. In 1956 an ex-Ted from Newcastle called Alan Perry registered as a conscientious objector. The 21-year-old was promptly released from a three-month prison sentence imposed for refusing to serve in the Army Reserve. Perry admitted that he used to go looking for trouble as part of a gang but was now a member of a church and aimed to make his old colleagues see the error of their ways. In 1959 another Evangelist, William Shufflebottom (alias Billy Highfield) from Stoke-on-Trent, Staffordshire, successfully appealed against his National Service. The former gang leader, who admitted to once carrying a gun and razor, claimed that he now had a conscientious objection to carrying arms and that his current work took him all over the country helping to convert Teddy Boys. He was instead allowed to work on a farm or in a hospital.

Nevertheless, for some a new-found love of religion was only a ruse, as King of the Teds Tony Reuter, who claimed to have been 'converted' after seeing evangelist Billy Graham at Wembley Stadium (see chapter 9), demonstrated.

25

TEDDY BOY INTERNATIONAL

'In different forms – and to different degrees – the Teddy boy problem and a serious increase in youthful lawlessness have in recent years affected a large part of the world.'

(T.R. Fyvel, 1961)

The 1950s were an era of worldwide youthful rebellion. T.R. Fyvel – whose book on the Teds was published in 1961 – speaks of 'the Teddy Boy International' to describe the growing destructive element. He attributes rising juvenile crime and aggression to a modern malaise linked to the breakdown of traditional authority, growing affluence and the negative images of youth portrayed in the media. These factors were said to lead to varying degrees of youthful cynicism and violent delinquency. In 1960, discussions at a United Nations Congress on Crime, held in London, centred on the worldwide rise in juvenile delinquency. Crime experts from eighty-six countries discussed their variations of the Teddy Boys.

Britain's Teds had contemporaries and counterparts not only in Europe but throughout the world. America, of course, led the way. From the late 1940s some fashion-conscious American youths styled their hair like Tony Curtis and wore white tee-shirts, black leather jackets, tight jeans with turn-ups and baseball boots. Unable to adjust to civilian life after the war, some ex-soldiers joined motorcycle gangs, particularly in California. These later became the Outlaw motorcycle gangs of the 1950s. The rebel image of the biker was popularised in the film *The Wild One*, featuring Marlon Brando as the leader of the The Black Rebels who ride from town to town drag-racing and drinking.

Numerous gangs, including The Bishops, The Jesters, The Streaks and The Dragons, sprang up in the projects and run-down tenements of New York boroughs such as Brooklyn, Manhattan, the Bronx and Queens. Gang members, or 'boppers', were mostly teenagers. Although many gangs were divided into ethnic groups, including Blacks, Italians, Irish and Puerto Ricans, some had a mixture of ethnic backgrounds. Often the gangs were highly organised with a President, Vice President and War Counsellor (who was responsible for setting up fights, scouting enemy territory and keeping the weapons inventory). Some of the larger gangs also fielded a 'junior' division. Younger members would 'graduate' to the 'senior' gang after proving their mettle in battle or when they came of age.

Gangs mostly fought over girls and 'turf'. Each had its own small strip of territory that they could call their own, where other gangs dared not intrude. Often there would be a 'no-man's land' between neighbouring areas. Gangs would stay on their own turf unless they were invading rival territory in search of a fight, or 'rumble'. This was a huge battle where twenty to fifty members on each side would meet at a pre-arranged location, often a park or school ground – with the battle often brokered by the 'war counsellors'. Another form of warfare was called 'japping'. This involved a small group of 'boppers' sneaking into enemy territory in order to beat up a lone rival gang member.

In the tough, overcrowded apartment blocks some gangs were formed purely to protect themselves. One Puerto Rican lad explained that he hadn't belonged to a gang until being harassed by The Gauls. In response the Puerto Ricans formed The Spanish Counts. The names of some of the gangs – Ambassadors, Phantom Lords, Viceroys, Dukes and Central Harlem's Noble Englishmen – suggest a craving for status, self-esteem and respectability that was at odds with their violent manner of gaining it. Despite the daily dangers of territorial warfare, members put gang loyalty before their own safety.

One lad explained, 'Sure, I'm scared of being knifed and maybe killed. But I'm more scared of being called chicken by the gang.'

In February 1956 Robert Kirby was stabbed to death for trying to date a girlfriend of one of the Corsair Lords. On the same day, after a fight with the Astoria Gents, James McGowan was stabbed in the chest. Fighting for his life in hospital the lad told a police officer pressing him for information that he hated all cops and would deal with the problem himself.

As well as the usual weapons of switchblades and knuckle-dusters, gangs also had access to baseball bats, spiked sticks, bullwhips, belts and rocks. Some gang members also wore shoes with metal cleats that cut into the victim's flesh. Those unable to afford guns used home-made firearms called 'zip-guns', sneakily constructed in school workshops. Stolen car radio aerials were also fired from elastic bands. In response some lads wore armour, such as square metal plates under their shirts.

Like British Teddy Boys the gangs were ably assisted by girlfriends and female followers, who were known as 'debs', with imitative names such as the Pythonettes and Campirettes. Since females were unlikely to be searched by the police, they were responsible for carrying the weapons: two-dozen girls held the guns when the Chaplains went to war with a rival gang.

Suggested solutions to the problem included 10 p.m. curfews, corporal punishment and the public humiliation of those convicted of gang violence. In Detroit a judge ordered two hoodlums to have their heads shaved. He explained that if the rowdies couldn't think any more than a billiard ball, then they might as well look like one.

* * *

In Australia they had Bodgies – and their female counterparts, Widgies. The first recorded Bodgies were seamen during the Second World War. The name means fake or bogus, a likely reference to the fact that these young men were impersonating

Americans who had recently occupied Australia as military personnel. The first Bodgie gang was the 'Woolloomooloo Yanks', based in the Sydney suburb of the same name, and by 1948 there were about 200 Bodgies hanging about Sydney's milk-bars. The seamy districts of Melbourne and Brisbane also had their own gangs. Lads dressed in leather jackets and drainpipe trousers and rode motorcycles and stolen cars. The Widgies wore bleached-blonde beehive hairstyles and tight, slit pencil skirts or narrow trousers called ski-slacks. The term Widgie stems from 'widgeon', meaning female teenager.

In April 1955 Melbourne police declared that the Bodgie cult was finished, an announcement that proved premature. A year later a Melbourne policeman estimated that more than 1,000 youths were members of the city's Bodgie gangs, with additional mobs in Bendigo, Ballarat and Geelong. Indeed, in 1956 about forty Melbourne Bodgies, cheered on by Widgies, fought a moonlit battle using fists, boots and sticks. In the November Brisbane experienced its first rock 'n' roll riot after a concert featuring local rockers Frankie Thornton and Barry Erickson. Bodgies and Widgies threw pennies at the police, smashed bottles on a police car and snatched policemen's hats.

In January 1957, outside Sydney's Paddington Town Hall, local Bodgies took on British sailor Teddy Boys from the liner *Orsova*. The next day about thirty Bodgies, riding in a convoy of six hot rods, went looking for their rivals. Spotting three seamen on the wharf, the Bodgies pounced. One sailor escaped but two were given a good kicking. A witness heard one of the attackers complain, 'I nearly broke my — foot on the —'. In April the Perth parents of a sixteen-year-old Bodgie dragged their hysterical son from a rock 'n' roll concert to hand him over to the police and have him charged as an 'uncontrollable child'. The following month at least 100 Bodgies and Widgies broke into a home in Melbourne while the owners were away and staged a five-day orgy of rock 'n' roll, sex, drink and destruction. The six-bedroomed house was wrecked and household goods either stolen or destroyed. In 1958 Melbourne police confronted a fifty-strong gang of young Bodgies aged between eleven and fourteen. Weapons confiscated included knuckle-dusters, a chain and stacks of pennies held together by adhesive tape to give added weight to their punches.

Press reporting of Bodgie outrages echoed British newspaper coverage of the Teds. Typical headlines included 'Savage Bodgie Brawls', 'Bodgie Razor Attack' and 'Bodgie in Bottle Attack' and, as in Britain, there were attempts to explain the phenomenon. Experts claimed that the Bodgies and Widgies were not lacking in intelligence or money but suffered from feelings of cynical hopelessness because their lives lacked purpose. They were also described as 'social boils' on the body of society.

Robust solutions to the menace also echoed those put forward in Britain. Some suggested sending the lads to do hard manual labour laying tracks with the rail gangs while others proposed putting them to sea under a tough naval skipper. Corporal punishment was another option. One sixteen-year-old Widgie was so penitent when she appeared before an Adelaide court that she begged to be flogged. She had recently joined a gang and indulged in immoral acts. Her wish was granted and she was given fifteen strokes of the birch.

By the early 1960s the Bodgies were finished, partly through the intensified actions of the police, partly through the taming of rock 'n' roll music and partly as a result of social remedies such as youth work. There was also less sensationalised coverage of youth disorder by the press and the term 'Bodgie' eventually faded from newspaper reports, replaced by 'larrikin', the old-fashioned and less glamorous term for a hooligan.

* * *

The Far East also had its fair share of rebellious cults, popularised in Japanese fiction. There was the colourful *Tayozoku* (Sun Cult or Sun Clan), who wore drainpipe trousers, sunglasses, Hawaiian shirts and sported crew-cut hairstyles. Some had their hair greased back in a style called *Shintaro*, after a character of the same name in a popular Japanese TV show. It was said that they drank whisky, brawled and made love with youthful and abandoned young women.

The Ducktails were a white South African delinquent group originating in the late 1940s in many urban areas. By 1958 they were notorious for acts of vandalism, car theft, assaults on innocent people and inter-gang warfare. Gangs took their names from their districts. Germiston, for example, boasted the Jeppe Gang, Fordsburg Deep Gang, North End Gang and the Primrose Boys. Distinguished by their ornate Brylcreemed hairstyles, the Ducktails wore a uniform of thick-soled shoes, worn with white or pastel socks and brightly coloured shirts with the tails flapping loosely outside their tight jeans. Gang members carried flick-knives, knuckle-dusters and revolvers, smoked *dagga* (marijuana) and beat up pedestrians after dark, particularly blacks, Indians and homosexuals. Reputations were often won by gatecrashing and trashing parties and beating up anyone who objected.

In 1958, after a rock 'n' roll show in Johannesburg's Selbourne Hall, a group of Ducktails stood on the balcony throwing empty bottles at the police outside. Inside, two policemen intervened as some lads tried to steal the takings from the female cashier. One lad jabbed an officer in the face with a fistful of knives and forks. Nine squad cars answered the call for help only to be met by a further hail of bottles from the balcony. The Ducktails then rushed down to fight the baton-wielding officers. The police fired twenty shots in the air to restore order.

Like their British counterparts the Ducktails had a violent relationship with the military. In 1957, after a soldier was beaten up and humiliated in a café in Pretoria, his colleagues banded together to ambush a gang of motorbike-riding Ducktails. They pulled a chain across the road to stop them before beating them up. Soldiers also entered the city and gave captured Ducktails a haircut.

* * *

It was in European countries, however, that variations of the Teddy Boys really thrived. An early inspiration on French youth was American cinema, particularly films such as *The Wild One* and *Rebel Without a Cause*, released in France in 1956. The arrival of rock 'n' roll music at around the same time had much the same invigorating effect as it did on British teenagers. Towards the end of the 1950s France had a new youth subculture in the *Blousons Noirs*, named after their black wind-cheater jackets. The term first appeared in the press in a report of a confrontation between gangs in the public gardens of Saint-Lambert, Paris. In July 1959 a large group of youths staged a riot on the seafront near Cannes. Armed with knives, sticks, buckled belts and bicycle chains they smashed property, harassed tourists and stoned the police. Their reason for beating up people was 'because we don't like their faces'. Similar riots broke out at other places on the French Riviera, culminating in an attack by Toulon youths on lads from the resort of Bandol ten miles away. In one incident twenty-six youths attacked a cafe. In the August, at Cannes, ten lads were arrested after causing trouble at an open-air dance, while in Paris a forty-strong gang used axes, bicycle chains and stones to assault innocent bystanders. After a disturbance in the Paris suburb of Drancy, 100 youths were taken into custody. In 1959 there were said to be seventy to eighty gangs operating in Paris alone.

Eventually the term *Blousons Noirs* fell out of favour, as black jackets were not universally worn, and the term was replaced by JVs – standing for *Jeune Voyou* (young hooligan). The girls were known as BBs after their attempts to look like the popular French actress Brigitte Bardot. Reasons offered for the wave of youth disorder included domestic overcrowding, which forced disaffected youths onto the streets, combined with a lack of public spaces and facilities for them.

In 1959, after motorists and several women were attacked in Milan, questions were tabled in the Italian Parliament about the activities of Teddy Boys. Holidaymakers were also attacked at resorts near Rome. A circular from the Minister of the Interior was sent to every police station ordering strong measures to combat the growing threat from gangs. The Italian Teds, who wore black leather jackets and blue jeans, were mostly from middle- and upper-class families. Concern was heightened after a nineteen-year-old girl stabbed to death a teenage boy after being accosted by five lads. It seems that she carried a knife for protection after previously being molested.

In 1960 tough action was declared on the Spanish equivalent of the Teds, the *Gamberros* (hooligans). Fines of between £6 and £30 (between £120 and £600 today) were proposed for anyone whose words or actions attacked others. The names of all *Gamberros* were also to be published in the press. In 1962 twenty-one were found guilty of disorderly behaviour at a bullfight and barred from returning for three months. They were forced to report to the police station an hour before each weekly fight and to stay until an hour after the event had finished. Because of such firm action there was said to be less hooliganism in Spain than in other countries.

The West German equivalent was the *Halbstarken* (Half-Strong or Half-Grown), a term that had been used for young working-class delinquents since the 1920s. As in France the*Halbstarken* found role models for their fashion and rebellious behaviour in movie stars such as James Dean and Marlon Brando. Lads sported quiffs, tight jeans (preferably authentic Levi's), checked shirts and leather jackets. Since tee-shirts were not widely available, youths wore their vests back to front to reveal the high-cut neck. Gangs followed Brando's lead by riding mopeds and motorbikes. Rock 'n' roll music also incited many youths to rebel. In 1956 Haley's 'Rock Around The Clock' reached number one in the German pop charts. In the same year Karin Baal and Horst Buchholz starred in the movie *Die Halbstarken* (also released under the title *Teenage Wolfpack*) about juvenile delinquents on the rampage. Due to a lack of leisure facilities, the *Halbstarken* spent a great deal of their spare time outdoors. Groups met on street corners, in parks or other public places. Such loafing behaviour wasn't appreciated by the older generation.

Although only about five per cent of German youths were involved in the movement, between 1956 and 1958 the *Halbstarkenkrawalle* ('Half-Strong riots') broke out in city after city throughout West Germany. These were spontaneous eruptions of youthful anger for no apparent reason, but sometimes blamed on the damaging influence of American popular culture or seen as a protest against the bleakness of post-war German society. The disturbances, however, were not thought to be directly politically motivated.

Usually they took the form of confrontations with the police, particularly at concerts or after watching movies. Youths would sometimes hold up traffic or take over public spaces, harassing people. In Hanover, in August 1956, groups of youths ran riot through the city smashing windows, stoning police cars and resisting arrest. The following month there were more widespread disturbances. Crowds of young people demonstrated on the streets of Frankfurt while in Brunswick police made baton charges to disperse a mob of 2,000. On 22 September 1956 *Rock Around the Clock* opened in the city of Duisburg to wild scenes. On 30 December, after another showing of the film, about 4,000 youths swaggered through Dortmund, insulting passers-by, rampaging and staging battles with the police. In the same year Austrian Teds raided a police museum at Graz and took their pick from the revolver exhibits.

Between March 1956 and March 1957 eighty-one riots were reported in West Germany, with a further nineteen disturbances by the end of 1958 – four of them involving over 1,000 youngsters. In Essen, in 1958, 8,000 teenagers rioted and tore up seats at a Bill Haley concert. By 1960 West Berlin had suffered 108 riots involving a total of 22,000 young people.

In September 1956 it was the turn of the Norwegian capital, Oslo, to experience riots connected with the showing of the Bill Haley film. Denmark also suffered rock 'n' roll-related disorder. As a result, in January 1957, Bill Haley was barred from playing in the country although the film *Rock Around the Clock* was eventually shown in Copenhagen on 5 August. There followed a week-long series of riots and a gun fight between the *Laederjackker* (Leatherjackets) and the police. It was the first time in Denmark that guns had been used by teenagers against the police.

In January 1960, in The Hague, capital of the Netherlands, the local version of the Teddy Boys began setting fire to Christmas trees discarded in the streets. When firemen tried to extinguish the flames they were pelted with stones and bottles. A riot erupted between police and youths which ended with up to forty people hospitalised and between 200 and 300 injured. A year later Teddy Boys once again began setting fire to unwanted Christmas trees. They then threw stones at the police, tore down traffic signs, smashed street lamps and damaged parked cars. Police drew their sabres to disperse the crowd. A sixteen-year-old boy was later found dead with two stab wounds.

Sweden's gangs were called the *Skinnuttar* (Leather Jackets) and *Raggare* (Picker Up), so-called after their practice of picking up girls in their flash cars. On the eve of the international motor race at Karlskoga in 1960, hundreds of *Raggare* met up to enjoy a night of violence and hooliganism. The lads, who wore leather jackets and their hair grown long, drove around Stockholm and other major districts in large, second-hand American cars picking up girls wearing tight slacks, sweaters and heavy make-up. The souped-up cars, which were customised with fox brushes attached to long aerials, boasted signs such as 'Live dangerously and die young' and 'Hell on wheels'.

Forty-five arrests were made after some youths camped near the race-track and set fire to a wood. Firemen trying to extinguish the fire were attacked by drunks wielding knives and broken bottles. Attempts were made to cut their hoses and a track watchman was hospitalised after trying to stop lads breaking into a racing depot. The disturbances were so bad that officials feared that the races might not be allowed to continue. The concern was justified. There was more trouble the following year. In all 107 youths were arrested at Karlskoga, all said to be members of Teddy Boy groups who had invaded the town once again for the motor races. To offset the threat, some municipal authorities installed their own race-tracks to occupy the lads.

In 1959 Greek Teddy Boys were responsible for a spate of anti-social behaviour. In one incident two lads, racing by in a stolen car, threw a cup of yoghurt in a woman's face. The culprits were caught, taken to the police station and later paraded through the streets wearing placards around their necks stating 'We are Teddy Boys'. Two other boys were arrested for throwing figs in a girl's face. The lads, who wore their hair long, were taken to the police barber who shaved their heads except for a patch in the middle. He also cut off the turn-ups of their narrow jeans. The lads were then paraded through the streets wearing placards stating 'I am an ass and a Teddy Boy'. Such unusual treatment did not seem to have any effect on their behaviour. Photos of the youths appeared in the press showing the lads smiling and looking quite unashamed.

Nevertheless, there were complaints about human rights infringements and accusations that the police were taking the law into their own hands – though when young men started attacking women in public parks and streets there were calls for tougher measures for convicted Teddy Boys. The Greek Minister of Justice called for Teds to be detained in isolated wards in provincial reformatories. Here they were to be subjected to a strict programme of education, physical training, manual labour and religious instruction. The minimum sentence available was also doubled so that youths could be given six months' imprisonment, including tough outdoor manual work. The Minister of Justice later reported that offences by Teddy Boys had dropped considerably.

Despite its Communist ideology the Soviet Union also had its own type of Teddy Boy. Fashion-conscious youths were known as *Stilyagi* (various translations include style boys, groomed boys and style hunter), an insulting label first used in 1949 in a satirical article in the journal *Crocodile*. The first *Stilyagi* had roots in the emotionally troubled generation which had endured the tough period of economic crisis and war. Behind the movement lay the struggle between Capitalism and Communism, between individual freedom and the uniformity of Stalinism. Alienated by enforced Soviet conformity, the *Stilyagi* became attracted to the delights of Western culture, particularly jazz music. Young men returning from military service also based their fashion ideas on British and American images they had found in films, newspapers and photographs. They wore long, greased hair combed straight back like Tarzan, draped jackets with padded shoulders, narrow trousers, ties with American motifs and thick crepe rubber-soled shoes, preferably in yellow or light tan.

By 1955 the *Stilyagi* had grown as an underground movement, attracting both respect and disapproval. Although the emerging Soviet upper-middle class, known as the 'intelligentsia', objected to the *Stilyagi*, they had become too large a group to be totally suppressed. Instead of trying to purge them, politicians and the media took to ridiculing their lifestyle and the *Stilyagi* became a target of official satire. *Izvestia* newspaper published an unflattering picture of Russia's shifty-eyed Teddy Boys with their trousers stuffed into their boots and sports caps tilted forward. Said to be partial to half a litre of vodka, they were accused of operating in gangs near dark entrances, hurling filthy abuse at passers-by, not to mention shoving women and insulting children.

The youth section of *Pravda* newspaper described the *Stilyagi* as wearing uniforms that turned them into monsters. In Moscow posters were displayed showing cartoon images of the Russian Teds and their girlfriends. The caption underneath declared: 'By foolish fashion they were captured ... they would be funny if they were not so pitiful.' In an echo of the humiliating treatment of the black-American Zooties, South African Ducktails and French *Zazous*, in 1958 members of the Communist Youth League patrolled the streets of Sverdlovsk and Ulyanovsk detaining and shaving the heads of the *Stilyagi*.

The World Festival of Youths and Students, held in Moscow in 1957, attracted thousands of people from 130 countries and resulted in the USSR becoming more open to the impact of modern Western culture. By the 1960s jazz music was no longer censured and recordings of popular music became increasingly available. These reforms helped dampen the youthful rebelliousness of the *Stilyagi*, who, like their British counterparts, slowly began to settle down into the dull routines of adulthood.

26

WHATEVER HAPPENED TO THE TEDS?

'Teenage rebellion? All my eye. Our memories are short. Mods and Rockers are exactly the same nine-day wonder as the Teddy Boys. The best thing is to take no notice of them.'

(A psychologist, 1964)

The Teds did not go quietly. In 1959 their swan song was to attract 3,000 newspaper headlines throughout the country – and the term Teddy Boy lasted well into the 1960s, usually in association with crime and violence. In 1965 a murder suspect claimed that the bloodstains on his clothes were caused by a fight with Teddy Boys. By the late 1950s, however, the Teds were already considered dinosaurs, mocked and caricatured in Colin MacInnes' novel *Absolute Beginners* by the 'primitive' figure of 'Ed the Ted', described by writer Jonathan Green as 'a knuckle-dragging Neanderthal'. In 1959 MacInnes wrote that although caricaturists continued to draw stereotypes, the absurd authentic Teddy style was now only to be found in remote locations. He claims to have last spotted it in a cafe in the picturesque village of Goring-on-Thames, Oxfordshire. By 1962 Worthing Museum, on the West Sussex coast, was asking for a Teddy Boy costume for its costume and textiles collection.

To be parodied, caricatured and displayed as an ancient relic was the cruel fate of the uniquely flamboyant and innovative Teddy Boys. Even hardened crime reporters seemed to suffer from amnesia. As the 1960s drew to a close and a new wave of drink- and drug-fuelled violence swept through the city, a *Liverpool Echo* journalist recalled reporting on the Teds years earlier. He explained, 'They were frightening enough but the 1969 pattern is more menacing. The Teddy Boys fought amongst themselves. Today the innocent bystander or pedestrian is the target for roaming gangs.' Already, the Teds were on their way to becoming beacons of morality in an increasingly savage world.

* * *

To the question 'what happened to the original Teds?', an obvious answer is that they grew up, got married and became parents. Liverpool MP Richard Bingham felt that once the Teds had sowed their wild oats, many of them would settle down to become useful citizens. For most the movement was simply a stage in life, a brief opportunity for working-class youths to enjoy themselves before graduating to lives of dull domesticity and boring jobs. On a 1965 radio programme called *The Teddy Boys Grew Up* one ex-Ted trotted out various reasons for lads giving up on the movement: courting, the demands of employment and becoming a parent. Indeed, a probation officer in the mid-1950s felt that sooner or later the Teddy Boy would have to leave his mates for marriage and find that he had to work hard to support his wife and children. A *Times* reader best summed it up: when the Teddy Boy has to provide for half a dozen children, he will take to wearing baggy trousers like the rest of us.

Even during the heyday of the Teds some were looking to the future and a different way of life. A Ted called Ron explained that he was going steady with a girl and wanted to get married. While not completely giving up on nights out with the boys he wanted 'to do something better'. What he wanted was a sense of responsibility along with somebody to love and look after.

Some questioned whether the Teds were capable of bearing that kind of responsibility. The Rev. W.J. Samuel, of Glamorgan, pondered what sort of parents the Teddy Boys would make, seeing that they were obsessed with spending all their money on their own pleasures. He felt that the problem could only get worse in another twenty years as their children grew up. Others disagreed. The Chief Constable of Lancashire thought that the Teds would become really tough parents and would not let their children behave as they had done. Perhaps he was right.

In 1968 the *Daily Telegraph* colour supplement ran a feature called 'Whatever Happened to the Teddy Boys?' Various ex-Teds from around the country were interviewed and photographed with their wives and children. They all appeared to have settled into happy domestic life. Dave Milward, from West Drayton, Middlesex, had swapped a love of fighting and Elvis Presley for marriage to a childhood sweetheart and was busy stocking up his home with the latest appliances. Dudley Noble, a commercial artist, lived with his wife and three children in Herne Bay, Kent. A veteran of the *Rock Around the Clock* disturbance at the Prince of Wales Cinema in Paddington, Noble was busy paying off his new radiators. Alan Endersby, a 32-year-old ex-member of the Catford Boys, lived on an estate in Stevenage, Hertfordshire, with his wife and two children. He admitted that marriage had changed him. Alan Wright, an ex-member of Midlands gang The Rebels (see chapter 8) was pictured in a woollen cardigan at his home on a Warwick estate. He was now married with two sons. Complaining of teenagers playing their transistor radios on the street corner, he expressed a desire to move to a quieter neighbourhood. His own wilder days were not forgotten and he still kept a wad of police court receipts, in lieu of a diary, detailing his former exploits.

That the Teds would inevitably experience the same generation gap that afflicted their own teenage years was a common theme in any interviews. In 1969 a documentary was shown on BBC2 called 'Where Have all the Teddy Boys Gone?' An interviewer spoke to five former Teds from Elephant & Castle. She found them responsible, hardworking family men who were beginning to show intolerance towards present-day youth. In 1970 Max Needham, from Tooting, South London, appeared in the *Sunday Times* with his thirteen-year-old daughter. Max, an original Ted, carried on the tradition by wearing a sky-blue drape with velvet collar and black-suede crepe-soled shoes set off by green luminous socks. Despite being force-fed rock 'n' roll music from birth, his daughter was into Skinhead clothes and loved reggae music. Her father was critical but tolerant. Interviewed in 2001, a 59-year-old former Teddy Girl who had married another Ted, a member of the Chiswick Mob, revealed that she had settled down after having children. She was now a pillar of the community and campaigned for the Conservative Party.

* * *

For the vast majority of young people growing up in the 1950s the Teddy Boy cult came and went, replaced by other working-class youth subcultures as decade followed decade. By 1959 some of the more well-off Birmingham Teds had begun to own 500cc motorbikes festooned with chrome accessories. Dressed in black skin-tight trousers, black leather jackets adorned with emblems, cravats and American-style helmets, they alternated between speeding along arterial roads for kicks and crawling along the pavement in search of girls. Social commentator Jeff Nuttall denies that these 'Teds on motorbikes', otherwise known as Rockers, were the direct descendants of the Teddy Boys: 'They were a younger generation who imitated the American pattern of rebellion.' Nevertheless both groups shared a love of rock 'n' roll music and had much more in common with each other than with the Rockers' legendary enemies, the Mods, who from the early 1960s followed an entirely different fashion trajectory.

Rather than looking back to the Edwardian past, some young Londoners looked forward – adopting a more modern, clean-cut Italian look, with shorter jackets and winkle-picker shoes. According to writer Simon Frith, 'The teds had, in the end, seemed like losers, desperate for attention.' For him the winners were the Mods, who made adults 'irrelevant' and became the 1960s 'symbol of consumption'. Later in the decade came the rise of the hippies, yet the peace and love movement, with its anti-uniform of patched denim jeans and long dishevelled hair, was the very antithesis of the ultra-smart and violent

Teds. For one commentator, Teds took a long time dying, but were finally kicked into the grave by the beatniks.

Although their style pre-dated rock 'n' roll the Teddy Boys became so bound up with the music that as the soundtrack of the 1950s changed so did the strength of the movement. By 1960, Buddy Holly, along with the Big Bopper and Ritchie Valens, had been killed in a plane crash; Gene Vincent had been injured in the same car crash that killed Eddie Cochran; Jerry Lee Lewis was still in disgrace after marrying his young second cousin; Little Richard had turned to religion; and Elvis had enlisted in the Army only to re-emerge as a film star with a broader appeal. In 1962, Chuck Berry was imprisoned after being found guilty of transporting an under-age girl across state lines for immoral purposes. As the music lost its big American stars, the record industry replaced them with an army of 'Bobbies' and 'Frankies', good-looking young men, often of Italian descent, who sang safe love songs such as 'Teenager in Love' and 'Bobby Sox to Stockings' aimed at adolescent girls. The raw edginess of rock 'n' roll had gone.

* * *

Despite this taming, the demand for 1950s-style rock 'n' roll never went away. Radio 1 DJ Tony Blackburn was allegedly sent a razor-blade sandwich through the post, accompanied by a message threatening to shove it down his throat if he didn't play a rocking record. Another disgruntled listener from Cardiff sent a blood-stained sock with a note promising to deliver another sock encased in a boot if Blackburn didn't play some rock 'n' roll.

It would also be wrong to give the impression that the Teds died away completely. Some of the originals continued wearing the clothes, enjoying the music and adopting the attitude throughout the 1960s and beyond. Ray Gosling claimed that he could spot a Ted walking down the street, even if he was a Ted fifty years ago, by the stride of his walk and his look of defiance. In the late 1960s the Black Raven pub in London's Bishopsgate began to host rock 'n' roll nights on

Fridays and Sundays. Some customers travelled forty miles to be part of the budding scene. The pub, with its jukebox packed with classic 1950s tunes, became an important centre for the national revival movement, although the pub's owner, Bob Acland, declared that it was impossible to revive something that had never died. Explaining the continuing popularity of the Edwardian style he was adamant that the Teds weren't a broken army, 'all gone down a hole like rats'. By 1972 the pub housed up to 300 Teds at weekends.

The surviving Teds stuck around long enough to enjoy the popularity. A more mean and moody Elvis had already made his comeback in 1968, the same year that Buddy Holly's 'Peggy Sue'/'Rave On' re-entered the charts, while Haley's 'Rock Around the Clock' became a hit again in March 1974. By the early 1970s rock 'n' roll music was undergoing a resurgence, culminating in a concert staged at Wembley in August 1972. A who's who of rock 'n' roll giants, including Bill Haley, Chuck Berry, Bo Diddley, Little Richard and Jerry Lee Lewis, turned up to thrill a crowd of 50,000, many wearing the original gear. In the same year, Savile Row tailor Lew Rose took nearly 1,000 orders for drape jackets and drainpipe trousers. He believed it was a reaction to the hippie movement.

A year later the film *That'll be the Day*, featuring David Essex and Ringo Starr, was released. Set in the 1950s and with a soundtrack of classic songs, the movie helped introduce the music to a younger audience. By the 1970s and 1980s, revivalist bands such as Showaddywaddy and Darts would go on to make frequent appearances on *Top of the Pops*, somewhat diluting the music but attracting a new generation to the movement. The image had become cuddly and safe, more teddy bear than Teddy Boy. Wearing brightly coloured drapes and covering some classic rock 'n' roll hits, Showaddywaddy popularised a sanitised version of the music and fashion. Meanwhile on TV, comedian Russ Abbott's sketch-show Ted was loveable but dim. All this was a far cry from the terror conveyed by the original Teds.

Unsurprisingly the original Teds sneered at the younger revivalists who, influenced by the current trend of glam rock, succeeded in getting the uniform all wrong, particularly the luminous colours. Older Teds mocked these teenagers by branding them 'plastic Teds'. Nevertheless these younger lads helped keep the tradition alive and many will have gone on to discover the original artists and a more authentic look. Meanwhile, the scene also thrived in the hands of less commercial but more authentic bands such as The Wild Angels, Matchbox, Crazy Cavan and the Rhythm Rockers, and the early Shakin' Stevens and the Sunsets.

Throughout Britain there were pockets of diehard Teds who kept the scene alive, often travelling to other districts for rock 'n' roll dance nights and performances. In the late 1970s Liverpool's Rumford Coach House held weekly rock 'n' roll nights, a trend repeated in pubs and clubs throughout the country. By now some Teds were wearing ever more flamboyant versions of the style, particularly brightly coloured drapes and thick crepe-soled shoes.

* * *

The birth of the Punk movement in 1976 sparked a number of town-centre skirmishes between the new generation of Teds and the Punks, clashes that were swiftly blown up by the press into a Mods versus Rockers-style war. In one incident, in Hammersmith, West London, a mob of Teds beat up some Punks outside the Tube station. There were also a few clashes in East London between Teds and Skinhead gangs in Brick Lane. During the summer of 1977, Teds and Punk Rockers fought ritual Saturday afternoon battles in the King's Road, Chelsea. One Ted explained that fifty colleagues had been done over by the Punks at Margate, Kent, on the Easter Bank Holiday. The Punks had also won a battle in King's Road. Since then, however, the Teds had evened the score.

In London's West End, in July 1977, Teds aged between fourteen and twenty-two went hunting for Punks, leaving a trail of destruction from Trafalgar Square through Chinatown and Soho into Oxford Street. They rampaged through the streets, throwing bottles at shop windows and forcing shopkeepers to close their doors. One stallholder was kicked. In another incident the next month, police moved seventy-five Teds from Sloane Square. There was no resistance but this did not stop the Punks kicking off and thirty youths later appeared in court. In an echo of certain press behaviour during the rock 'n' roll cinema riots of 1956, one Punk claimed that he knew people who were offered money by a photographer to throw bricks at the Teds. It seems that Teds were also offered the same incentive in a bid to manufacture some news.

The trouble continued sporadically for a few more years. In April 1979, Teds and Punks clashed at the Southend seafront in Essex. And in March 1980, 200 youths, a mixture of Teds, Skinheads and Punks, converged on Neasden underground station in North West London. A driver was injured as they rampaged through a waiting train, smashing windows and doors. Sledgehammers and shovels were also seized from a storeroom and used as weapons.

* * *

The early 1980s saw an unlikely Rockabilly revival, boosted by the British success of American band the Stray Cats. Rockabilly was the white southern country wing of rock 'n' roll, first popularised by Elvis Presley and other artists on the legendary Sun Records label in Memphis, Tennessee. The Teddy Boy movement was by now splitting into different factions, with some of the younger lads becoming Rockabillies or Hepcats and wearing a more American look of tee-shirts or check shirts, jeans and work boots. From the mid-1980s there was a counter-drive to return to authentic clothing roots, culminating in 1993/94 in the formation of The Edwardian Drape Society (TEDS), which promotes the original pre-1955 image of the Teds. The development of the internet also allowed Teds far and wide to communicate with each other, share photographs and memories and promote gigs and reunion weekends. In 2004, minus their leader Bill Haley who died in

1981, the remaining Comets, with a collective age of 445, were still performing and producing albums such as *You're Never Too Old to Rock*. In the mainstream clubs rock 'n' roll nights continue to the present day, some attended mostly for the opportunities for jive dancing as a more energetic alternative to the line-dancing craze. Although dismissed as 'jive bunnies' by the more authentic Teds, these enthusiasts help keep rock 'n' roll music alive in the clubs.

'Plastic Teds' and 'jive bunnies' are some of the more harmless terms that have been attached to newer followers of the Teddy Boy movement. The original Teds were called far worse. Over the years they have been labelled rebels, hooligans, reactionaries and xenophobic racists. The Ted has at times been the victim of press hysteria and misrepresentation. He has been analysed by psychologists, condemned by politicians and barred from cinemas but thankfully forgiven by churchmen.

Although during their heyday the Teds were seen simply as mindless thugs, social commentators and critics have now established the vital importance of the movement in British history. Teddy Boys were by no means the first violent youths, nor will they be the last. The Mods might have been more obsessed with clothes. The Skinheads might have been more obsessed with violence. The Teds, however, were style trendsetters and cultural innovators. For Alexander Plunket Greene, the husband and business partner of fashion designer Mary Quant, Teds 'started everything'. Once they had opened the floodgates, everyone else could follow. Pop culture simply exploded. Writer Jonathan Green claims that the Teds must be credited with sparking the 'whole teenager epic'. If that were not enough, Ray Gosling believes that the Teddy Boy movement was the most important rebellion in the hearts of the common people since the Protestant Nonconformist revolution of the seventeenth century. Nevertheless, it was an often bloody revolution, kick-started by the tragic death of seventeen-year-old John Beckley near Clapham Common. Over sixty years later, the fashions have changed but gang violence continues.

INDEX OF GANGS

British Gangs

Latchmere Lot (London)
Long Jackets (Greenock)
Mambo Boys (Bradford)
Mau Mau (Bradford)
Midnight Blue Gang (Liverpool)
Moss Side Gang (Manchester)
Mussies (London)
Nick's Lot (Bradford)
Nuneaton Boys (Glasgow)
Paddington Boys (London)
Peaky Blinders (Aston/Birmingham)
Plough Boys (London)
Putney Gang (London)
Quinton Lot (Birmingham)
Razor Boys (London)
Rebels (Warwick)
Rosehill Mob (London)
Salford Gang
Scuttlers (Manchester/Salford)
Snyder's Gang (West Bromwich)
Stick It Boys (Glasgow)
Swallow Gang (Liverpool)
Valleyfield Gang (Fife)
Walham Green Gang (London)
Walworth Gang (London)
Wythenshawe Gang (Manchester)

International Gangs

Ambassadors (United States)
Astoria Gents (United States)
Bishops (United States)
Blousons Noirs (Black Windcheaters – France)
Bodgies (Australia)
Campirettes (United States)
Chaplains (United States)

Dragons (United States)
Ducktails (South Africa)
Dukes (United States)
Fordsburg Deep Gang (South Africa)
Gamberros (Hooligans – Spain)
Gauls (United States)
Halbstarken (Half-Strong – West Germany)
Jeppe Gang (South Africa)
Jesters (United States)
Jeune Voyou (Young Hooligan – France)
Laederjackker (Leatherjackets –Denmark)
Noble Englishmen (United States)
North End Gang (South Africa)
Phantom Lords (United States)
Primrose Boys (South Africa)
Pythonettes (United States)
Raggare (Picker Up – Sweden)
Skinnuttar (Leather Jackets – Sweden)
Spanish Counts (United States)
Stilyagi (Style Boys – Russia)
Streaks (United States)
Tayozoku (Sun Cult – Japan)
Viceroys (United States)
Widgies (Australia)
Woolloomooloo Yanks (Australia)
Zazous (France)
Zooties (United States)

REFERENCES

To cut down on thousands of references to newspaper articles, I have decided to omit references to incidents involving Teddy Boys, as well as comments made about them, reported in the newspapers listed below, which are now available online and accessible in many libraries via the following platforms: the British Newspaper Archive (British Library), Gale NewsVault, ProQuest Historical Newspapers and UK Press Online. Each platform offers cross-searching of relevant newspapers. Articles are easily searched using dates, names and keywords.

British Newspaper Archive includes: *The Citizen*; *Courier and Advertiser*; *Evening Express* (Aberdeen); *Kensington News and West London Times*; *Reading Mercury*; *Somerset County Herald and Taunton Courier*; *West London Observer*; *Yorkshire Post and Leeds Mercury*

Gale NewsVault includes: *Daily Mail*; *Picture Post*; *The Sunday Times*; *The Times*

ProQuest Historical Newspapers includes: *Manchester Guardian*; *The Observer*

UK Press Online includes: *Church Times*; *Daily Express*; *Daily Mirror*

Brief references to all other printed paper sources are given in the following notes. Full bibliographic details are given in the bibliography.

Preface

Father of Ted in *Somerset County Herald*, 10 August 1957. Crime statistics in *The Times*, 1 March 1993 and Morris, *Crime and Criminal Justice Since 1945*, p. 96. Fyvel, *Insecure Offenders*, p. 75.

Chapter 1 – The Clapham Common Murder

Cohen in *Folk Devils*, p. 114. Nuttall, *Bomb Culture*, p. 29. This chapter is heavily indebted to Parker, *Plough Boy*.

Chapter 2 – Cosh Boys

Opening quote and cosh boy description in *Illustrated*, 24 Jan 1953. On the need for Teds to imitate Edwardian behaviour see *Liverpool Echo*, 10 May 1954 and *Nottingham Evening Post*, 28 February 1955. Jackson in *Crewe Chronicle*, 28 July 1956. *Salford City Reporter* on scuttlers, 9 September 1955. For history of scuttlers see Davies, *Gangs of Manchester*. Northern Irish Teds in Fowler, *Youth Culture in Modern Britain*, p. 110. For traditional gang behaviour see Pearson, *Hooligan*, p. 202. Parliamentary references in *Hansard*, 31 July 1952, 3 February 1949, 16 February 1950, 9 March 1950, 23 March 1950, 9 November 1950, 24 July 1952 and 31 July 1952. Pre- and post-war comparative criminal statistics in Hopkins, *The New Look*, p. 207, *Hansard*, 24 July 1952. Moore in *Hansard*, 6 May 1954. Leather straps in Collins, *The Likes of Us*, p. 153. Fabian in *London After Dark*, pp. 101, 107. Bentley and Craig in Yallop, *To Encourage Others*, p. 47. Spooner in *Velvet Collar*, issue 6, Sept-Oct 1998. 'Mantle of terror' in (Leicester) *Illustrated Chronicle*, 14 April 1956. For Teds worse than racecourse gangs see *Brighton and Hove Herald*, 20 November 1954. Birmingham Ted in *John Bull Illustrated*, 14 March 1959. Griffiths in Fyvel, *Insecure Offenders*, pp. 76-77.

Chapter 3 – The Origins of the Teddy Boy Style

Opening quote from *Derby Evening Telegraph*, 26 September 1956. Alternative history of Ted origins in Rushgrove, *Fashionable, Foolish or Vicious*, p. 3 and Ferris and Lord, *Teddy Boys,* p. 10. *Men's Wear*, 3 October 1953, p. 34. For zoot suits see Cosgrove, 'The Zoot-Suit and Style Warfare' and *Velvet Collar*, issue 13, April-June 2000. *Chicago Defender*, 14 November 1942. Gee in Cohn, *Today There Are No Gentlemen*, p. 20 and Chibnall, 'Whistle and Zoot', p. 68. Wain, *Hurry on Down*, p. 179. *Tailor and Cutter* cited in *Manchester Guardian*, 14 November 1953. *Zazous* claim in *The Times*, 11 August 1959. *Blousons Noirs* in Polhemus, *Street Style*, pp. 27-28. Alternative views of the geographical spread of Ted fashion in Cohn, *Today There Are No Gentlemen*, p. 29 and Springhall, *Coming of Age*, p. 199. Stucley, *Teddy Boys' Picnic*, pp. 120-21.

Chapter 4 – The Look

Opening passage from Pearson, *Sex, Brown Ale and Rhythm & Blues*, p. 10. Hair perms in Fyvel, *Insecure Offenders,* p. 45. Rose in *Picture Post*, 13 November 1954. Pountney in Kynaston, *Family Britain*, p. 80. Gosling, *Personal Copy*, pp. 42, 43. Powe in *The Sunday Times*, 5 June 1960. Eckler in *West London Observer*, 29 March 1956. McCullin, *Unreasonable Behaviour*, p. 30. Morris and arrested Liverpool Teds in (Liverpool) *Evening Express*, 24 & 26 May 1955. Ted called Robert in Kerr, *The People of Ship Street*, p. 115. For Western image of Teds see Jefferson, 'Cultural Responses to the Teds', p. 86 and Frith, *Sound Effects*, p. 185. Glasgow father in *Bulletin and Scots Pictorial*, 18 April 1956. Braddock in (Liverpool) *Daily Post*, 17 February 1958. Milward in Sandilands, 'Whatever Happened to the Teddy Boys?', p. 20. Cohn, *Today There Are No Gentlemen*, p. 31. Walham Green Gang in Scala, *Diary of a Teddy Boy*, p.16. Liverpool gang in *Liverpool Echo*, 9 February 1956. For parents' disapproval of

Edwardian uniform see Akhtar and Humphries, *The Fifties and Sixties*, p. 41 and Cohn, *Awopbopaloobopalopbamboom*, p. 68. Fabian, *London After Dark*, p. 104. Blantyre House in Home Office, *Report of the Commissioners of Prisons for the Year 1955*, p. 110. Melly, *Revolt into Style*, p. 170. Douglass in *Geordies – Wa Mental*, p. 203.

Chapter 5 – Delinquents in Drape Jackets

Nuttall, *Bomb Culture*, p. 29. Binder, *Peacock's Tail*, p. 385. Stucley, *Teddy Boys' Picnic*, pp. 120-21, 109. Woman from West Ham in Binder, *Peacock's Tail*, p. 384. Melly, *Revolt into Style*, pp. 37-38, 34. Birmingham Youth leader in *John Bull*, 14 March 1959. Reuter in *The People*, 5 & 12 June 1955. Irish observer on homosexuality in Fyvel, *Insecure Offenders*, pp. 64-65. Kerr, *The People of Ship Street*, pp. 167-68. Cohn, *Today There Are No Gentleman*, p. 33. Ford, *Delinquent Child*, pp. 159, 165. Lowson, 'Delinquency in Industrial Areas', pp. 53-54. Lambeth Teddy girl in *Daily Sketch*, 6 November 1954. For more of the meaning of the Edwardian style see Schulz, *The Function of Fashion and Style*, p. 13. Links between Edwardian style and homosexuality in Cole, *'Don We Now Our Gay Apparel'*, pp. 22-24. Parents' alarm at effeminacy in Montgomery, *The Fifties*, p. 157. Dunn in Kynaston, *Family Britain*, p. 380. Woolfenden and Liverpool passages in (Liverpool) *Evening Express*, 23 May 1955. O'Connor, 'The Youthful Offender', p. 88. Knife bully story in *Reading Mercury*, 29 March 1958. Harrogate Mayor and Southend youth councillor in Rock and Cohen, 'The Teddy Boy', pp. 291, 298. Scotland Yard's call for reports of Teddy incidents in *News Chronicle*, 1 May 1954. Kettering solicitor in *Velvet Collar*, issue 13, April-June 2000. Penge solicitor in *Evening Standard*, 7 May 1959. *Sunday Chronicle*, 28 February 1954. *The Star*, 7 & 8 May 1954. Liverpudlian on demonisation of Teds in *Liverpool Echo*, 13 July 1956. Prendergast in *Daily Sketch*, 7 May 1954. Blishen, *Roaring Boys*, pp. 177-80. Pupil's essay in *King's Norton Parent-Teacher Association Magazine* quoted in *Daily Mail*, 28 June 1955. Chapman in *Birmingham Mail*, 2 October 1958. For Teds having grudge against society see Fyvel, *Insecure Offenders*, pp. 54, 130.

Chapter 6 – Weapons

Opening quote from (Liverpool) *Evening Express*, 26 May 1955. Fabian, *London After Dark*, pp. 104, 101-102. Probation officer in *West London Observer*, 15 February 1957. Rogers in *Hansard*, 31 October 1958, 24 July 1952. Newcastle Ted in (Newcastle) *Evening Chronicle*, 29 November 1957. Metropolitan Police report in *Velvet Collar*, issue 12, January-March 2000. 'Shivs' in Marchant, 'The Making of Boy Gangsters', p. 42. Morley Ted in *Yorkshire Evening News*, 14 November 1955. Potato weapon in *Evening Standard*, 25 January 1956. Great Barr incident in *Birmingham Mail*, 29 October 1958. Shovel in *Manchester Evening Chronicle*, 17 February 1956. Forks in *Bulletin and Scots Pictorial*, 12 July 1954. Mattersey Thorpe brawl in *Nottingham Evening News*, 28 February 1955. Dumfries Ted in (Glasgow) *Sunday Mail*, 30 October 1955. Rhyl Ted in *Liverpool Echo*, 11 June 1956. Peachment in *Daily Sketch*, 18 October 1957. Slough incident in *Slough Observer*, 4 February 1955. Holloway gang in Rushgrove, *Hold the Front Page, Final Years*, p.13. Razor tattoos in *Dundee Weekly News*, 29 November 1958. 'Midnight Blue Gang', Liverpool shopkeeper and modified belt buckle in (Liverpool) *Evening Express*, 14 March 1956, 23 May 1955 and 21 April 1955. Liverpool cosh pockets in *Today: the New John Bull*, 20 August 1960. Banbury incident in *Banbury Advertiser*, 19 September 1956. Michael Davies' colleague in Parker, *Plough Boy*, pp. 245-55. Regent Dance Hall incident in *Sunday Chronicle*, 21 November 1954 and *Brighton and Hove Herald*, 20 November 1954. Leicester Teds and Harding in (Leicester) *Illustrated Chronicle*, 9 and 23 July 1955. Ex-Ted's view of knife crime upon leaving Navy and lavatory chain weapon in Fyvel, *Insecure Offenders*, pp. 61, 129. Lowestoft incident in *Fashionable Foolish or*

Vicious. Brynmawr incident in *South Wales Echo*, 18 August 1958. Lead belt in *Essex Chronicle,* 3 April 1959. Studded belts in (Wolverhampton) *Express & Star*, 24 June 1958 and 23 April 1959. Moston Ted in *Manchester Evening Chronicle*, 3 February 1958. Bonner and Liverpool's 'jungle law' in *Liverpool Echo*, 11 July 1956. Fish-hooks behind lapels in Akhtar and Humphries, *The Fifties and Sixties*, p. 41. Stucley, *Teddy Boys' Picnic*, p. 38. Ford, *Delinquent Child*, p. 164.

Chapter 7 – Gangs

Somerset County Herald, 13 December 1958. Symons, *Progress of a Crime*, p. 45. For insignificance of British delinquent gangs and fashion uniformity interpreted as social uniformity see Rock and Cohen, 'The Teddy Boy', p. 299, 293, 295. Brislington shooting in *Bristol Evening Post*, 3 November 1955. Girl shot in *Daily Sketch*, 9 November 1955. Revolver incident in *Yorkshire Evening Post*, 27 February 1956. 'Natural' leader in Marchant, 'The Making of Boy Gangsters', p. 17. Huddersfield solicitor in *Yorkshire Evening News*, 12 September 1957. Figures about London gangs, Fyvel on gang leaders, Ted crying in cell, revelations of bus conductor, planning of revenge missions and London probation officer on boys joining gangs in *Insecure Offenders*, pp. 69, 106, 145, 53-55, 63. Downes, *Delinquent Solution*, p. 117. Plough Boy quotes from Parker, *Plough Boy*, pp. 24-25, 28. Birmingham gangs in *John Bull Illustrated*, 14 March 1959. *Sunday Graphic*, 1 March 1959. Fabian, *London After Dark*, p. 103. Unfavourable views of Liverpool Teds and New Brighton Arcade incident in (Liverpool) *Evening Express*, 23 & 25 May 1955. Lambeth Boys in Hoggart, 'Lambeth Boys', p. 107. Melly, *Revolt into Style*, p. 34. Johns in Akhtar and Humphries, *The Fifties and Sixties*, p. 41. Philips in *Yorkshire Evening News*, 1 July 1957. Endersby and Wright in Sandilands, 'Whatever Happened to the Teddy Boys?', pp. 22, 23.

Chapter 8 – Pitched Battles

MP for Brighton Kemptown in Rock and Cohen, 'The Teddy Boy', pp. 29. Brighton battle in *Sunday Chronicle*, 18 April 1954. Marmaduke St and other Liverpool incidents in *Liverpool Echo*, 30 August 1954 and 26 & 31 May 1958. Shoreham-by-Sea incident in *Sussex Daily News*, 11 April 1955. Scots and Irish Teds in *Coventry Evening Telegraph*, 21 April 1955. 'Bingo Boys' in *Daily Record*, 3 May 1955. Nuneaton Boys in *Bulletin and Scots Pictorial*, 7 April 1956. Clydebank incident in *Daily Record*, 13 April 1956. Smethwick incident in *Smethwick Telephone*, 6 July 1956. Hebburn incident in (Newcastle) *Evening Chronicle*, 16 June 1956. Whitley trouble in *Whitley Bay Guardian*, 6 April 1956. Shepperton incident in *Evening Standard*, 11 June 1956. Battersea lads in *Evening Standard*, 27 June 1956. Burton's Dance Hall in *Liverpool Echo*, 24 February 1956. Southport battles in *Southport Guardian*, 7 & 31 March 1956. Wythenshawe incidents in *Manchester Evening News*, 16 & 29 June and 5 July 1956. Wythenshawe fight in *Wythenshawe Recorder*, 27 July 1956. Blandy, *Razor Edge,* pp. 11-12. St Albans incident in *Herts and St Albans Times*, 22 November 1957. Breward incident in *Velvet Collar*, issue 13, April-June 2000. Hockley and Snyder gangs in (Wolverhampton) *Express & Star*, 9 December 1957. For more on Marwood see Kirby, *Death on the Beat*, pp. 30-48. Glossop incident in *Manchester Evening News*, 23 September 1958. Wavertree and Bootle incidents in (Liverpool) *Evening Express*, 20 May 1955 and 14 March 1956. Watford disturbance in *Daily Herald*, 21 March 1959. Wallington incident in *Evening Standard*, 2 October 1957. Tamworth incident in Rushgrove, *Teddy Boy Violence 40 Years Ago*. Ratby incident in *Leicester Mercury*, 28 April 1958. Dagenham versus Canning Town feud in Fyvel, *Insecure Offenders*, pp. 86-88. Dean versus Budd mob in *Evening Standard*, 7 January 1959. Stourport battles in *Birmingham Evening Dispatch*, 31 March 1959 and (Wolverhampton) *Express & Star*, 23 April 1959. Hedley Wood incident in *Barnett Press*, July 11 1959.

Express, 4 February 1955. Black Widows in *Sunday Post*, 20 November 1955. Turner in (Glasgow) *Evening News*, 5 May 1959. Richardson, Howards store, Harrow magistrate, Wicker Cinema, Everton vigilantes, Tooting broken nose and Stowmarket usherette in Rushgrove, *The Truth About Teddy Girls* and *Velvet Collar*, issue 41, July-December 2009. Warwick schoolgirl in *Leamington Morning News*, 29 November 1956. Lichfield girl in *Lichfield Mercury*, 12 April 1957. Psychiatrist in *Weekly News*, 16 April 1960. Shrewsbury girl in *Shrewsbury Chronicle*, 16 September 1955. Griffiths in *Sunday Pictorial*, 9 May 1954. Dagenham girls in *Essex Chronicle*, 27 August 1954. Eagle tattoo in *Sunday Mercury*, 11 December 1955. Wolverhampton Chief Constable in *Daily Sketch*, 19 April 1958. Birmingham girls in *John Bull Illustrated*, 14 March 1959. Hainault dance in *Ilford Pictorial and Guardian*, 10 November 1955. Alhambra Theatre in *Manchester Evening News*, 30 May 1959. Ford, *Delinquent Child*, p. 163. *South London Advertiser*, 13 May 1954. *Banbury Guardian*, 9 February 1956. Blackpool Tower in *Manchester Evening News*, 12 January 1955. North East aggressive girls in *Daily Sketch*, 16 October 1953. Kingston girls in *Daily Sketch*, 9 August 1954. Portsmouth seventeen-year-old in *Bulletin and Scots Pictorial* , 17 July 1954. Ipswich girl in *Evening Standard*, 17 October 1957. Teddy girl and grandfather in *Porth Gazette*, 19 July 1958. Knives in hand-bags in Parker, *Plough Boy*, pp. 245-55. South London Girls carrying knives in *South London Advertiser*, 6 June 1958. Black Angels in *Daily Sketch*, 20 August 1954. Reading incident in *Reading Standard*, 13 December 1954. Heckmondwike girl and Galleon Gang in *Heckmondwike Herald*, 4 March 1955. Bath incident in *Daily Herald*, 30 May 1955. Tooting loss of teeth in *Tooting Advertiser*, 13 August 1955. Widnes girls in *Widnes Weekly News*, 26 August 1955. Pontypridd fight in *Empire News and Sunday Chronicle*, 22 January 1956. Dike in *Bristol Evening World*, 3 May 1957. Halifax girl in *Yorkshire Evening News*, 2 February 1959. Shoplifting girls in *Weekly News*, 16 April 1960. Riches in *Brentford and Chiswick Times*, 31 January 1958. Southampton girls in (Southampton) *Advertiser and Gazette*, 17 October 1958. Milnrow incident *Manchester Evening News*, 10 June 1959. Dundee usherette in *Dundee Weekly News*, 8 August 1959.

Chapter 11 – Teds Versus the Military

Ford, *Delinquent Child*, p. 160. Teds' anti-Americanism in Fyvel, *Insecure Offenders*, pp. 138-39. Bootle fun-fair incident in (Liverpool) *Evening Express*, 2 & 10 March 1955. Cowglen incident and 'Tiffies' in *Bulletin and Scots Pictorial*, 10 May 1954 and 12, 13 & 16 April 1956. Petty officer in *Dundee Courier and Advertiser*, 10 April 1956. Manchester cadets in *Manchester Evening Chronicle*, 17 February 1956. Speke cadets in (Liverpool) *Evening Express*, 31 October 1956. Ear bitten off in *Portsmouth News*, 19 October 1956. Train incident in *Manchester Evening News*, 26 September 1958. Brentwood incident in (Liverpool) *Daily Post*, 15 October 1958. East Anglians in *Essex Chronicle*, 3 April 1958. Kane in Rushgrove, *Dangerous Youth*, p. 3. Newberger, Monckton and Kilmarnock incidents in (Glasgow) *Evening Times*, 10 December 1954, 21 November 1955, 12 August 1955. Colindale incident in *Hendon and Finchley Times*, 15 July 1955. Greenwich incident in *Kentish Mercury*, 6 January 1956. Fountainbridge in *Velvet Collar*, issue 6, September-October 1998. Chelmsford attack in Rushgrove, *Teddy Boy Violence 40 Years Ago*, p. 4. Casino Ballroom and Warrington Station incidents in *Liverpool Echo*, 12 January 1956 and 26 January 1957. Braintree incident and Fell in *Evening Standard*, 14 June 1958 and 23 January 1956. Bruningthorpe airmen in Rushgrove, *Hold the Front Page, Final Years*. Prescot bus in *Prescot and District Newspaper*, 17 November 1955. Liverpool bus crash in *Liverpool Echo*, 13 October 1955. Judo training in *Dundee Courier & Advertiser*, 19 November 1955. Teds dodging bus fare and Nottingham Teds on bus in Fyvel, *Insecure Offenders*, pp. 55, 20. Boyd-Carpenter in *Hansard*, 9 November 1961. Bus groping incident in Langford diary quoted in Kynaston, *Family Britain*, p. 499. Wavertree bus incident in (Liverpool) *Evening Express*, 7 November 1955.

Chapter 12 – 'Long Jackets and Short Tempers'

Title taken from *Manchester Evening News*, 5 July 1956. *Smethwick Telephone*, 9 May 1958. Victimised Ted, response to 'Cocky', man heaved through window and Wilkie incident in Fyvel, *Insecure Offenders*, pp. 45, 66-67, 16, 20. Tamworth Teds in *Nuneaton Evening Tribune*, 28 October 1959. Workington incident in *Cumberland Evening Star*, 22 October 1958. West Earlham youth in *Eastern Evening News*, 1 July 1958. Edinburgh stabbing in (Glasgow) *Evening Times*, 21 February 1956. Birmingham Ted in *John Bull Illustrated*, 14 March 1959. Boy butted in face in (Liverpool) *Evening Express*, 31 October 1956. One-armed man in (Newcastle) *Evening Chronicle*, 28 May 1956. Gosling, *Personal Copy*, pp. 34-35. Battersea Teds in *South London Press*, 17 April 1956. Goose Fair in *Nottingham Evening News*, 8 October 1956. Collins in *Kilburn Times*, 17 January 1958. Loughborough gang in *Yorkshire Evening Post*, 6 November 1957. Series of Liverpool incidents in (Liverpool) *Evening Express*, 23 May 1955. Stoning of dog in Rock and Cohen, 'The Teddy Boy', p. 309. Choirboy in *Manchester Evening Chronicle*, 9 March 1959. Colne vandalism in *Blackburn Evening Telegraph*, 15 August 1958. Southend to London train incident in Steele-Perkins and Smith, *The Teds*, [p. 3]. London schoolteacher in *Evening Standard*, 24 January 1956. Smashing of train bulbs in Sandilands, 'Whatever Happened to the Teddy Boys?', pp. 26-27.

Chapter 13 – Just Rock 'n' Roll

Pickett in *Bury Times* 30 May, 1958. Fyvel on dancing, on adverse effects of music, validity of musical careers for Teds, Teds not having to think while listening to jukebox and London probation officer on the danger of cafes in *Insecure Offenders*, pp. 53, 126, 99, 63. Jive corner in *Eastbourne Gazette*, 12

January 1955. Bill in Akhtar and Humphries, *The Fifties and Sixties*, p. 36. New Brighton doormen and fair in (Liverpool) *Evening Express*, 23 & 16 May 1955. Foxtrot reminiscence in Gosling, *Personal Copy*, p. 43. Dene in Turner, *Halfway to Paradise*, p. 118. Early dance hall trouble and Glasgow fair in Rushgrove, *Fashionable, Foolish or Vicious*, pp. 13, 19, 25. Rowntree and Lavers, *English Life and Leisure*, p. 282. Cardiff Teds in *South Wales Echo*, 8 March 1955. 'Black Duffle Coat Gang' in Steele-Perkins and Smith, *The Teds*, [p. 7]. Batley fight in *Batley News*, 12 October 1957. Barnsley dance in *Sheffield Telegraph*, 14 March 1959. Croydon incident and London journalist in *Evening Standard*, 16 March 1959, 25 January 1956. Hill and Wooler in Leigh, *The Best of Fellas,* pp. 54-57. 60-61, 78-79. Leazes fair and Tynemouth's Chief Constable in (Newcastle) *Evening Chronicle*, 3 & 17 April 1956. Greenock fair in *Bulletin and Scots Pictorial*, 10 May 1958. Leicester fair in *Leicester Mercury*, 11 May 1959. 'Pagan altars' in *House of Lords Debate over Magistrates Powers and Control of Clubs.* Jukebox statistics in *Daily Mirror*, 26 June 1956 and Horn, *Juke Box Britain,* p. 169. Number of espresso bars in Hopkins, *The New Look*, pp. 459-60. Descriptions of jukebox cafes and milk bars in *The Observer*, 19 June 1955 and Fyvel, *Insecure Offenders*, pp. 97-104, 128. Protection money in *Sunday Graphic*, 1 March 1959. Probation officer's criticism of coffee bars in *Illustrated Magazine*, March 1958, quoted in Everett, *You'll Never be 16 Again*, p. 31.

Chapter 14 – Cinema Wars

Opening quote from *Manchester Guardian*, 13 November 1956. Isaacs in *Hansard*, 21 November 1955. Fyvel on Teds in cinemas in *Insecure Offenders*, pp. 107-108. Trouble at Huyton and Prescot cinemas in (Liverpool) *Evening Express*, 4 March 1955. Gosling's reminiscences in *Personal Copy*, pp. 31-32. Scala, *Diary of a Teddy Boy*, p.21. Melbourne Cinema in *Leicester Mercury*, 9 November 1955. Queen's Gaumont in (Newcastle) *Evening Chronicle*, 23 August 1956.

Favourable reactions from boy and cinema manager to *Rock Around the Clock* in Kynaston, *Family Britain*, pp. 654-55. Warning about Gaumont, Shepherd's Bush in Whitcomb, *After the Ball*, pp. 226-27. Croydon incident in Bicat, 'Fifties Children: Sixties People', pp. 324-25. *News Chronicle* letters quoted in Kynaston, *Family Britain,* pp. 654-55. Experts' views on disturbances in *Daily Mirror*, 12 September 1956. Lloyd's broker quoted in *Velvet Collar*, issue 8, January-March 1999. Stevenage seat burner in Montgomery, *The Fifties*, p. 165. Fletcher in 'Beat and Gangs on Merseyside', p. 153. Liverpool doctor and Liverpool ban in *Liverpool Echo*, 13 & 15 September, 1956. 'Ginger' incident in *Derby Evening Telegraph*, 25 September 1956. Venue without seats quoted in Rushgrove, *Teddy Boy*, p.33. Bootle and Colne incidents in Akhtar and Humphries, *The Fifties and Sixties,* pp. 42-43. Burnley incident in *Crosby Herald*, 7 September 1956. Riots in European cities and use of police dogs at Cleveleys in Rock and Cohen, 'The Teddy Boy', pp. 310, 308. Figures about the number of incidents at cinemas in Whitcomb, *After the Ball*, p. 226 and *The Times*, 15 September 1956. Official reactions to disturbances in Home Office file on the impact of Rock 'n' Roll, HO 300/6 quoted in Travis, *Bound and* Gagged, p. 109. Journalist at Bethnal Green in (Newcastle) *Sunday Sun*, September 16th, 1956. Loog Oldham, *Stoned*, pp. 28-29.

Chapter 15 – Race Wars I: Nottingham

Fountaine in *Daily Express*, 17 August 1977. *Bravo* quote in 'Die Ganze Welt Rockt und Rollt', *Bravo*, 30 September 1956, in Poiger, *Jazz, Rock and* Rebels, p. 89. Harrison in *Evening Standard*, 27 July 1957. Teds as racial group, tough Cypriot cafe owner, Walworth Road incident, Teds' racial abuse of West Indians in the street and getting off buses in Fyvel, *Insecure Offenders*, pp. 56, 102, 40, 16, 44. Gosling, *Personal Copy*, pp. 34-35. Wolverhampton sign in *Daily Herald*, 7 February 1956. Smethwick incident in *Birmingham Evening Dispatch*, 8 October 1956. Brighton march in (Brighton) *Evening Argus*, 3

September 1956. Singh attack in *Leamington Morning News*, 15 February 1958. Sheffield fairground in *Sheffield Star*, 20 May 1958. Night watchman in Montgomery, *The Fifties*, p. 165. Statistics about Cypriots in *Picture Post*, 14 June 56, p. 11. Walker, *Cosh Boy*, pp. 157-58. Figures about the number of black people in Britain from Walvin, *Passage to Britain*, p. 111. Braithwaite, Scobie and Irons in Phillips, *Windrush*, pp. 162, 167, 168-69. Nottingham racial population figures in Glass & Pollins, *Newcomers*, p. 131. West Indian with torn suit in Hiro, *Black British White British*, p. 39.

Chapter 16 – Race Wars 2: Notting Hill

Teddy Boy 'creed' courtesy of Institute of Race Relations in Wickenden, *Colour in Britain*, p. 38. Young boy's views on the Queen in *The Observer*, 7 September 1958, quoted in Glass, *Newcomers*, p. 145. Ex-Ted's views on black people and youth club leader on cause of racial attacks in Fyvel, *Insecure Offenders*, pp. 79, 85. Hamm quoted in Skidelsky, *Oswald Mosley*, p. 510. Mosley in *European*, October 1958, also quoted in Skidelsky, p. 511. On Teds turning to peer leaders see Ellis, 'The Younger Generation', p. 215. May in *Gloucester Citizen*, 3 April 1959. Blackheath incident in *Oldbury Weekly News*, 9 April 1959. Pakistani cafe in *Wednesbury Borough News*, 18 April 1959. 'Darkie gets chivved' in *Manchester Guardian*, 4 September 1958. BBC radio interview with 'Teds' and threat of more trouble in Glass, *Newcomers*, pp. 261-69, 263. Adams, Anderson, Braithwaite and Weekes reminiscences in Phillips, *Windrush*, pp. 183, 166, 174-75. Ages of those arrested, Teds deflecting attention from the authorities and Teds jumping on the bandwagon in Pilkington, *Beyond the Mother Country*, pp. 129. Denning in *Hansard*, 8 April 1959. Pannell in *Hansard*, 5 December 1958. Rogers in *Hansard*, 30 October 1958. Teds as scapegoats in Rock and Cohen, 'The Teddy Boy', p. 314. Shepherd's Bush cafe discussed in *Velvet Collar*, issue 6, October 1998.

Chapter 17 – Teds and the Media

On Teds as scapegoats see Osgerby, *Youth in Britain Since 1945*, p. 121. Edelman in *Hansard*, 16 March 1959. Dunn in Kynaston, *Family Britain*, p. 381. On the effects of the press presence on the disturbances see Fryer, *Staying Power*, p. 377. 'Self-appointed guardians of the peace' in *Nottingham Evening News*, 26 August 1958. Reaction to 'conception' of Teds, press treatment of Teds after 1954 and boy thrown into the Thames in Rock and Cohen, 'The Teddy Boy', pp. 300, 302, 312. Braddock in (Liverpool) *Daily Post*, 17 February 1958. Steele-Perkins and Smith, *The Teds*, [p. 9]. Birmingham Ted in *Velvet Collar*, issue 8, January-March 1999. 'Three Disc Spinners' in (Newcastle) *Evening Chronicle*, 13 September, 1956. 'That's us brother' in *Manchester Guardian*, 11 September 1956. For the creation of moral panics see Cohen, *Folk Devils*. Home Office files, HO 300/6 quoted in Travis, *Bound and Gagged*, pp. 109-10. Knight incident in *Bournemouth Times*, 8 June 1956. Journalist threatened in *Walthamstow Guardian*, 21 September 1956. *Widnes Weekly News*, 22 April 1955. Bromley conference in *Bromley and Kentish Times*, 18 March 1955. Fyfe's response and Teds blamed for crime in Springhall, *Coming of Age*, pp. 204-6. Melly, *Revolt into Style*, p. 34. Young Conservatives in Leech, *Youthquake*, p. 2. *Tailor and Cutter*, November 1953. 'Teddy Boys in army uniform' in *News Chronicle*, 10 December 1956. Edwardianism as synonym for 'thug' in *Daily Sketch*, 7 May 1954. Alleged damage to youth club by Teds and press behaviour after Marwood execution in Fyvel, *Insecure Offenders*, p. 21, p. 90. Mistiming of authority's response to Teds in Rock and Cohen, 'The Teddy Boy', p. 306. Mazzetti in Hewison, *In Anger*, p. 193. Macalister Brew, *Youth and Youth Groups*, pp. 136-37.

Chapter 18 – Defending the Teds

'New Elizabethans' in Bentley 'New Elizabethans', p.18. Martin in *Liverpool Echo*, 24 October 1957. Debating Society in *Herts Advertiser and St Albans Times*, 14 March 1958. Domestic Teds in Northern Ireland and Haughton in Child Welfare Council, Minutes, 15 March 1957 discussed in Fowler *Youth Culture in Modern Britain*, p. 110. Huyton youth and Teds as 'misplaced angels' in (Liverpool) *Evening Express*, 3 November 1955, 23 May 1955. Bury Teds in *Manchester Evening News*, 5 September 1956. Drummond's views in Turner, *Halfway to Paradise*, p. 44. Lewes councillor in Rock and Cohen, 'The Teddy Boy', p. 304. Isaacs in *Hansard*, 18 March 1957. Exeter floods in *Hansard*, 11 November 1960. Harry in *Daily Mirror*, 4 September 1954. Teds and skiffle in Bradley, *Understanding Rock 'n' Roll*, p. 127. Leach in *Rocking City*, pp. 18-19. Hornsby in Fowler, *Youth Culture in Modern Britain*, p. 108. Ford, *Delinquent Child*, p. 159.

Chapter 19 – Understanding the Teds

Whittington-Egan, (Liverpool) *Daily Post*, 3 January 1956. Henriques in (Liverpool) *Evening Express*, 30 September 1950. Family doctor in *Evening News*, 12 May 1954. Dance in *Hansard*, 26 November 1958. Fyvel views paraphrased by Downes, *Delinquent Solution*, p. 124. Avey in *County Express*, 25 January 1958. Drifting youth of the Welfare State in Jephcott, *Some Young People*, pp. 6-7. Teds being the result of boredom and affluence in Leech, *Youthquake*, pp. 2-3. Montgomery on children overcoming greed and the welfare state diminishing responsibility of parents in *The Fifties*, pp. 167, 163. Paget in *Hansard*, 11 April 1961. Conservative Party's view on prosperity in Cooper & Nicholas, *Crime in the Sixties*, pp. 12-14. Consumerism 'sapping moral fibre' in Morris, *Crime and Criminal Justice Since 1945*, pp. 94, 95. Working-class consumer spending in Abrams, *The Teenage Consumer*. Barstow, *Desperadoes*, p. 173. For Ted as a bogeyman on which adults projected anxieties see Davis, *Youth and the Condition of Britain*, p. 149. BMA on welfarism in *The Adolescent*, p. 5. Cumella in (Liverpool) *Evening Express*, 24 May 1955. Burt in *News Chronicle*, 5 May 1954. Plough Boys on war in Parker,

Plough Boy, pp. 26, 25. Rogers in *Hansard*, 16 February 1956. Ford, *Delinquent Child*, pp. 161-62. Stucley, *Teddy Boys' Picnic*, p. 55. War Museum and gangs in *Special Report and First, Second and Third Reports from the Committee of Public Accounts*, 1956-57, p. 18 (Evidence of L.R. Bradley). Crime figures in Morris, *Crime and Criminal Justice Since 1945*, p. 90. Wilkins also in Rock and Cohen, 'The Teddy Boy', p. 315. Scott in *Bulletin and Scots Pictorial*, 2 December 1954. Griffiths in *Daily Mirror*, 1 April 1952. Walker, *Cosh Boy*, p. 135. Borstal officer on offenders' hellish backgrounds in Fyvel, *Insecure Offenders*, p. 123. One Nation Group, *The Responsible Society*, p. 58. Economic Research Council, *Social Problems of Post War Youth*, p. 8. National Union of Conservative and Constitutional Associations. Conservative Political Centre, *Youth Astray*, p. 42. Conservative Political Centre, *The Responsible Society*, p. 60. Influence of social factors on crime in Mays, *Growing Up in the City*, p. 73 and Cohen, *Delinquent Boys*.

Chapter 20 – Class Wars: Work, National Service and Education

Liverpool headmaster, Bootle employment officer, Martin and sending Teds to Cyprus in *Liverpool Echo*, 9 February 1956, 20 January 1956, 24 October 1957, 11 July 1956. Moore in *Evening Standard*, 23 January 1956. Prendergast in *Daily Sketch*, 7 May 1954. Midlands interview ban in *Sunday Mercury*, 21 December 1958. Tipton Ted in (Wolverhampton) *Express & Star*, 21 August 1956. 1958 report on shortage of jobs in *Manchester Guardian*, 7 December 1958. Idwal Jones in *Hansard*, 28 October 1958. Merchant Navy Teds in King, *No Paradise*, p. 69. National Union of Seamen in *Velvet Collar*, issue 13, April-June 2000. Shipping company ban in *Daily Herald*, 10 April 1956. Paget in *Hansard*, 11 April 1961. Begg in *Leamington Spa Courier*, 30 May 1958. Bristol's Lord Mayor in *Bristol Evening World*, 30 May 1958. For working-class youths' lack of aspirations see Downes' views paraphrased in Rock and Cohen, 'The Teddy Boy', pp. 316-17. Fighting qualities of Teds in *The Sunday Times*, 6 November 1958. Relf in *West Bromwich Chronicle*, 9 May 1958. Delinquency in the army in Spencer, *Crime and the Services*. Birmingham airman in *Birmingham Evening Dispatch*, 13 May 1955. Nesscliffe Teds in *Oswestry Border Advertiser*, 5 September 1956. Cumella in (Liverpool) *Evening Express*, 24 May 1955. Teds as 'morons' in Montgomery, *Fifties*, p. 164. Blantyre House in Home Office, *Report of the Commissioners of Prisons for the Year 1954*, p. 86. Ford on conscription and wearing Ted uniform as compensation in *Delinquent Child*, pp. 160, 159. *The Star*, 8 May 1954. King George's Jubilee Trust in *Citizens of Tomorrow*, pp. 17-18. Mays, *The Young Pretenders*, pp. 26, 169. Semi-heroic status of Teds in Springhall, *Coming of Age*, pp. 195-96. Teds buying status through clothes in Jefferson 'Cultural Responses to the Teds', p. 85. Hopkins, *The New Look*, p. 428. The Ted as 'yob' in Brake, *Comparative Youth Culture*, p. 73.

Chapter 21 – Punishment

Blantyre House in *Report of the Commissioners of Prisons for the Year 1954*, p. 86. Excerpts from Conservative Party speeches from 78th Annual Conference, pp. 95-102. Radio programme discussed in *Church Times*, 15 January 1965. Borstal figures from Ellis, 'The Younger Generation', p. 214. Pre- and post-war reactions to Borstals in Shichor & Delos, *Critical Issues in Juvenile Delinquency*, p. 293. Stamford House Remand Home and Midland probation officer in Fyvel, *Insecure Offenders*, pp. 178-79, 73. Heswall Nautical Training School, Liverpool cinema manager, probation officer, Ted clothing maxim, Assistant Recorder of Liverpool City Quarter Sessions and Waterhouse in (Liverpool) *Evening Express*, 27, 23 & 26, 25 May 1955. Joyce and the banning of Edwardian clothing in Ward, *The Hidden Boy*, pp. 71-72. Blackburn headmaster in *Blackburn Evening Telegraph*, 14 October 1959. Brighton Regent Dance Hall in *Brighton and Hove Herald*, 20 November 1954. Marlborough magistrate in

The Star, 7 May 1954. Grafton in Adams, *Hard Nights*, p. 105. Palais de Danse incident, Blackpool cinema manager, Bristol parent, British Army of the Rhine uniform ban and Acton and Newcastle-upon-Tyne magistrates in Rock & Cohen, 'The Teddy Boy', pp. 297, 303, 305, 298-99, 304, 303. Brankin in *Halifax Daily Courier*, 23 June 1955. Speed in (Bradford) *Telegraph & Argus*, 31 March 1956. Wolverhampton magistrate in (Wolverhampton) *Express & Star*, 8 May 1959. Dartford Juvenile Court in *Evening Standard*, 24 February 1954. Hendon magistrate in Binder, *Peacock's Tail*, p. 384. Stevens' Bill in *Hansard*, 7 March 1958. Dance's in *Hansard*, 16 May 1958. Lipton in *Hansard*, 6 May 1954. Anonymous police officer in *Police Chronicle and Constabulary World* also discussed in (Liverpool) *Evening Express*, 23 December 1955. Hicks-Beach in *Hansard*, 2 May 1958. Fallon in (Liverpool) *Daily Post*, 25 May 1954. Effect of the 1948 Act on the subsequent crime figures in Cooper and Nicholas, *Crime in the Sixties*, p. 29. Arbuthnot in *Hansard*, 28 June 1956. Haddon letter in Kynaston, *Family Britain*, p. 381. Heckstall-Smith, *Eighteen Months*, pp. 118-19.

Chapter 22 – Policing

Fabian in *Empire News*, 9 May 1954. Petition in *Chingford Guardian*, 9 November 1956. Colchester campaign in *Essex County Standard*, 2 December 1955. Newcastle action in (Newcastle) *Evening Chronicle*, 17 August 1955. Alloa action in *Glasgow Evening Citizen*, 17 August 1955. Policing of Teds in Liverpool and Huyton in (Liverpool) *Evening Express*, 23 May 1955 and *Liverpool Echo*, 11 July 1956. Wavertree funfair in *Liverpool Echo*, 18 June 1955. 'War' on Teds and 'Operation Teddy Boy' in *Sunday Dispatch*, 27 June 1955. Kingston police dog in Rock and Cohen, 'The Teddy Boy', p. 303. Liverpool dogs in *Daily Herald*, 6 April 1956. Sussex Alsatians in (Brighton) *Evening Argus*, 16 October 1958. Oldbury action in *Sunday Mercury*, 5 January 1958. Manchester action in *Manchester Evening News*, 26 September 1958. Birmingham Ted in *John*

Bull Illustrated, 14 March 1959. Bristol police harassment in *Western Daily Press*, 23 September 1961. Gillingham vigilantes in *Sunday Dispatch*, 26 June 1955. Liverpool vigilantes in (Liverpool) *Evening Express*, 26 May 1955 and *Liverpool Echo*, 11 July 1956. Toreador in *Sheffield Star*, 6 November 1958. Use of the stocks in Conservative Party, 78th Annual Conference, pp. 95-102. Convicted Northern Irish Teds in O'Connor, 'The Youthful Offender', p. 89. Family doctor in *Evening News*, 12 May 1954. MacInnes, *Absolute Beginners*, p. 144. Use of chlorpromazine in Rock and Cohen, 'The Teddy Boy', pp. 307-8.

Chapter 23 – Youth Work

Youth worker in Gillis, *Youth and History*, pp. 198-99. Diamond in *Hansard*, 11 February 1958. Leather in *Hansard*, 28 October 1959. Fyvel's tour of desolate night life, 'Lower stratum' of Teddy Boy society and Griffiths in *Insecure Offenders*, pp. 97, 125, 57. 'Prayers and table tennis' in Marchant, 'The making of Boy Gangsters', p.42. 'Leicester experiment' in *Lady Albemarle's Boys*. Teen Age Canteens in Brew, *Youth and Youth Groups*, pp. 160-61. Bristol Social Project in Spencer, *Preliminary Report of the Bristol Social Project*. Morris and Baker, Bootle YMCA and Everton Teds in (Liverpool) *Evening Express*, 26 May 1955, 27 June 1958, 8 August 1955. Reuter in *The People*, 5 & 12 June 1955. Butterworth in *Evening Standard*, 23 January 1956. Noble in Sandilands, 'Whatever Happened to the Teddy Boys?', p. 21. Lockway Club in *Thames Valley Times*, 3 December 1958. Camberwell youth centre in Rock and Cohen, 'The Teddy Boy', p. 294. Discussion about Teds' rejection of youth clubs in Jefferson, 'Cultural Responses to the Teds', p. 83. Griffiths on life's tameness in *Youth and Crime*, quoted in *Daily Mirror*, 1 April 1952. Sussex doctor in *Lancet*, quoted in *Daily Mirror*, 12 June 1959. Townsend, *The Young Devils*, pp. 203-4. Liverpool FC Teds in (Liverpool) *Daily Post*, 31 March 1956. Golf hut in *Birmingham Evening Dispatch*, 4 November

1956. Skating incidents in *Wood Green and Southgate Weekly Herald*, 27 April 1956 and *Romford Times*, 19 November 1958. Outward Bound in *John Bull Illustrated*, 14 March 1959. Somerset annual meeting in *Herts Advertiser and St Albans Times*, 29 May 1959. Girl Guides needing rescuing in *Leigh Chronicle*, 1 May 1959. Dundee Boys' Brigade in *Dundee Evening Telegraph*, 2 August 1958.

Chapter 24 – Religion

Gosling, *Lady Albemarle's Boys*, p. 13. Church ban on Teds in *Picture Post*, 4 June 1955, pp. 37-38. Scutt in *Daily Sketch*, 23 March 1956. Liverpool parson in (Liverpool) *Evening Express*, 26 May 1955. Mirfield Teds in *Yorkshire Evening News*, 23 June 1958. Manchester Teds in *Manchester Evening News*, 18 & 27 September 1956. Keighley minister in *Yorkshire Evening News*, 10 October 1956. Greenock minister in *Bulletin and Scots Pictorial*, 2 & 9 April 1956. Royston vicar in *Barnsley Chronicle*, 9 July 1955. St Paul's vicar in *Velvet Collar*, issue 6, September–October 1998. Gillingham vicar in *Chatham News*, 15 July 1955. Salvation Army's mission to Teds and jukebox in church in Hylton, *From Rationing to Rock*, p. 56.

Chapter 25 – Teddy Boy International

Fyvel on Teddy Boy international in *Insecure Offenders*, pp. 233, 34. Detroit judge in *Reveille*, 19 November 1954. All other American material from *Evening Standard*, 4 February 1956. Bodgies in Moore, 'Bodgies, Widgies and Moral Panic in Australia, 1955-1959', pp. 3-4. Number of Melbourne Bodgies in *Melbourne Herald*, 9 April 1955 and *Sun-Herald*, 17 June 1956. Brisbane incident in *Sydney Morning Herald*, 22 November 1956. *Orsova* incident in (Australian) *Daily Mirror*, 22 January 1957. Uncontrollable child in *Sydney Morning Herald*, 9 April 1957. Melbourne rock 'n' roll party in (Liverpool) *Evening Express*, 15 January 1957. Improvised knuckle-dusters in *Melbourne Herald*, 4 May 1957. Bodgie headlines from (Australian) *Daily Mirror*, 30 April 1957, 22 January 1957 and *Melbourne Herald*, 7 January 1956. Bodgies as 'social boils' in Manning, *The Bodgie*, p. 68. Solutions to the Bodgie problem in *Perth Daily News*, 7 October, 16 November 1957. Widgie begging punishment in *News of the World*, 8 July 1956. Ducktails in Mooney, 'Ducktails, Flick-Knives and Pugnacity'. Drancy incident and Hanover riot in Montgomery, *The Fifties*, pp. 166-67. *Halbstarken* and figures on number of German riots in Poiger, *Jazz, Rock and Rebels*, pp. 78-81. Copenhagen riots in Blevgad, 'Newspapers and Rock and Roll Riots in Copenhagen', p. 154. *Stilyagi* in Ball, *Imagining America*, pp. 185-86. *Izvestia* article discussed in *The Times*, 6 June 1957.

Chapter 26 – Whatever Happened to the Teds?

Psychologist in *Evening Standard*, 19 May 1964. Green, *All Dressed Up*, p. 8. MacInnes, 'Sharp Schmutter' in *England, Half English*, p. 150. Liverpool crime reporter in *Liverpool Echo*, 1 December 1969. Bingham in *Velvet Collar*, issue 6, September-October 1998. Ex-Ted Ron in Fyvel, *Insecure Offenders*, p. 46. BBC 2 programme, 'Where Have all the Teddy Boys Gone?' discussed in *The Times*, 4 August 1969. Nuttall, *Bomb Culture*, p. 35. Frith, *Sound Effects*, p. 220. Beatnik quote in Hamblett & Deverson, *Generation X*, p. 146. Punks and Teds being offered money by photographer in Everett, *You'll Never be 16 Again*, p. 137. Plunket Greene in Cohn, *Today There Are No Gentlemen*, p. 35. Green, *All Dressed Up*, p. 5.

ACKNOWLEDGEMENTS

The author would like to thank the editors and publishers of the following newspapers for permission to quote passages: *Banbury Guardian*; *Bristol Evening World*; [Brighton] *Argus/Evening Argus*; *Bury Times*; *County Express*; *Dundee Courier*; *Dundee Weekly News* (D.C. Thomson); *Eastern Daily Press*; *Evening Standard*; *The Guardian*; *Heckmondwike Herald*; *Herts Advertiser*; *Liverpool Echo*; *Liverpool Daily Post*; *News of the World/News Syndication; Nottingham Post*; *Porth Gazette*; *Sheffield Star*; *Shrewsbury Chronicle*; *South Wales Echo*; *Western Daily Press*; *Wolverhampton Express and Star.*

Quotations from *The Citizen*, *Courier and Advertiser*, [Aberdeen] *Evening Express*, *Kensington News and West London Times*, *Reading Mercury*, *Somerset County Herald and Taunton Courier*, *West London Observer* and *Yorkshire Post and Leeds Mercury* reproduced with kind permission of The British Newspaper Archive (www.britishnewspaper-archive.co.uk)

Newsquest Media Group Limited kindly allowed permission to quote from *Bournemouth Times*; *Brentford and Chiswick Times*; *Sussex Daily News* and *Walthamstow Guardian.*

The author would also like to thank the following individuals, publishers and organizations for permission to quote material: Christie Books for D. Douglass *Geordies – Wa Mental*; George Pearson for *Sex, Brown Ale and Rhythm & Blues*; Dewi Lewis Publishing for C. Steele-Perkins and R. Smith *The Teds*; Economic Research Council for *Social Problems of Post War Youth*; McGraw-Hill and Open University Press for D. Bradley *Understanding Rock 'n' Roll: Popular Music in Britain 1955-1964*; Oxford University Press and Institute of Race Relations for J. Wickenden, *Colour in Britain*; British Medical Association for *The Adolescent*; Constable and Robinson for D. Ford, *The Delinquent Child and the Community* and S. Frith, *Youth, Leisure, and the Politics of Rock*; Joseph Rowntree Charitable Trust for B.S. Rowntree and G.R. Lavers, *English Life and Leisure: A Social Study*; Elsevier for J. R. Gillis, *Youth and History: Tradition and Change in European Age Relations, 1770 – Present*; British Film Institute for *Sight and Sound*; I.B. Tauris for E. Pilkington, *Beyond the Mother Country: West Indians and Notting Hill White Riots*; Taylor and Francis for S. Cohen, *Folk Devils: the Creation of the Mods and Rockers* and D. M. Downes, *The Delinquent Solution: a Study in Subcultural Theory*; Macmillan for V. Bognador and R. Skidelsky, *The Age of Affluence, 1951-1964*, M. Akhtar and S. Humphries, *The Fifties and Sixties: a Lifestyle Revolution* and R. Skidelsky, *Oswald Mosley;* Random House for T.R. Fyvel, *The Insecure Offenders: Rebellious Youth in the Welfare State*; Deputy Keeper of the Records, Public Records Office of Northern Ireland for Child Welfare Council Minutes (HA/13/113); Conservative Party for National Union of Conservative and Constitutional Associations. Conservative Political Centre, *Youth Astray: A Report on the Treatment of the Young Offender*; One Nation Group, *The Responsible Society*; *78th Annual Conference.*

The following libraries and organisations kindly posted material: Newcastle Library, Staffs, Glasgow Life, Bradford Local Studies, Sandwell Council Community History and Archive Service, Leeds Local and Family History Library. The Document Supply staff at Liverpool John Moores University also provided research material.

A big thanks to Peter Walsh for helping resurrect this project after I had spent many years gathering material on the Teds. The huge newspaper research project undertaken and published periodically by Teddy Boy historian and archivist Brian A. Rushgrove has also been invaluable. Brian's task has been to index and record every British newspaper article on

Standard; *Evening Argus* (Brighton); *Evening Chronicle* (Newcastle);*Evening Express* (Aberdeen); *Evening Express* (Liverpool); *Evening News*; *Evening News* (Glasgow); *Evening Sentinel* (Stoke); *Evening Standard*; *Evening Times* (Glasgow); *Express & Star* (Wolverhampton); *Glasgow Evening Citizen*; *Gloucester Echo*; *Halifax Daily Courier*; *Heckmondwike Herald*; *Hendon and Finchley Times*; *Herts Advertiser and St Albans Times*; *Ilford Pictorial and Guardian*; *Illustrated Chronicle* (Leicester); *Izvestia*; *Kensington News and West London Times*; *Kentish Mercury*; *Kilburn Times*; *Leamington Morning News*; *Leamington Morning Spa*; *Leamington Spa Courier*; *Leicester Evening Mail*; *Leicester Mercury*; *Leigh Chronicle*; *Lichfield Mercury*; *Liverpool Echo*; *Manchester Evening Chronicle*; *Manchester Evening News*; *Manchester Guardian*; *Melbourne Herald*; *News Chronicle*; *News of the World*; *Nottingham Evening News*; *Nottingham Evening Post*; *Nuneaton Evening Tribune*; *The Observer*; *Orpington & Kentish Times*; *Oswestry Border Advertiser*; *The People*; *Perth Daily News*; *Politiken*; *Portsmouth Evening News*; *Pravda*; *Prescot and District Newspaper*; *Reading Mercury*; *Reading Standard*; *Reveille*; *Reynolds News and Sunday Citizen*; *Romford Times; Salford City Reporter; Sheffield Star*; *Sheffield Telegraph*; *Shrewsbury Chronicle*; *Slough Observer; Smethwick Telephone*; *Somerset County Herald and Taunton Courier*; *South London Advertiser*; *South London Press*; *South Wales Echo*; *Southport Guardian*; *The Star*; *Sun-Herald*; *Sunday Chronicle*; *Sunday Dispatch*; *Sunday Empire News*; *Sunday Graphic*; *Sunday Mercury*; *Sunday Mail* (Glasgow); *Sunday Pictorial*; *Sunday Post*; *Sunday Sun* (Newcastle); *Sunday Times*; *Sussex Daily News*; *Sydney Morning Herald*; *Telegraph and Argus*; *Thames Valley Times*; *The Times*; *Tooting Advertiser*; *Walthamstow Guardian; Wednesbury Borough News*; *Wednesbury Times*; *Weekly News*; *West Bromwich Chronicle*; *West London Observer*; *Western Daily Press*; *Whitley Bay Guardian*; *Widnes Weekly News*; *Wolverhampton Chronicle*; *Wood Green and Southgate Weekly Herald; Wythenshawe Recorder*;

Yorkshire Evening News; *Yorkshire Evening Post; Yorkshire Post.*

Journals

Bravo; *Esquire*; *The Face*; *Family Doctor*; *European*; *Illustrated Magazine*; *John Bull Illustrated*; *King's Norton Parent-Teacher Association Magazine*; *Lancet*; *Outfitter*; *Man about Town*; *Men's Apparel Reporter*; *Picture Post*; *Police Chronicle and Constabulary World*; *Tailor and Cutter*; *Today: the New John Bull Illustrated; Tribune*; *Varsity*; *Velvet Collar.*

Parliamentary papers

PP 1956-57, *Special Report and First, Second and Third Reports from the Committee of Public Accounts.*

PP 1955-56 Cmnd. 9547 Home Office. *Report of the Commissioners of Prisons for the year 1954.*

PP 1956-57 Cmnd. 10 Home Office. *Report of the Commissioners of Prisons for the year 1955.*

Hansard

House of Lords Debate over Magistrates Powers and Control of Clubs in House of Lords, 1 June 1960, vol. 224.

Unpublished theses

Watson, Jonathan Paul, '"Beats Apart": A Comparative History of Youth Culture and Popular Music in Liverpool and Newcastle upon Tyne, 1956-1965', PhD thesis, University of Northumbria, 2009.

Documentary films

Reisz, Karel, *We Are the Lambeth Boys.*

British Pathé, *Teddy Boys Help Church.*

Radio programmes

BBC, *Any Questions?*

BBC, *Black and White.*

BBC, *The Teddy Boys Grew Up.*

TV programmes

BBC, *About Religion.*

BBC, *Special Enquiry* [into the Teddy Boys].

BBC, *Where Have All the Teddy Boys Gone?*

Novels

Barstow, Stan, *The Desperadoes*, London: Corgi, 1973. Originally published in 1961.

Blishen, Edward, *Roaring Boys*, London: Panther 1972. Originally published in 1955.

Burgess, Anthony, *A Clockwork Orange*, London, Heinemann, 1962.

MacInnes, Colin, *Absolute Beginners*, London: MacGibbon & Kee, 1959.

Ryman, Ernest, *Teddy Boy*, London: Michael Joseph, 1958.

Symons, Julian, *The Progress of a Crime*, London: Thriller Book Club, 1961.

Wain, John, *Hurry on Down*, Harmondsworth: Penguin, 1960. Originally published by Secker & Warburg, 1953.

Walker, Bruce *Cosh Boy*, London: Harborough Publishing Co., 1959.

Semi-published material

Rushgrove, Brian A., *Dangerous Youth.*

Rushgrove, Brian A., *Fashionable, Foolish or Vicious.*

Rushgrove, Brian A., *Hold the Front Page, Final Years.*

Rushgrove, Brian A., *Teddy Boy*, 1994.

Rushgrove, Brian A. *Teddy Boy Violence 40 Years Ago.*
Rushgrove, Brian A. *The Truth About Teddy Girls.*

Reports and surveys

Abrams, Mark, *The Teenage Consumer*, London: London Press Exchange, 1959.

British Medical Association, *The Adolescent*, London: BMA, 1961.

Cooper, Beryl Phyllis and Garth Nicholas, *Crime in the Sixties*, a Bow Group pamphlet, London: Conservative Political Centre, 1963.

Economic Research Council, *Social Problems of Post War Youth*, London: ERC, 1956.

Gosling, Ray, *Lady Albemarle's Boys*, London: Fabian Society, 1961.

Griffiths, Douglas, *Youth and Crime*, London: Epworth Press, 1952.

Home Office, *Penal Practice in a Changing Society: Aspects of Future Development (England and Wales)*, London: HMSO, 1959. Cmnd.645.

Home Office Research Unit, *Delinquent Generations: a Paper Based on a Communication to the British Association for the Advancement of Science (Section J) at Their Meeting in Glasgow, 1958*, Studies in the Causes of Delinquency and the Treatment of Offenders; 03, by Leslie T. Wilkins, London: HMSO, 1960.

Jephcott, Pearl, *Some Young People*, London: Allen & Unwin, 1954.

King George's Jubilee Trust, *Citizens of Tomorrow: A Study of the Influences Affecting the Upbringing of Young People*, London: Odhams, 1955.

LPA, *Youth Commission Papers*, YC. 12.

Ministry of Education, *The Youth Service in England and Wales*, London: HMSO, 1960.

Moore, Keith, 'Bodgies, Widgies and Moral Panic in Australia, 1955-1959'.

Paper presented to the Social Change in the 21st Century Conference, Centre for Social Change Research, Queensland University of Technology, 29 October 2004.

National Union of Conservative and Constitutional Associations. Conservative Political Centre, *Youth Astray: A Report on the Treatment of the Young Offender*. London: Conservative Political Centre, 1946.

One Nation Group, *The Responsible Society*, London: Conservative Political Centre, 1959.

Rowntree, B.S. and G.R. Lavers, *English Life and Leisure: A Social Study*. London: Longmans, 1951.

Spencer, J.C. et al., *Preliminary Report of the Bristol Social Project*, 1961, unpublished.

Books

Adams, Roy, *Hard Nights: My Life in Liverpool Clubland*, Southport: Cavernman Publications, 2003.

Akhtar, Miriam and Steve Humphries, *The Fifties and Sixties: a Lifestyle Revolution*, London: Boxtree, 2001.

Ball, Alan M., *Imagining America: Influence and Images in Twentieth Century Russia*, Oxford: Rowman & Littlefield, 2003.

Binder, Pearl, *The Peacock's Tail*, London: Harrap, 1958.

Blandy, Mary, *Razor Edge: The Story of a Youth Club*, London: Victor Gollancz, 1967.

Bognador, Vernon & Robert Skidelsky (eds), *The Age of Affluence, 1951-1964*, London, Macmillan, 1970.

Bradley, Dick, *Understanding Rock 'n' Roll: Popular Music in Britain 1955-1964*, Buckingham: Open University Press, 1992.

Brake, Michael, *Comparative Youth Culture: the Sociology of Youth Cultures and Youth Subcultures in America, Britain and Canada*, London: Routledge & Kegan Paul, 1985.

Brew, Josephine Macalister, *Youth and Youth Groups*, London: Faber, 1957.

Cohen, Stanley, *Folk Devils: the Creation of the Mods and Rockers*, Routledge Classics, 3rd ed., London: Routledge, 2011.

Cohn, Nik, *Awopbopaloobopalopbamboom: Pop from the Beginning*, London: Paladin, 1970.

Cohn, Nik, *Today There Are No Gentlemen*, London: Weidenfeld and Nicolson, 1971.

Cohen, Albert K., *Delinquent Boys: the Culture of the Gang*, London: Routledge & Kegan Paul, 1956.

Cohen, Phillip & Harwant S. Bains (eds), *Multi-Racist Britain*, Basingstoke: Macmillan, 1988.

Cole, Shaun, *'Don We Now Our Gay Apparel': Gay Men's Dress in the Twentieth Century*, Oxford: Berg, 2000.

Collins, Michael, *The Likes of Us: A Biography of the White Working Class*, London, Granta, 2005.

Conservative Party, *78th Annual Conference*, Conservative Political Centre, 1958.

Davies, Andrew, *Gangs of Manchester: the Story of the Scuttlers: Britain's First Youth Cult*, Wrea Green: Milo Books, 2008.

Davis, John, *Youth and the Condition of Britain: Images of Adolescent Conflict*, London: Athlone Press, 1990.

Donoghue, Albert, *The Enforcer: the Secrets of My Life With the Krays*, London: John Blake, 2002.

Douglass, Dave, *Geordies – Wa Mental*, Newcastle upon Tyne: Tups Books, 2000.

Downes, David M., *The Delinquent Solution: a Study in Subcultural Theory*, International Library of Sociology and Social Reconstruction, London: Routledge & Kegan Paul, 1966.

Everett, Peter, *You'll Never be 16 Again: an Illustrated History of the British Teenager*, London: BBC Publications, 1986.

Fabian, Robert, *London After Dark*, London: Naldrett Press, 1954.

Ferris, Ray and Julian Lord, *Teddy Boys: a Concise History*, Wrea Green: Milo Books, 2012.

Ford, Donald, *The Delinquent Child and the Community*, London: Constable, 1957.

Fowler, David, *Youth Culture in Modern Britain, c.1920-c.1970: From Ivory Tower to Global Movement: A New History*, London: Palgrave Macmillan, 2008.

Frith, Simon, *Sound Effects: Youth, Leisure, and the Politics of Rock*, Communication and Society, London: Constable, 1983.

Fryer, Peter, *Staying Power: the History of Black People in Britain*, London: Pluto Press, 1984.

Fyvel, T. R., *The Insecure Offenders: Rebellious Youth in the Welfare State*, London: Chatto & Windus, 1961. Also published as *Troublemakers: Rebellious Youth in an Affluent Society*, New York: Schocken Books, 1964.

Gildart, Keith, *Images of England Through Popular Music: Youth and Rock 'n' Roll, 1955-1975*, London: Palgrave Macmillan, 2013.

Gillis, John R., *Youth and History: Tradition and Change in European Age Relations, 1770 – Present*, London: Academic Press, 1974.

Glass, Ruth (ed.) **assisted by Harold Pollins,** *Newcomers: the West Indians in London*, London: Centre for Urban Studies and Allen & Unwin, 1960.

Glinert, Ed, *The London Compendium: A Street by Street Exploration of the Hidden Metropolis*, London: Penguin, 2003.

Gosling, Ray, *Personal Copy: A Memoir of the Sixties*, London: Faber, 1980.

Green, Jonathan, *All Dressed Up: the Sixties and the Counter Culture*, London: Pimlico, 1999.

Hall, Stuart & Tony Jefferson (eds), *Resistance Through Rituals: Youth Subcultures in Post-War Britain*, London: Hutchinson, 1976.

Hamblett, Charles and Jane Deverson, *Generation X*, London: Tandem Books, 1964.

Heckstall-Smith, Anthony, *Eighteen Months*, London: Wingate, 1954.

Hennessy, Peter, *Having It So Good: Britain in the Fifties*, London: Penguin, 2007.

Hewison, Robert, *In Anger: British Culture in the Cold War 1945-60*, New
York: Oxford University Press, 1981.

Hiro, Dilip, *Black British White British*, London, rev. ed., Harmondsworth: Penguin, 1973.

Hopkins, Harry, *The New Look*, London: Secker & Warburg, 1964.

Horn, A.M., *Juke Box Britain: Americanisation and Youth Culture, 1945-1960*, Manchester: Manchester University Press, 2009.

Hylton, Stuart, *From Rationing to Rock: the 1950s Revisited*, Stroud: Sutton Publishing, 1998.

Jefferson, Tony, *The Teds: a Political Resurrection*, Stencilled occasional paper, Sub and popular culture series; SP 22, Birmingham: Centre for Contemporary Cultural Studies, University of Birmingham [1973].

Kerr, Madeline, *The People of Ship Street*, International Library of Sociology and Social Reconstruction, London: Routledge & Kegan Paul, 1958.

King, Robin, *No Paradise: a Chronicle of the Merchant Navy*, London: Arthur Barker, 1955.

Kirby, Dick, *Death on the Beat: Police Officers Killed in the Line of Duty*, Barnsley: Pen & Sword Books, 2012.

Kynaston, David, *Family Britain, 1951-57*, London: Bloomsbury, 2009.

Leach, Sam, *The Rocking City: the Explosive Birth of the Beatles*, Gwynedd: Pharaoh Press, 1999.

Leech, Kenneth, *Youthquake: the Growth of a Counter-Culture Through Two Decades*, London: Sheldon Press, 1973.

Leigh, Spencer, *The Best Of Fellas: the Story of Bob Wooler*, Liverpool: Drivegreen, 2002.

McCullin, Don, *Unreasonable Behaviour: an Autobiography*, London: Vintage, 1992.

McDonald, Brian, *Elephant Boys: Tales of London and Los Angeles Underworlds*, Edinburgh: Mainstream, 2000.

MacInnes, Colin, *England, Half English*, London: MacGibbon & Kee, 1961.
Manning, Arthur E., *The Bodgie: a Study in Psychological Abnormality*, Sydney: Angus and Robertson, 1957.
Mays, John Barron, *Growing Up in the City: a Study of Juvenile Delinquency in an Urban Neighbourhood*, Social Research Series, Liverpool: Liverpool University Press, 1964.
Mays, John Barron, *The Young Pretenders: a Study of Teenage Culture in Contemporary Society*, Live Issues, London: Michael Joseph, 1965.
Melly, George, *Revolt into Style: The Pop Arts in Britain*, Harmondsworth: Penguin, 1972.
Montgomery, John Morais, *The Fifties*, London: Allen & Unwin, 1965.
Morris, Terence, *Crime and Criminal Justice Since 1945*, Making Contemporary Britain, Oxford: Basil Blackwell, 1989.
Nuttall, Jeff, *Bomb Culture*, London: Paladin, 1968.
Oldham, Andrew Loog, *Stoned*, London: Secker & Warburg, 2008.
Opie, Iona & Peter, *The Lore and Language of Schoolchildren*, Oxford: Oxford University Press, 1959.
Osgerby, Bill, *Youth in Britain Since 1945*, Making Contemporary Britain Series, Oxford: Blackwell, 1998.
Parker, Tony, *The Plough Boy*, London: Hutchinson, 1965.
Pearson, Geoffrey, *Hooligan: A History of Respectable Fears*, London: Macmillan, 1983.
Pearson, George, *Sex, Brown Ale and Rhythm & Blues: The Life That Gave Birth To The Animals*, Darlington: SnagaP Publishing, 1998.
Phillips, Mike & Trevor Phillips,*Windrush: the Irresistible Rise of Multi-Racial Britain*, London: HarperCollins, 1998.
Pilkington, Edward, *Beyond the Mother Country: West Indians and the Notting Hill White Riots*, London: I.B. Tauris, 1988.
Poiger, Uta G., *Jazz, Rock and Rebels: Cold War Politics and American Culture in a Divided Germany*, Studies on the

History of Society and Culture, Berkeley: University of California Press, 2000.

Polhemus, Ted, *Street Style*, new ed., London: PYMCA, 2010.

Powell, Nosher with William Hall, *Nosher*, London: Blake, 1999.

Raison, Timothy (ed.), *Youth in New Society*, London: Rupert Hart-Davis, 1966.

Sandbrook, Dominic, *Never Had It So Good: a History of Britain from Suez to the Beatles*, London: Abacus, 2005.

Scala, Mim, *Diary of a Teddy Boy: a Memoir of the Long Sixties*, Dublin: Sitric Books, 2000.

Schulz, Susanne, *The Function of Fashion and Style in the Formation of Self-Help and Group Identity in Youth Subculture*, University of Manchester Sociology Working Papers, 6: University of Manchester, Department of Sociology, 1998.

Shichor, David & Delos H. Kelly (eds), *Critical Issues in Juvenile Delinquency*, Lexington, Mass.: Lexington Books, 1980.

Skidelsky, Robert, *Oswald Mosley*, London: Macmillan, 1975.

Spencer, John C., *Crime and the Services*, International Library of Sociology and Social Reconstruction, London: Routledge & Kegan Paul, 1954.

Springhall, John, *Coming of Age: Adolescence in Britain*, 1860-1960, Dublin: Gill & Macmillan, 1986.

Steele-Perkins, Chris and Richard Smith, *The Teds*, Stockport: Dewi Lewis Publishing, 2002.

Stucley, Elizabeth Florence, *Teddy Boys' Picnic*, London: Anthony Blond, 1958.

Townsend, John, *The Young Devils: Experiences of a School Teacher*, London: Chatto & Windus, 1958.

Travis, Alan, *Bound and Gagged: a Secret History of Obscenity in Britain*, London: Profile Books, 2000.

Turner, Alwyn W., *Halfway to Paradise: the Birth of British Rock*, London, V&A Publishing, 2008.

Ward, R.H., *The Hidden Boy: the Work of C.A. Joyce as Headmaster of an Approved School*, London: Cassell, 1962.

Whitcomb, Ian, *After the Ball: Pop Music from Ragtime to Rock*, Baltimore MD, Penguin, 1974.
Wickenden, James, *Colour in Britain*, London: Oxford University Press, 1958.
Yallop, David, *To Encourage Others*, London: W.H. Allen, 1971.

Essays in books

Bicat, Anthony, 'Fifties Children: Sixties People' in Bognador and Skidelsky (eds), *The Age of Affluence*, pp. 321-38.
Fletcher, Colin, 'Beat and Gangs on Merseyside', in Raison, *Youth in New Society*, pp. 148-59. Originally published in *New Society,* 20 February 1964.
Jefferson, Tony, 'Cultural Responses to the Teds', in Hall & Jefferson, *Resistance Through Rituals*, pp. 81-86.
MacInnes, Colin, 'Sharp Schmutter', in MacInnes, *England, Half English*,
pp. 148-57. Essay originally published in *Twentieth Century*, August 1959.
Rock, Paul and Stanley Cohen, 'The Teddy Boy', in Bognador and Skidelsky, *The Age of Affluence,* pp. 288-320.

Journal articles

Bentley, Nick, '"New Elizabethans": The Representation of Youth Subcultures in 1950s British Fiction', *Literature & History*, vol. 19(1), Spring 2010, pp. 16-33.
Blevgad, Britt-Marie, 'Newspapers and Rock and Roll Riots in Copenhagen', *Acta Sociologica*, vol. 7, 1963, pp. 151-78.
Carney, Brian, 'The Mysterious Cult of the Teddy Boys and Girls', *John Bull Illustrated*, 14 March 1959.
Chibnall, Steve, 'Whistle and Zoot: The Changing Meaning of a Suit of Clothes', *History Workshop*, no. 20, Autumn 1985, pp. 56-81.
Cosgrove, Stuart, 'The Zoot-Suit and Style Warfare', *History Workshop*, no. 18, Autumn 1984, pp. 77-91.

Cross, Robert J., 'The Teddy Boy as Scapegoat', *Doshisha Studies in Language and Culture*, 1-2, 1998, pp. 263-91.

Ellis, Catherine, 'The Younger Generation: The Labour Party and the 1959 Youth Commission', *Journal of British* Studies, vol. 41(2), 2002, pp. 199-231.

Hoggart, Richard, 'Lambeth Boys', *Sight and Sound*, vol. 54(2), 1985, pp. 106-109.

Lowson, David, 'Delinquency in Industrial Areas,' *British Journal of Criminology*, vol. 1(1), July 1960, pp. 50-55.

Marchant, Hilde, 'The Making of Boy Gangsters', *Picture Post*, 10 October 1953, issue 2, pp. 16-18, 42.

Marchant, Hilde, 'The Truth About the Teddy Boys and the Teddy Girls', *Picture Post*, 29 May 1954, issue 9, pp. 25-26.

Mitchell, David, 'What's Wrong with Teddy Girls?', *Picture Post*, 4 June 1955, issue 10, pp. 37-40.

Mooney, Katie, '"Ducktails, Flick-Knives and Pugnacity": Subcultural and Hegemonic Masculinities in South Africa, 1948-1960', *Journal of Southern African Studies*, vol. 24(4), December 1998, pp. 753-74.

O'Connor, James, 'The Youthful Offender', *Studies: An Irish Review Quarterly*, vol. 52(205), Spring, 1963, pp. 87-96.

Sandilands, J., 'Whatever Happened to the Teddy Boys?', *Daily Telegraph Magazine*, no. 217, 29 November 1968, pp. 20-27.

Savage, Jon, 'Teds', *The Face*, 26 June 1982, pp. 12-15.